D1031794

Religion in the South

John B. Boles, Series Editor

When Slavery Was Called Freedom

Evangelicalism, Proslavery, and the Causes of the Civil War

John Patrick Daly

THE UNIVERSITY PRESS OF KENTUCKY

Publication of this volume was made possible in part by a grant
from the National Endowment for the Humanities.

Copyright © 2002 by The University Press of Kentucky

Scholarly publisher for the Commonwealth,
serving Bellarmine University, Berea College, Centre College of Kentucky,
Eastern Kentucky University, The Filson Historical Society, Georgetown College,
Kentucky Historical Society, Kentucky State University, Morehead State University,
Murray State University, Northern Kentucky University, Transylvania University,
University of Kentucky, University of Louisville, and Western Kentucky University.
All rights reserved.

Editorial and Sales Offices: The University Press of Kentucky
663 South Limestone Street, Lexington, Kentucky 40508–4008

06 05 04 03 02   5 4 3 2 1

Library of Congress Cataloging-in-Publication Data

Daly, John, 1964-
    When slavery was called freedom : evangelicalism, proslavery, and the causes of the
Civil War / John Daly.
        p.   cm.—(Religion in the South)
    Includes bibliographical references and index.
    ISBN 0-8131-2241-4 (alk. paper)
    1. Slavery—Moral and ethical aspects—Southern States—History—19th century.
2. Slavery—Moral and ethical aspects—United States—History—19th century.
3. Slavery —Southern States—Justification. 4. Evangelicalism—Political aspects—
Southern States—History—19th century. 5. Evangelicalism—Political aspects—United
States—History—19th century. 6. Southern States—Politics and government—
1775-1865. 7. Southern States—Intellectual life—19th century. 8. Southern States—
Moral conditions. 9. Antislavery movements—United States—History—19th century.
10. United States—History—Civil War, 1861-1865—Causes. I. Title. II. Series.
E449.D23 2002
973.7'11—dc21   2001007143

This book is printed on acid-free recycled paper meeting
the requirements of the American National Standard
for Permanence of Paper for Printed Library Materials.

Manufactured in the United States of America

For Elizabeth McCarthy Daly

Contents

Acknowledgments

Many individuals and institutions have contributed to the production of this book. A special thanks is due the staffs at the many libraries and archives where I have worked, in particular the staffs of the Southern Historical Collection in Chapel Hill and the Historical Foundation of the Presbyterian and Reformed Churches at Montreat, North Carolina. Crucial financial support was provided by the Farish Fellowship, the Mellon Foundation, the McGinty Foundation, and the James and Carolyn Fitz-Gerald Foundation. All of my history colleagues and students in the various colleges and universities in which I have taught in the past seven years offered welcome support: Rice University, Texas Southern University, University of St. Thomas, University of Houston, Austin College, and Louisiana Tech University. My current colleagues in the History Department of the State University of New York, College at Brockport, provided an ideal atmosphere for the completion of the project. Three mentors and friends—Thomas L. Haskell, John B. Boles, and Stephen Webre—have contributed so much to my professional, intellectual, and personal development that this book's completion is only a minor example of all they have done for me. I cannot begin to thank them enough. Kendra Winkelstein, Robert L. Daly, Robert W. Daly, and Bertram Wyatt-Brown all read the manuscript closely and offered key suggestions, though any errors are, of course, mine alone. Finally, the book is dedicated to the master editor and Scrabble player who has always been there for me.

Introduction

Evangelical Proslavery and the Causes of the Civil War

The year 1831 marked a new epoch in proslavery. America's fiercest moral debate erupted over the issue of slavery and was intimately linked to the sectional crisis that brought civil war thirty years later. The nearly suicidal violence of that conflict implies that the combatants disagreed about the nature of morality itself, but that was not the case. Deep political divisions, after all, do not necessarily stem from deep cultural divisions.[1] Antebellum political debates *were* moralized, and moral debates were politicized as the sectional crisis deepened, but, as David Potter has noted, America at the outset of the Civil War had more "cultural homogeneity" than ever before.[2] An analysis of the dominant southern proslavery position confirms this cultural convergence and thereby dissolves the truism that "the South became increasingly isolated from the progressive ideology of the Western World."[3]

For a hundred years after the Civil War, politicians and historians analyzing the period made much of the antebellum South's alleged departures from national ideals. Their emphasis on aberration salvaged the continuity of the nation's history and moral mission.[4] Some critics held that southern culture had deviated not only from the tenor and progressive course of *American* institutions but from modern global patterns of development as well.[5] Such thinking was common both among scholars who were horrified at the backwardness of the South and among

1

southerners who believed their region had, with characteristic and commendable stubbornness, resisted the cultural power of a postbellum world that held it in scorn.[6] Recent studies demonstrate, however, that the antebellum South participated in mainstream nineteenth-century moral, intellectual, and socio-economic developments. The region's leaders were often proponents of current doctrines.[7] Southerners, then, sought to compete with the North for economic power in a thoroughly contemporary spirit. A modern foundation for the South's moral position was laid out in pamphlets and pulpits before the war began, as southerners explained how slavery had arisen in keeping with the "genius of the age."[8]

The South and the North drew different practical conclusions from the same evangelical moral premises. As religious historian Samuel Hill has noted, "only a society so united could be so divided."[9]

Antebellum cultural unity was particularly evident in the northern and southern use of religious and moral language. In an era of national "evangelical hegemony," Hill found the vocabularies of the regions to be "nearly indistinguishable."[10] How then did moral disagreements occur? How did southerners preach equality and democracy and not feel like hypocrites? How did they disclaim responsibility for the plight of their slaves? Why did northerners feel threatened by a slave economy that did not directly involve them? And why did Americans fight and die, so violently and with so much commitment, for causes that began in a moral debate about these issues? Evangelical moralism, which dominated the era, solves the riddle of these questions.

The book that follows studies the content and influence of evangelicals' proslavery ideas. The first chapter defines my use of the term "evangelical" and the central place of the evangelical impulse in antebellum American culture. I argue that the movement characterized the era. I therefore employ the term "evangelical" to denote a sweeping cultural movement that celebrated individualism and moral self-discipline, rather than to denote technical aspects of certain Protestant churches and their theology. The chapter also describes the distinctive role of evangelicalism in the South.

The second chapter surveys the history of proslavery thought in the United States and the new tradition of proslavery ideology that coalesced after the year 1831. History textbooks often repeat the facile and inaccurate argument that the South defended slavery as a "necessary evil" before 1831 and then became defensive, after abolitionist assaults, and argued after 1831 that slavery was a "positive good." I found little support for this argument in the voluminous proslavery documents produced by evangelicals.[11] Southerners typically defended slavery only as it was practiced in the southern states and rarely argued that slavery would last forever or that it was a feature of an ideal society.

The arguments the South produced after 1831, however, differed significantly from Revolutionary and Early National Era positions. New spokesmen, with new social and moral outlooks, addressed the morality of slavery after 1831. There also were simply far more outspoken defenders of slavery after that date, and after 1831 proslavery ideology became much more self-conscious, more thoroughly articulated, and more central to white southerners' identity. The growth of the slave economy (and territory) and southern revivalism between 1787 and 1831 changed the region's entire outlook. Even if the abolitionist challenge had not forced southerners to examine and articulate their moral identity in 1831, the South would have undergone an ideological revolution around this time. Two coalescing events, and complimentary intellectual movements to explain them, dominated the region at this point: the growth of evangelical religion and material prosperity. Naturally, antebellum southerners applied evangelical moral concepts and free market economic science to the question of slavery. These intellectual tools could hardly have been employed to defend slavery prior to 1830. Only after that date did mature evangelical religion dominate the region and the scale of the cotton boom and modern economic and technological innovation (especially steam and rail) become clear. In 1832 Thomas R. Dew of Virginia applied the developing economic science and religious assumptions of the era to the question of the moral status and the future of slavery. Evangelical ministers would popularize similar (and less academic) versions of his arguments throughout the antebellum South. The second chapter examines Dew's contribution and the evolution of the southern religious perspective on slavery prior to 1831, via the 1822 writing of the Reverend Richard Furman of South Carolina, as well as other ministers.

The third chapter describes the southern response to the abolitionist criticism of slavery. Abolitionists attacked slavery on the basis of Christian principles and American assumptions about freedom. Southern ministers answered them on the same basis. Southern evangelicals found ample passages in the Bible that had been used to support slavery for hundreds of years. I hope, however, that this chapter makes it clear that southern evangelicals did not defeat the antislavery argument or have a "stronger" biblical argument. I am not interested in or capable of handing out grades to dead Christians for their biblical interpretations (and it is an intellectually fallacious project by definition). Antebellum evangelicals did not believe in biblical literalism as twenty-first century Americans understand it. The frequency of positive biblical references to slavery definitely bolstered southern confidence, and southern evangelicals had no doubts that the Bible supported their position and that abolitionism had been defeated. But the southern evangelicals expected the Bible to be in perfect harmony with beliefs about contemporary science, history, political freedom, economics, and even current events. Southerners did not simply stamp slavery "Bible approved." They articulated how slavery fit into the "genius of the American system," and how slavery was only right as part of that system.

The fourth chapter explores the evangelical proslavery vision of the South, its economic future, and its racial order. This is by far the longest chapter in the book because it catalogues the proslavery writings produced for consumption inside the South after the three evangelical churches had split by 1846 into separate northern and southern organizations. These documents reveal the mind of the South and growing southern sectionalism better than any other historical artifacts.

The chapter argues that evangelical ministers built the southern identity during this era. After 1831, evangelicals told the region it was blessed and destined for great things. Southern identity, southern unity, southern belligerence, the sectional crisis, secession, and civil war followed, with evangelical ministers cheering each new step. Southern ministers reflected and enhanced the culture they came from. Evangelical ministers served in populist churches and had to win and keep their audiences. They gave expression and a degree of coherence and logic to the grassroots assumptions and cultural baggage of Dixie. Their defense of the morality of slavery dominated the regional culture after 1831, and no account of the momentous events of the following thirty years can ignore evangelical proslavery ideology.

The fifth chapter focuses on the 1850s and the height of the sectional crisis. The South faced a new and more serious enemy than the abolitionists in this era: the free soil movement and its moderate antislavery. Southern ideology matured further in these last years before the Civil War, producing a wide variety of ingenious proslavery writing on the meaning of "free labor" for the South. Some isolated scholars, George Fitzhugh, James Henry Hammond, and Henry Hughes chief among them, departed from evangelical nostrums and did support slavery as a general labor system and basis for proper social order. Historians have dwelt on their arguments since they speak to twenty-first-century academic concerns (and their proslavery writings have a depth and interest that rewards continuing scholarly analysis), but the popular evangelical proslavery of the 1850s reveals the dominant trends in southern society and the causes of the Civil War at the end of the decade. Southern evangelicals argued that free labor theory did not threaten the South, not because slavery was a superior economic system to a free economy but because the South had a free economy and because slavery constituted a form of free labor. Some ministers took this argument farther than others in the 1850s, but the ideological position differed little from that popularized by Thomas R. Dew in 1832. Southern slavery was in harmony with the development of freedom and a freely operating economy. The Republican Party and, increasingly during the decade of the 1850s, public opinion in the North rejected the southern position. Northerners believed that slaveholders undermined a free, fair, and prosperous economy.

The final chapter chronicles the fate of proslavery ideology and the evolution of southern religion during the Civil War and the demise of slavery. With the defeat of the Confederacy, white southern religion lost much of its emphasis on secular, this-worldly, material signs of God's favor, and the South lost nearly all of its religiously based optimism in human progress. Evangelical proslavery ideology, however, sustained secession and the war effort and survived the war. The white South became, if anything, more convinced of the righteousness of their cause after the cause had died. And the defense of slavery, since it was based in ideals Americans still hold dear and still use to address twenty-first-century moral problems, has yet to die.

1

Freedom and Evangelical Culture in the South

Southern morality was an amalgam of Protestant traditions and blunt materialism, because evangelical ministers tended to sacralize the American institutions under which their denominations expanded. It is no surprise, therefore, that southern evangelicals reached seemingly self-interested conclusions on what they deemed wholly religious grounds.[1] The Protestant work ethic had established worldly success as a sign of divine favor since at least 1630 when the Puritans reached American soil. In the two hundred years that followed, and especially since the individualistic and democratic American Revolution of the 1770s, the subtleties of the Puritan theology of success had diminished, where they had not disappeared. In the atmosphere of the early nineteenth-century South's populist, frontier revival, the equation of individual and national success with moral superiority and divine favor lost even more of its theological and intellectual sophistication.[2] The evangelicals who came to dominate the South promoted this moral tradition on new soil and elaborated on it in ways that would not have been possible in any other social setting.[3] One key social fact, slaveholding, became a sacred badge of success as a result of the evangelicals' saturating the South in their religion and its moral outlook on success and power.

"Evangelicalism," as applied to the mid-nineteenth century, denotes a proselytizing Christian insistence on individual moral power.[4] When southerners advanced the antebellum truism that "the American mind thus far is cast in a religious mold," the mold referred to was the evangelical idea of individual moral autonomy and accountability. The southern Methodist minister and president of Randolph-Macon College, William A. Smith, gave a typical definition of antebellum religion when describing the basis of a public education: "It must be a strictly Protestant education—Protestant, at least, in its main feature: that is, every citizen [whatever his gospel] . . . is still individually and personally responsible to God and his country."[5] Similarly, Smith argued, "He is within the limits of his capacity a cause within himself, strictly a self-acting agent, and hence accountable."[6] The mid-nineteenth century was characterized by a popular religious culture in which the autonomy Smith demanded was taken for granted and moralized. It was on the basis of these assumptions that historians call the period an evangelical age.

Evangelicalism, however, was primarily and technically a style of Protestantism centered on the conversion experience and on a theology that stressed heartfelt individual proximity to God over communal or doctrinal definitions of piety.[7] In America, this movement was associated with the advent of Methodism and with Baptist and Presbyterian participation in the Great Awakening of the eighteenth century. Theological flexibility and simple appeals to the "word and heart" allowed various denominations to participate in a general movement: southern revivalism.[8] There was, for example, room for Unitarians and Episcopalians under the "evangelistic" rubric because they tried, as New Orleans Unitarian and proslavery minister Theodore Clapp put it, to "adopt a plan of preaching the simple doctrines of the gospel, instead of distinguishing the tenets of Calvin, Arminicus, Edwards or Wesley."[9] The simple message of conversion mattered most to evangelicals, not theological or denominational distinctions. The nondenominational spirit of the evangelical movement had a profound practical reality in revivals and church building, especially in recently opened frontier areas. Evangelical preachers won souls throughout the South, but not necessarily for their own churches. Presbyterian Daniel Baker, a leading revivalist who worked the Old Southwest, remarked how he would sometimes win hundreds of converts at a single meeting, not one of whom became a Presbyterian. In a frontier community in east Texas, he once joined a Methodist and a Baptist in preaching a revival, whose converts proceeded to form an Episcopal church.[10]

This popular ecumenical spirit necessitated a de-emphasis of doctrine; indeed, it excused many ministers from intellectual rigor, enabling them to dismiss the theological contradiction between the power of the individual and the power of God, between absolute moral autonomy and accountability. Echoing Calvin, they preached human depravity, insufficiency, and dependence on Providence, thereby implying that individual salvation was uncertain, while simultaneously assuring believers that human effort could carry the day (an accommodation to a uniquely American pelagianism—glorification of free will, or an explicit avowal of free will in the case of Methodist Arminianism).[11] Episcopal bishop Stephen Elliot of Georgia unashamedly trumpeted this precarious doctrine: "There is no inconsistency in calling on God and then telling you to do it."[12] Had evangelicals emphasized doctrinal issues, they might not have celebrated the power of individuals so easily. There was, however, a compensation for, perhaps even a solution to, this intellectual contradiction in the conversion experience. The preachers insisted that new believers be cognizant of their depravity and their powerlessness to overcome sin before leading them into the presence of a God who would grant them the confidence and power they needed to make sanctified lives on their own.

Evangelicals offered believers knowledge of their personal justification much earlier in their lives than did traditional Calvinism. Evangelicalism claimed that after regeneration the unaided self (with the presence of God) could transcend its own passions, tame its own instincts. Such an ethic was consonant with the secular mood of the day and offered a solution of sorts to keenly felt secular moral problems. In its assurance that man could apprehend and fulfill his responsibilities, evangelicalism mirrored Jacksonian America's confident sense of national destiny.[13] In a mobile and fast-changing society with few authoritative institutions to provide roles or moral signposts, it offered a model of "right" behavior to nonbelievers who knew that they had selves but were not sure what to do with them. Evangelicals promised such people that, with some help from God, they had "self-power" and that they controlled their own destinies. In considering the 1830s, it is hard to draw any clear lines between promoters of the evangelical movement and Americans seeking secular success, order, unity, and reform. Reform and the creation of a nation of self-controlling individuals obsessed the era. And with good reason. America in the antebellum era still radiated youthful energy and faced potential chaos.

In the early nineteenth century, America was a republic of the young. Demographic trends and geographic mobility produced a landscape overrun with youth. Transcendental pundits and educational reformers sought to direct immature energies through calls for moral self-discipline and adult responsibility. These campaigns coincided with explosions of evangelical conversions. Ministers in frontier and rural southern communities were frank about the social meaning of conversion, calling it the beginning of "self-dependence."[14] Conversion often marked the moment when young people ceased to work for their parents and set out on their own. For young women, the experience prepared the way for and eased the transition to the responsibilities of married life and motherhood. Whatever their marital state, religion provided rural women with one of their only social outlets. Hyper-emotional and deeply personal conversions also steeled young southerners for the drudgeries most of them would face. Conversion, however, was not simply a form of initiation, training, or social control, although it contained elements of all three. The experience invested the sacrifices of common folks' lives with a moral and spiritual grandeur, an element of self-direction and choice.[15]

Evangelical conversion served to socialize those who experienced it; in convincing them of their powers of self-direction, it made them more effective citizens of a nation whose institutions did not define social roles. Over and above the typical teenage transgressions that preceded his conversion, Presbyterian James Henley Thornwell, one of the South's leading theologians, said he had been guilty of a fundamental sin—telling himself that he was not culpable because he "was born without any agency." His conversion as a young man dispelled this evil and convinced him that "we all must be brought to see that all—under God—depends on ourselves."[16] Another southern minister described the "most salutary influence of human agency" in more socially explicit terms: "It is in it we see the foundation God has laid for pure individualism."[17] Baptist minister Jeremiah Jeter was converted as a youth in a rural Virginia revival in 1818. He echoed Thornwell in noting that, before regeneration, "it had seemed unreasonable that I should bear a self-imposed yoke."[18]

American individualism, much propounded throughout the period, was an invitation to self-control. The growth of the young Republic demonstrated the wisdom of personal restraint and the inevitability of the achievement of its moral mission. It was therefore easy for southern evangelicals to assume that the problem of personal autonomy had been solved in the new land. Evangelical arguments for individual responsibility were compelled and confirmed by social experiences and so appeared self-evident, irresistible. An isolating personal moral responsibility, not freedom, was the first principle of American public culture in the early nineteenth century.[19] The history of the period makes little sense if this is not understood, as the assumption that simple "personal freedom" was the core American value makes popular southern moral acceptance of slavery appear as self-contradiction, self-delusion, simple dishonesty, a mark of regional deviance, or a product of stupidity on a massive and odious scale.[20] The horrors of slavery and racism aside, such readings grossly misrepresent southerners, whose fundamental understanding of morality and veneration of "freedom" were not at variance with that of their northern countrymen.[21]

In his lectures at Randolph-Macon, William A. Smith, a leading proslavery philosopher, regularly told southerners that "self-control is the abstract principle of freedom." In this aphorism, potential disparities between southern preaching and practice were neatly resolved, and the gulf between northern and southern ideals narrowed. As a form of freedom, self-control—self-restraint—was attainable by women, inmates, blacks, and paupers.[22] As historian of freedom Orlando Patterson has indicated: "The fact that people consider freedom the most important thing in life is in no way inconsistent with a tolerance for the institution of slavery or, what amounts to the same thing, a lack of interest in promoting a policy of manumission."[23] This manner of espousing of freedom describes the attitude of most Americans in both sections of the country in the first half of the nineteenth-century.

Southern Presbyterian James Henley Thornwell said that "true Freedom" was "discipline," and that as such it was universally available. He noted that "the lesson is the same however different the textbooks from which it has been taught."[24] In their discussions of freedom, echoed by fellow southern ministers, Thornwell and William Smith paraphrased Francis Wayland, the northern Baptist minister and leading antislavery lecturer who wrote the nation's most popular book on moral philosophy.[25] Wayland, in his more philosophical vein, said, "The truth that every man is responsible for all his actions to God, presupposes the right to universal freedom."[26] Evangelical moralists battled over the practical implications of individual restraint, but they agreed that it was the cardinal element of freedom. They believed that anyone capable of practicing moral self-control had obtained true freedom and therefore could enjoy the good life regardless of material conditions.

Such reasoning on freedom is not as preposterous as it appears if one's first premises are theistic. Freedom had long since been established as America's great good—its founding principle and social compass. Goodness, for evangelicals, derived from and was directed toward God. Freedom was properly construed, therefore, not as liberty to do as one chose, but as the ability to choose what Providence intended. The satisfaction of Providence with the social status quo was evident in the blessings it continued to bestow on the United States. Blessings would continue to flow only if the individuals comprising the nation exercised the power, won through ecstatic conversion, to curb instinctual desires. Freedom as unrestraint was therefore anathema to ministers North and South, who agreed that under such definition "freedom is incompatible with a state of accountability."[27]

Evangelical terms seemed to be at odds with broader and more obvious interpretations of "freedom." To listeners not schooled in moral theology, the Evangelical message appeared as this: "You are free to contain yourselves within the roles society has set for you and, in mature acceptance of your fates, to justify yourselves to God. You are autonomous, not in that you have a range of options from which to select, but in that nobody else can win salvation for you. You are alone." If restraint produced freedom, freedom might mean any social condition that taught lessons of self-control and that encouraged willed acceptance of self-denial. Evangelicals did say that women enjoyed such a form of Christian freedom.[28] Likewise, this traditional understanding of freedom gave evangelicals a basis for tolerating almost any form of labor exploitation without blanching. Some important early nineteenth-century moralists and social theorists, particularly in Great Britain and the South, did take brutal positions on the benefits of social depravation and personal abnegation. The pleasures of autonomy and rewards of self dependence, however, were not often subsumed under so limited a concept of liberty.

Many antebellum Americans described the choices of women, the poor, and "inferior" races in highly constricted terms, but their stances rarely paralleled general social thought and were not attuned to the vague optimism of Jacksonianism, popular evangelicalism, and, indeed, the national civil religion. All cultural languages, especially in their rendering of religious myths, obscure or make unexaminable some social realities. While this is achieved in most cultures through the restriction of options, it was accomplished in the United States through the appearance that all options were open. The myths of unlimited opportunity for improvement and of powerful individuals who overcome any obstacles implied that Americans need not attend too closely to social forces. In ethico-religious terms, antebellum Americans were rarely called to make direct choices between submission to social roles and individual autonomy, between personal sacrifice and collective reward, or between traditional values and material progress. As cultural historian Sacan Bercovitch asserts, from at least the time of late Puritan homiletics on the American mission, American public religious doctrine had long been cast such that the "terms are not *either/or* but *both/and*."[29]

James Henley Thornwell, as one of the South's leading intellects, demonstrated that his evangelical program could call for both self-restraint and pursuit of power, thereby satisfying his southern audience's taste for "both/and" solutions. In 1861, on the eve of secession, he noted that "Virtue is power, vice is weakness," condensing the pervasive ideas of the era and making religious morality appear practical.[30] During the same period, proslavery political and moral scholar Beverly Tucker said much the same thing, although less pithily, to a Virginia audience, "power . . . Be assured, its ripening fruit waits to reward the votary of virtue."[31] If Protestant virtue—self-restraint—was power, it followed that the release of *God-fearing* citizens from social restraint and the growth of material prosperity would not result in an explosion of sin and selfishness. Evangelical insistence that absolute individual moral agency and responsibility before God were conducive to power, which would in turn breed further virtue, made ongoing expansion of economic prosperity and individual liberty not only unthreatening, but desirable—not only desirable, but mandated by heaven. William Smith of Randolph-Macon held that even the masses of Europe would be driven toward democracy and prosperity by "the power *itself*, which their improved moral and social condition has rendered."[32]

Under the "virtue is power" schema, of course, growth could only occur if Protestant godliness were increasing in the South. The message made evangelical profession and religious morality attractive, even essential. They were, as Thornwell put it, the only "conditions upon which we are authorized to hope for success."[33] Pro- or antislavery Protestant clergymen sought, like Thornwell, to point the way to ethical material prosperity. "Virtue is power" promised both that autonomy would conduce to moral order and that moral order would yield wealth. R.N. Sledd, the proslavery pastor of the Market Street Methodist Church in Petersburg, Virginia, during the height of the Civil War, put the matter bluntly: "perfect submission to the disposal of God . . . [offered the] surest way to secure the accomplishment of the end we seek. It is thus that we have access to his sympathy and exhaustless resources."[34] A success ethic, in other words, was not at odds with the evangelical ethic of self-restraint. Such credos came very close to the crassness of "justification by outcome" associated with utilitarianism and the secular success ethic of the capitalist industrial order. Yet, Thornwell, Sledd, and others arrived at and preached their message on religious grounds. Such a belief was possible because evangelicals had assimilated the materialism of utilitarian ethics into Protestant theological categories. Nineteenth-century evangelicals moralized economic rewards, linking morality with utility and self-interest. In so doing they dramatically modified important doctrines of the ethical self bequeathed by both the American Revolution and eighteenth-century Protestantism. After the Great Revival of 1801, southern evangelicals began to embrace a more expansive, near boundless, and rigidly moralistic view of national and individual potential than had been entertained by prior generations. "Force of character" became a southern evangelical and American obsession.

With the development of the market economy and spread of democratic ideology in the Jacksonian period,[35] evangelical and southern culture moved to a system of values based on this standard of *character*. A sense of the power of the individual to master passions and mold a distinct moral self dominated the cultural landscape. Southern ministers trumpeted their assurance that "nowhere on the face of the globe is so much energy of character displayed."[36] They preached that passions were to be subdued, if not crushed, by the "true" self. The character ethic demanded internalized moral control. Force of will would produce a conquering moral wholeness.

The evangelical character ethic anticipated hitherto unimaginable material and moral rewards. Like most antebellum moralists, North Carolina's inspector of public schools, Calvin Henderson Wiley, was not subtle about the nature of rewards that accrued to the virtuous. In "Protestant America," he wrote, the "Church [is] immediately paid in temporal benefits for its services: it receives an instant reward even in worldly blessings."[37] More typically, ministers bypassed the church and placed worldly rewards directly in the hands of individuals displaying moral character. "I repeat: every person who does his duty receives a perfect recompense this side of the grave," was the blunt refrain of Theodore Clapp.[38] Clapp, a theological radical in New Orleans, identified himself as a Unitarian and an evangelical defender of slavery. On the issue of rewards accruing to character, however, his position was indistinguishable from that of conventional evangelicals. H.A. Holmes, a Baptist proslavery minister from Virginia, echoed Clapp: "An act performed . . . from a sense of duty—God's favor and God's authority being properly recognized, cannot fail of its reward."[39] R.N. Sledd, in a widely circulated proslavery and pro-Confederate sermon, gave an even less qualified directive: "Godliness is profitable unto all things."[40]

The evangelicals' cheerful confidence in material rewards for virtue may seem paradoxical in light of the common perception of their disapprobation of worldly prosperity. Evangelicals' suspicion of wealth (particularly their own), of growth, and of control or distinction over others has often been exaggerated by historians who have taken their critiques of selfishness and materialism at face value.[41] Ubiquitous antebellum denunciations of selfishness rarely constituted normative critiques of wealth. Warnings were instead issued against the wrong *kind* of *self*: the weak-willed self that gave in to desire and the self of misguided will, as represented by those who did not acknowledge dependence on God for the power they attained. Lack of will and the case of the powerful man who "pretends to a character to which he is really a stranger,"[42] then, were perceived as the chief threats to the marriage of power and theistic virtue. Revivalist Daniel Baker preached a "both/and" solution to combat both dangers: "1.) It is the duty of every Christian to be a man of business. 2.) It is the duty of every man of business to be a Christian." Baker was a Calvinist. His message on the call to Christian commerce might well have taken on an absolutist and retributive tone. But Baker amended his statement above by assuring listeners that "it is a mistake that duties of religion conflict with life: they are perfectly harmonious."[43] Fellow Presbyterian proslavery minister and father of president Woodrow Wilson, Virginian Joseph Wilson, provided a more direct reconciliation of Christian faith and worldly life. "Christianity," he said, "made everything the best of its kind."[44]

Other evangelicals did not always share the Presbyterian educational background or need to address Calvinist doctrines, but they reached similar conclusions about wealth and moral duty. Plain-spoken Virginia Baptist

Jeremiah Jeter admired backwoods revivalists he had known in his 1810s childhood but criticized them for insisting on "preaching without fee or reward." Jeter thought the early revivalists' greatest strength—the simplicity of their message of faith and heartfelt emotion—was also a liability for ethical understanding.[45] By the time Jeter began to preach, southern Baptist leaders like Richard Furman were preaching "the importance of diligent improvement of all the means at our command." Furman's doctrine of wealth was little different from that of Presbyterian evangelicals like Baker. Furman said that "talents are to be improved. One has the talent of wealth. God has prospered him in the world."[46] Accompanying most antebellum moral pronouncements on selfishness was an obsession with the nature of this "right" to prosperity for the normatively positive self.

Evangelicals held that the real purpose of individual effort was the attainment not of wealth but of moral merit. Americans were not to amass fortune at the expense of building moral character. Evangelicals insisted that God never rewarded pursuit of self-interested ends nor of secular godless diligence even if it resulted in otherwise morally acceptable ends. By contrast, Revolutionary Era utilitarian ethics had generally held that private vice (self-interest) could lead to public virtue. Parts of the Constitution had reflected Madison's utilitarian outlook, an outlook shared in large part with southern Founding Fathers Washington and Jefferson, as well as New England Founders like Franklin. Selfish competition checked selfish competition in the separate branches of the federal government. Vice—selfishness—ended up producing virtue and a better government. For the Founding Fathers there was such a thing as a necessary, even beneficial, evil.

The post-Revolutionary generation of the 1830s modified Revolutionary formulas. Antebellum evangelicals removed vice from the picture altogether. Private virtues would produce public rewards. A scriptural proslavery tract written by Howell Cobb of Georgia described the theological mind set that supported the evangelical's ethical ideal: "However prudent and skillful we may be in the affairs of life, unless God's blessing be upon our efforts we cannot succeed; whenever therefore success attends our efforts we are to remember we are indebted to Providence for it."[47] This providential mind-set let evangelicals see themselves as moral agents engaged solely in acts of will that built character. They believed, therefore, that any success that came to them was wholly ethical. Rewards were morally earned through the virtue-power of character, morally obtained from God's providential hand. These carrot-and-stick theological ideas, with emphasis on the carrot, had an enormous impact on antebellum social relations and conflicts. Had so many Christians not been uncritically convinced that God's hand routinely dispensed material rewards, more realistic analysis of and practical steps to overcome moral, economic, and political dilemmas might have been possible before the Civil War. However, it is hard to imagine antebellum Americans (anymore than Americans in subsequent eras) abandoning a moralistic approach to social problems. Yes, the slavery crisis might have been less disastrous, but only if the whole development of American culture had been different. The laissez-faire evangelical ideology was just one version of Americans' suspicion of secular social analysis and planning. Antebellum evangelicals often sounded like later free market capitalists, indeed much like late nineteenth-century Social Darwinists who advocated laissez-faire policies. For antebellum ministers, "Providence" itself often came to denote the operation of divine social laws that must not be interfered with or questioned. The entire evangelical ethical imagination turned on the pivot of providentialist assumptions.

Evangelicals had a powerful sense that God was not an ineffable, airy phantom but an immanent governing power. They proclaimed that Providence worked in perfect harmony with free will. Georgian Howell Cobb's description of Providence was a typically flexible synthesis of God's and the individual's sovereign powers: "Providence may be defined to be God's care manifested in every circumstance and event, over and above all human sagacity and prudence. . . . Providence is a subject requiring the profoundest study: it neither forces human conduct nor prevents it."[48] Providentialism reflected the prevalent theory that God not only had created the universe but sustained it moment to moment.[49] Nothing occurred by chance. God handed out success and spankings in perfect accordance with the individual's moral choices. God's scheme of rewards and punishments, Providence, almost *was* God to antebellum evangelicals. Providence stood at the center of popular religious belief. Even Presbyterian James Henley Thornwell, the South's most sophisticated theologian, defined "atheism" as "ascribing to luck or chance or fortune, what has been brought about by the dispensations of His providence," and also as "worshiping self" by having "ascribed to myself, the Good I have received."[50] Southerners could worship this God of Providence and their own power and ambitions just so long as they "ascribed" the outcomes to God. A theologically minded Presbyterian or an ambitious plantation lord (though often one and the same person, or aspiring to be) could easily share the same providential language. Between 1831 and 1861 southerners solidified a culture that accomplished just that end—fuzzy moral ideology that brought regional unity and confidence. Theologically minded ministers did the bulk of the ideological work and sometimes had to accommodate their providential traditions to the tenor of the times.

While making adjustments to individual power, educated Presbyterian ministers, in particular, strove to maintain a Calvinist Providence and thereby turned a few theological cartwheels. Thornwell, like other Presbyterians, adhered to the Calvinistic Westminister Creed (1647) that stated, "God the great creator of all things, doth uphold, direct, and dispose, and govern all creatures, actions and things from the greatest to the least by His most wise and holy Providence." Presbyterians in the nineteenth-century South had accommodated their creed to increased autonomy and natural theology. Thornwell's colleague, Thomas Smyth of Charleston, echoed Howell Cobb in his insistence that even the men who wrote the Bible "were acted on by the spirit, were acted upon as free and intelligent agents, and not as unconscious and senseless tools."[51] Calvinists had never been as resigned to visitations of divine will as their opponents imagined. God may have brought storms, bountiful crops, or the death of a child, but the faithful had always looked for the *meaning* in these events rather than treating them with fatalistic acceptance. Calvin himself had asked, "What avails it, in short, to know a God with whom we have nothing to do? . . . Ignorance of providence is the greatest of all miseries and the knowledge of it the highest happiness."[52] Evangelical Calvinists extended their interpretation of divine intervention to the lives of individuals. James Henley Thornwell, the central figure in the southern branch of Old School Presbyterianism, presented the issue in stark terms and made theological concessions in his application of Providence to daily life. "Providence of God" to him was a "scheme" that was "not fixed but progressive" and spoke to the "circumstances of individuals."[53] Fellow Presbyterian Daniel Baker showed how this idea worked in practice. When a man he had just converted was killed by lightning while leaving a camp meeting, Baker gloried in how his convert had been rewarded and "called to heaven." When a popular Richmond theater, which Baker considered vulgar, burned to the ground killing 100 persons in 1811, he declaimed with evident satisfaction, "Hear ye the rod and who hath appointed it."[54]

Neither in public nor in their own writings did even conservative Presbyterians observe careful distinctions between God's intervening hand and natural law. They switched back and forth (often unconsciously) between the two depending on the lesson to be taught. In isolated communities, pockets of real providential fatalism certainly remained before the Civil War. Most evangelicals, however, rarely applied fatalistic or Calvinistic interpretations of Providence.[55] Evangelicals rarely expected miraculous divine intervention in events. God had a plan to teach individuals self-government, so Providence operated via consistent, practical principles that did not violate natural laws. Episcopal evangelical Stephen Elliot of Georgia flatly stated at the height of the Civil War, "God works by means, we must not expect in these days to receive help from Him through miracles."[56] In a popular vein, proslavery moralist John Fletcher of Louisiana simply said, "The Providence of God to man is practical."[57]

Evangelicalism's doctrinal flexibility allowed for a synthesis of Calvinist providentialism and the Revolutionary Era's emphasis on free will, natural law, and utility. William Buck, editor of *The Baptist Banner* of Kentucky, laid out this synthesis in stark form: "God has beneficent designs . . . to employ human instrumentalities."[58] God's design, in other words, involved precisely the plan to give self-disciplining Americans their free will and the individual power that went with its proper use. Like evangelicalism, providentialism was a descendant of both Puritanism and the eighteenth-century American Enlightenment, and therefore was not a precise phenomenon. Ambiguity allowed ministers from various denominations to emphasize different aspects of God's agency in the world, while compiling, despite the gamut of providential beliefs and attitudes in the antebellum period, a series of common conclusions about ethics. Individual moral choices and Providence worked together. Moral character found its reward from Providence; loss of character its punishment. Personal character, for the evangelicals, played as important a role in determining individual fate as did Providence.

A life, after all, was an arena in which Providence instructed character through a series of moral trials. An individual could be as powerful as Providence, if through self-control he aligned himself perfectly with God's will. For the man of character, therefore, the trial was relatively easy to bear and to uninitiated observers might even have appeared to be rigged.

The righteous would not find their ends frustrated by social forces greater than themselves, nor would they run up against "natural" barriers that checked their development.

The "righteous" in the evangelical system sound much like the "rich" or the "free market capitalists" of late nineteenth-century Social Darwinist economic theories. Antebellum evangelicals not only casually attributed market forces to Providence, but they thought of economics in providential terms. The antebellum evangelical outlook fostered later Darwinism (and its forerunner Malthusianism) and later capitalist ideology in America, but antebellum evangelicals did not understand what free market modern economists understand, nor did they think in their secular terms. They had blended some Revolutionary Era utilitarian theories and natural philosophies, like Adam Smith's, into their religious message, but secular economic doctrines were not compatible with their providential obsessions. Economic literacy eluded antebellum Americans of even the more sophisticated backgrounds. Religion still permeated education, and the industrial and free market systems still awaited their full blossoming (and intellectual scrutiny)—to come in the postbellum era. Ignorance bred license. The free market ethic lurked in evangelical moralizing and in providentialism, unchecked by strict analysis. Evangelicalism paved the way for later capitalist free market ideology, but antebellum ministers did not create apologies for the free market that they hardly knew was there. Evangelicals' economic innocence allowed their providential and moral speculations about American progress to be both rigidly didactic and almost miraculously exuberant about material prosperity. Providence and character stood at the center of the evangelical economic imagination. Secular free-market economics, based solely on the analysis of the selfish competition of individuals for material rewards in the marketplace, puzzled and offended southern evangelicals. Antebellum evangelicals accepted doctrines of Providence and traditions of natural theology that posited an immanent God within all practical processes and outcomes. Only God could bring virtue out of vice, good out of evil. Only He could design this benefit-generating economic machine that was neither intended by nor entirely understandable by any individual.

According to evangelicals, God used competing personal instincts and self-interested social competition to direct depraved men to virtue and the moral law. Amateur moral philosopher and proslavery pundit John Fletcher of Louisiana gave a careful description of how, under Providence, apparent "evils" were in fact "laws which are found to have a direct tendency to progressive improvement."[59] Because God was perfectly good, the "Chastenings of the Lord operate for the moral and mental and physical improvement of the chastised." Believing that God issued punishment but was always benevolent, Fletcher continued: "our idea of punishment is inadequate to express the full idea. . . . The law of God clothes the effect [of chastisement] in mercy and positive good . . . as schoolmaster to lead men back to virtue . . . if the mind cannot perceive the chastenings of the Lord are blessings, let it regard them as lessons. The whole Providence of God to man is upon this plan."[60] With recourse to the doctrine of Providence, evangelicals were able to insist that God was both absolutely benevolent and unfailingly just. Like the conversion experience, Providence overcame the conflict of evangelicals' simultaneous emphasis on human inadequacy (rooted in original sin) and on individual power in building character. "Let no one imagine that this position [agency] conflicts with the well-known fact that man is a fallen being. For although fallen he is still accountable," warned W.A. Smith of Virginia.[61] Calvin Henderson Wiley asserted that this aspect of Providence taught "a moral lesson, manifesting the innate depravity of man . . . and still advancing the general good of the world."[62]

Once the requisite moral lesson had been learned, an evangelical society could bypass the vice and the wasteful striving to satisfy the desire that Revolutionary Era utilitarians, like Madison and Adam Smith, had taken for granted. God's moral law, as revealed in the natural world through human striving, was more efficient than utilitarianism or the free market because it required less sinful blundering. Having willed himself into alignment with the moral law, evangelical man was no longer required to slam blindly into walls while working out his destiny through trial and error. Evangelicals bordered on positing a utilitarian God. Thornwell held that providences "have all been ordered for wise and beneficent results."[63] Fletcher likewise concluded that "providences of God collectively . . . terminate in the greatest good."[64] A local denominational paper, *The Baptist Banner* of Kentucky, was less philosophic about this point: "*God approves of that system of things which under the circumstances, is best calculated to promote the holiness and happiness of men.*"[65] Religious southerners admitted that they were often overwhelmed by "how directly God was working for their interest."[66]

As popular evangelicalism bluntly and often banally equated moral behavior and power, it stressed the unity of truth in almost all intellectual categories: reason and faith, science and exegesis, nature and theology, moral and political economy. In the antebellum period, even theologically orthodox ministers made casual concessions to rational doctrines.[67] Presbyterian Thomas Smyth, like most evangelicals, proved his points by appealing to "Natural causes ... or ... all-wise God leaving our readers to adopt either or both methods."[68] Smyth was flexible on this point because like all evangelical intellectuals he was sure "the Bible will be found equally harmonious with reason and science."[69] Protestant intellectuals assumed that all natural processes would manifest God's providential hand and that therefore few respectable scholars would embrace radical conclusions. All was well.

Evangelicals concluded that the will of God could be known through personal experience. Virginian W.A. Smith put it this way: "The will of God is the only rule of right. . . . That which in itself is *the right* is the will of God. . . . What then does he will? In regard to the present subject of inquiry, we can only judge that which he wills from that which he has done."[70] Physical and social phenomena were not a higher authority on the law than the Bible, but supplements through which God made known his ongoing plans for mankind. There were "two sources of the will of God . . . 1) revelation and faith. 2) . . . the observation of the facts uniformly developed in the material and moral world."[71] Like biblical and physical facts, moral "facts" could never contradict each other.

Evangelicals thought that punishment followed directly upon sin (or error), and reward upon virtue. Antebellum moralists believed that "Sins and afflictions are well understood to be always and inseparably connected as cause and effect."[72] The trained mind, in apprehending the cost of wrong action (sin), could apprehend a moral law from experience. The sinful was the impractical: every time I do X or see X done, bad consequences follow; therefore, doing X is a violation of God's moral law. In this way experience would eventually build up an accurate picture of the moral law. If character developed in accordance with it, personal improvement would inevitably follow. James Henley Thornwell cited such Scottish Common Sense philosophy as the basis of his claim that "Religion may be introduced as a matter of *science*." Thornwell thought this common-sense system was particularly useful for the teaching of "moral science" in public schools because "schools have a higher object, the formation of character."[73] Reason discovered laws of cause and effect—

the design of the physical world—but conscience or "moral sense" was the key to discovering the ethical laws through which nineteenth-century Providence acted specifically on *individuals.* The only moral law apprehended was, of course, "self-government."[74]

Evangelicals, like previous theological innovators, rewrote the moral lexicon. Character was the quality of self-control, the will that overcame desire. Conscience was the faculty that chose correctly between alternative selves. Conscience coordinated the operations of the mind and indicated the right and wrong selves for character to build on or destroy. Evangelicals' uncompromising denunciations of self-will and selfishness made little sense without this doctrine. Evangelical character, after all, was a powerful will and preoccupation with oneself. Conscience contained these energies and directed them to moral pathways. Conscience was "the moral and responsible agency" of the mind.[75]

By the 1830s American evangelicals had become preoccupied with combating moral and social disorder. Democratic self-reliance offered an opportunity for the practice of private vices. Evangelicals sensed a potential explosion of sin within strangers and explosion of chaos within the Republic, but their confident energies were directed toward raising a generation of disciplined Protestants, armored to face temptations. Jacksonian America directed moral and political campaigns against speculation, fashion, Sabbath breaking, ignorance of the Word of God, dueling, cruelty, idleness, secret societies, sexual indulgence, crime, disordered minds, and drunkenness.[76] Jacksonian evangelicals understood these problems not as demographic or economic phenomena but as the aggregate expression of the sinfulness of individuals. Their literature therefore emphasized moral cause and effect over analysis of social or material conditions. The strategy made sense on its own terms, for, as has been shown, evangelicalism offered believers direct access to and understanding of a God who had a specific plan for their every action. As their everyday project, evangelicals thought of themselves as moral agents building their powers of personal betterment. The rectification of society would be won, not through reasoned strategies or incremental programs, but through each convert's constant, intense study of himself. God came down to stand before each man and woman, walking beside them, writing on the blackboard of events, wielding the rod, pointing to opportunities for improvement. Increasingly self-conscious and independent Americans sustained a sense that God's Providence was directly involved in every individual's acts. They did not concentrate on His practical power to send storms or envision Him as a puppeteer controlling their actions, but rather stressed His constant moral guardianship.

Evangelical ethics absorbed the implications of political individualism as well as ethical individualism. Particularly in the South, members of evangelical denominations had participated in the American Revolution and absorbed the Lockean and Jeffersonian-Republican critique of centralized government.[77] In the 1850s southern evangelicals still routinely appealed to the authority of "the immortal Locke."[78] Baptist Iveson Brookes of South Carolina, typical in the antebellum period, denounced Jefferson's religious experimentation, but of "Mr. Jefferson's views on government," he maintained, "I have always been an admirer." They were, for Brookes, the foundation of "rational liberty . . . based in scripture." He rendered this judgment because Jefferson's political ideas had allegedly been influenced by his study of a Baptist church in Virginia.[79] Many evangelical ministers exaggerated the significance of this incident in Jefferson's intellectual heritage. They likewise accepted an exaggerated and moralized version of the Revolutionary attack on centralized authority and institutions.

For evangelicals and Jeffersonians alike, institutional structures necessarily undermined the efficacy of individuals. Institutions were government-created organizations (such as established churches) through which citizens passed and by which they were shaped.[80] Institutions, evangelicals feared, would diminish not liberty, but individual moral responsibility. This seeming rejection of liberty was countered by evangelical confidence that the American Revolution and Republican experiment had opened an institution-less field in which individual acts of moral self-denial would attain providential rewards. But even still, Godless thoughts, indulgence of passions, would of course bring punishment, which taught self-discipline. In short, the "natural" character of America's limited institutions mirrored Providence's system of rewards and punishments.

For southern evangelicals, the more obvious lesson taught by the Revolution was that institutional thought, to say nothing of institutions and institutional innovation, was no longer necessary. Individuals could make it on self-dependence alone. W.A. Smith proclaimed that "*Self-control*"[81] was the "influence of our free institutions or rather the tendency of the great principle of liberty (as embodied in our civil and religious institutions) which, with all true Americans, is a kind of instinctive belief."[82]

John Adger, an even more conservative antebellum proslavery minister and southern Presbyterian critic of human-rights philosophy, worshiped this aspect of the Revolution:"This progress of liberty it may well be the will of the Almighty Ruler to extend until free institutions become universal."This was practical wisdom. "Men," for Adger, were "nowhere on earth governed mainly by force. Moral means are mightiest."[83]

Moderate and less scholarly evangelicals, like Methodist minister Samuel Dunwoody of Kentucky, skipped anti-institutional poetics and cut right to the point:"the government of these United States . . . are of God."[84] Baptist William Buck, also of Kentucky, believed that "self-government" was "the Great Founder of nature's law." America could rest secure that in "Republics . . . in all ages of the world, God has intimated his preference for that system of government. . . . Moses gave to Israel the first model of representative government."[85] Political self-government was no more than the necessary first condition of establishing Providence as the only national institution. Methodist R.N. Sledd encouraged southerners in this work with descriptions of the rewards to follow:"If . . . we be qualified for self-government, and for the appreciation and enjoyment of the blessing of freedom: then we have an inalienable moral right to that state, and to the unmolested fruition of its advantages."[86] After the Revolution, the American political landscape was aligned with Providence, the dispenser of lessons, the perpetual motion machine designed at the creation but hindered throughout history by a myriad of flawed institutions. Once the Revolution had established a free providential government, Americans had only to behave well and then watch what was good prosper, and what was wicked decline.

Ministers took comfort in the belief that punishment for decreases in moral zeal would drive fallen citizens back to religious faith and moral responsibility.[87] An institution-less landscape offered no source of compulsion but God, and no locus of blame but the self. For many southern evangelicals, however, the development of liberty in America was not the progressive freeing of the self from institutions but the unfolding of revelation. Reverend John Adger, writing in the conservative *Southern Presbyterian Review* in 1849, explained the freedoms cited in Revolutionary documents:

All mankind have an inalienable right to obey God rather than man. This right can be invaded innocently by none—it can be surrendered innocently by none. If all mankind have a right to obey God, they have also a right to learn God's will, and so far it is true, as Doctor Wayland says, that "everyman's mind is his own."[88]

"Free my people from institutional dependence," Adger seemed to say, "that they may know God."

In the nineteenth century, as generations of evangelical Americans grew up under free institutions, the revolutionary experiment embodied in these institutions was often taken for granted. It had become a sacred reality—a cultural myth. One component of the myth, selected for sacralization by evangelicals, was America's free economy. This was the nation's great anti-institution. Before the Civil War few Americans thought of the economy as a free institution. Much as the Revolution had disestablished religion and put citizens under the governance of God's will, evangelicals assumed that economic systems had also been disestablished. Providence would unfailingly allocate the fruits of moral exertion and penalties of improvidence in the Republic. The economy was not an institution; it was simply God's economy. "The Divine Economy" was exactly the term William A. Smith attached to the providential system of worldly reward and punishment. The term "Divine Economy" was commonly used during the entire era. At the height of the disasters for the South during the Civil War in 1864, the Reverend W.E. Warren in Georgia was still promising southerners a "Vindication of the Divine Economy."[89] If Reverend Warren could be optimistic about the material rewards to come from the divine economy in Georgia in 1864, then the economic rewards imagined by southerners before the war must have been exuberant. They were, and the continuation and extension of slavery constituted only a part of a grander system of evangelical expectations about the divine economy and its providential rewards.

By the 1830s, westward expansion, the rapid development of infrastructure, and the burgeoning market economy provided overwhelming material evidence in support of evangelical confidence in the capacity of moral character to receive its reward from God.[90] It comes as no surprise, therefore, that evangelicals were obsessed with the providential and moral aspects of economics. For most Americans, Christian economics were the basis for understanding the political economy and for calculating self-interest.[91] The doctrine of Providence constituted the convention through which putatively self-less and otherworldly evangelicals could discuss their interests, responsibilities, and agency in the worldly economic universe. By and large, the same practical conclusions could be reached from "the principles of the divine economy" as from those of political economics and expediency.[92] The equation of these two modes of thought became apparent in the Jacksonian period and was expressed in the popular assertion that morality was power, that virtue brought reward.[93]

Southern evangelical ministers saw political economy as yet another branch of science manifesting the unity of truth. The absolute morality and rationality of God extended to America's economy. The economy was therefore a source of authority.[94] In his religious tracts and moral philosophy W.A. Smith settled controversies on this basis. "Principles of political economy alone considered . . . settle this question,"[95] as he was fond of pointing out. He shored up his evangelical credentials, however, by adding that "from well-established principles of political economy, it is *morally* certain."[96] Factual and moral certainty appeared together in every evangelical argument.[97] Most ministers appealed directly to the divine economy, bypassing political theories. The natural, providential economic system was the only legitimate system: "By the sphere of fervid and rigid economic systems, the most salutary influence of human agency is destroyed," an anonymous southern minister told the *New York Daily Times*. "It is sheer tyranny to interfere with its spontaneous operation. It is the steady corrective if left to its direct agency."[98] Many whose names *are* known would heartily agree.

In an America free of institutions, individual and national benefits—economic, political, and even religious—were automatically received in direct proportion to the individual's degree of alignment with God's will. "In a free country, upright, generous, pure, disinterested principles must of necessity triumph over those which are narrow, selfish and unrighteous,"[99] as Louisianian Theodore Clapp insisted. This applied as well to religion: "It is perfectly safe in a free country to tolerate all forms of religion, because the principle of reverence in man, uninfluenced by coercion, can never lead to any species of immorality. If Roman Catholics become more numerous in this republic than any other sect, the fact will prove conclusively the superiority of their teachings." He added, of course, that such an outcome was "hardly possible" and that the "protestant denominations" would carry the day.[100]

The obvious material and physical success of Protestant morality, rather than its number of church members, captured the imagination of the generation.[101] Josiah Priest, a self-educated harness maker and popular publisher of proslavery exegetical guides in the South, included hosannas in his books for the situation he perceived in America: "In the short period of a day . . . the magic wand of science and Christianity are waved over the great wilderness," which has thereby "disappeared."[102] Antebellum southern evangelicals were not like the Bible Belt fundamentalists who rejected and feared progress and technology in the early twentieth century. Many southern antebellum ministers used technological metaphors to illustrate the power of Providence against human efforts to seek, analyze, or dictate economic outcomes. "Steam, in all its applications, was argued against and rejected; yet it has prevailed. So the electric telegraph," Frederick Ross reminded Alabamians.[103] Virginia Baptist Jeremiah Jeter tried to settle a biblical dispute over whether or not laughing was forbidden by scripture (Jesus never laughed) with an appeal to a familiar, more acceptable act: "He never traveled in a railway car or in a steamboat, but that fact furnishes no reason why we should not do it."[104] Such logic defies refutation.

Material and economic advancements were important primarily because of their illustration of individual moral progress. "If we are teachable," Calvin Wiley told southerners, "this wilderness will lead us to our vineyards."[105] As the wilderness dramatically disappeared, the conclusion that Americans were learning their moral lessons well was hard to resist. Material advances were further proof, hardly needed by ecstatic converts, that "it is in the moral view that our national superiority stands forth prominent." As one proslavery evangelical put it: to "the great question: Is man capable of self-government?" the answer "of the generation [was] – Onward!"[106] Evangelicals described America as a naturally operating and fully moralized meritocracy.

Southerners assumed that the Revolution had established an institution-less order in which God and the individual were the only loci of social power. The economic inequities bred by this order were not merely assumed to be "natural," as Marx pointed out, but were taken as the index of individual moral power. Cultural and ideological analyses derived from European categories and social divisions, whether Marxian or otherwise, never yield satisfying representations of "conservative" Americans.[107] This is particularly true in descriptions of the early nineteenth century, when many southern conservatives subscribed to democratic and progressive doctrines that gave pause to some British liberal intellectuals and reformers. Southerners were conservative insofar as they thought the divine economy to be an uncomplicated reality not requiring analysis. They were satisfied with the status quo, but the status quo had a progressive, individualistic, and almost anarchic character. Southern ministers, however, exuded confidence that God held it all together and guaranteed both the moral and practical progress of the American system—it was God's system. The majority of southerners, like antebellum Americans in general, wanted progress, but they inflexibly insisted on the preeminence of character and did not really know how the engines of technology and the market ran. They merely preached the "practical points of morality, such as justice, sobriety, chastity, fidelity, honesty, industry, obedience," and assumed that the divine economy would allocate compensation fairly.[108] Evangelicals claimed that unfettered American institutions and individual improvement would by their very nature overcome any difficulty. This was the dominant *national* position. The evangelical culture of simple faith in a divine economy did, however, resonate most widely in the South.

Southern culture, for the most part, was evangelicized after the American Revolution. As a result, early nineteenth-century religious doctrines became the cornerstone of the region's popular morality and social thought. The groundwork had been laid for unquestioning acceptance of personal conversions and understandings of scripture. The apologies of natural theology and Common Sense philosophy bolstered evangelical theology with similarly simple articles of faith. Most important, the American Revolution established belief in a starkly individualistic society as the hallmark of national character. Evangelical ministers amended this belief with their assumptions about God's providential power. These doctrines were more than elitist pronouncements, more than pulpit aphorisms. They were rooted and revealed in popular culture. Southerners who had neither heard of W.A. Smith, Theodore Clapp, or James Henley Thornwell, nor listened very carefully to a local minister, knew that they could make moral judgments based on the pure force of their individual character. More fundamentally, they knew that no earthly source of judgment was superior to their own. The unity of truth assured that faith, the moral rules of the Bible, and the material world would justify their position. God, the moral good, and the material goodies flowed one from the other through the conduit of the individual.

A national or regional worldview based on evangelical morality may appear to have been too riddled with the potential for anarchical disaster; too laced with confused, crass reasoning; too dependent on individual character; and too optimistic to have ever been espoused by rational men. But it is important to remember that the leading religious and academic minds of the age were even *more* likely to present moral and social ideas in these terms than were stump preachers and politicians or self-interested slave traders. Evangelical moralists endowed these individualistic American doctrines with the authority of philosophic science and incontrovertible theological laws.[109] Henry May, the great intellectual historian of the twentieth century, reached the inevitable conclusion when he analyzed this didactic form of moral science—based in evangelical cosmology and democratic free enterprise—that dominated America in the 1830s: "At its worst American moralism could justify anything."[110]

Evangelical ministers categorically stated, of course, that the divine economy would never serve a secular end, especially one that undermined individual agency. Still, their faith that God would never vindicate selfishness allowed them to come very close to legitimizing an ethic of pure self-interest. The distinction between "virtue is power" and "outcomes of power are virtuous" was never drawn carefully prior to the Civil War. A sacralization, not a mere defense, of slaveholding was implicit in the moral discourse that promoted this confusion.

2

The Post–1831 Birth of
Evangelical Proslavery

Americans regarded slaveholding as a vaguely moral sign of success long before the antebellum period. Slaves first arrived in the colonies in 1619, and by the time of the Revolution there were slaveholders in twelve of the thirteen colonies. From Aristotle to Locke, from Moses to George Whitefield, slaveholding had been accepted as a legitimate exercise of power; the burden of proof was therefore on those who opposed it.[1] Abolitionists had to articulate every step of their outrage for themselves, whereas by the end of the eighteenth century all theoretical elements needed for the defense of racial slaveholding were already available to the prospective Western apologist.[2] In the nineteenth century, the case for the defense was advanced further by thorough and zealous advocates from south of the Mason-Dixon Line.[3] Evangelical language of morality and concepts of power gave new life to the claim that good men could hold slaves. Slaveholding was a traditional mark of success, and a moral defense of slavery was implicit whenever Americans who considered themselves good Christians held slaves. By the 1830s, such men lived primarily below the Mason-Dixon Line. Evangelical moral ideology coalesced and attained ascendancy in the South between 1801 and 1831, sacralizing regional realities.

The southern proslavery ideology evolved through a process involving self-recognition, gradual declaration of long-implicit attitudes, historic developments, and everyday experience in the slaveholding states.[4] Beginning slowly after the American Revolution and unfolding with increased visibility and intensity between 1831 and the Civil War, a self-conscious proslavery society arose in the Cotton South. Although a forth-right and intense attachment to slaveholding appeared at times as a remnant of an outdated patriarchal ideal, the unique feature of southern proslavery was its emergence within the antebellum culture of competitive indi-vidualism. A Protestant culture founded on individuals with strong per-sonal commitments to slaveholding existed nowhere else on earth. The addition of the moral energy and intensity of evangelicalism to the southern formula made it more remarkably unique. Moral and biblical justifica-tions of slaveholding constituted the first, and remained the most widely disseminated, foundation of southern proslavery.[5] It would be hard to exaggerate the importance of ethical and exegetical arguments in solidi-fying the South in defense of slaveholders' rights and righteousness. Such arguments were the basis for a popular proslavery bond, the heart of the consensus which made the sectional crisis possible.[6]

Most ministers who galvanized southern moral support for slaveholding denied that they were "proslavery."[7] The moniker fits none-theless. These men repeatedly insisted that good Christians could hold slaves, that slaveholding was moral, and that virtuous acts could result in one's becoming a slaveholder. Secular proslavery spokesmen also held that slaveholding often had progressive, practical results. Good slaveholders, they maintained, gave the institution its character—that is, goodness. As moral individuals, they were more powerful than institutions. This for-mulation allowed proslavery spokesmen to denounce the historically evil institution of slavery while defending southern practices: slaveholders in the evil form of slavery were bad men; the southerners were good, and the source of their wealth therefore untainted.[8] Good—and especially evangelical—slaveholders supposedly redeemed the institution of slavery. The consequences of this simple apology for individual slaveholders were profound. Any understanding of antebellum proslavery must begin here.

Evangelical proslavery centered on the moral defense of slaveholders— a stance that still provides the clearest distinction between proslavery and antislavery camps. Racism was at the heart of southern proslavery, but it was also at the heart of antebellum culture South and North. Antebellum white Americans defined and denigrated blacks in ways that advanced their own interests and confirmed their understandings of themselves.[9]

Virulent racism did not prevent Americans from opposing slavery, but a belief that slaveholders had good, Christian character usually did prevent a citizen—North or South—from attacking slavery.[10] Biblical accounts of God's ordination of slavery among his chosen people in the Old Testament and of righteous men's holding of slaves impressed Jews, Catholics, Lutherans, Congregationalists, and a variety of biblically traditional sects with and without attachments to slavery.[11]

The first concession of evangelical denominations to the morality of slavery appears in an eighteenth-century decision that converted slaveholders were not necessarily committing sin.[12] In 1831 abolitionists declared themselves by refusal to grant this concession. These pressures came to a head and divided the nation when the question arose as to whether slaveholding would be allowed in western territories. Protestant moralism had been providing the language used by antebellum Americans to discuss power and wealth. Now erstwhile theoretical debates concretely focused on the status of new territory and the acquisition of wealth. Was slaveholding, then, a natural, moral form of success? Could a region occupied by slaveholders and slaves be consistent with Providence? Could slavery coexist with, even promote, self-government? These were the practical points on which Americans divided into opposing camps.

Southerners' affirmative answers to these questions were, in the main, pragmatic, even eclectic, rather than theoretical and dogmatic. They reflected a surprising variety of positions, rarely defending slavery in the abstract or as a positive good, but abandoning the plea, influenced by the Enlightenment and dominant during the Revolution, that slavery was a necessary evil.[13] The rubrics of the Enlightenment meant little to southerners, influenced as they were by evangelicalism. For them, slavery as an abstract "social system" could never be a good in itself; good was the attribute of a particular sort of converted individual. Revolutionary-era and political moralists spoke of "necessary evils," but in evangelicals' uncompromising moral cosmology, evil was neither necessary nor tolerable. Necessity was dictated by Providence, to which no evil could be attributed.

Evangelical moral philosophy led the antebellum shift toward a less compromised, more ideological defense of slaveholding. This new stance constituted a practical, logical advancement of the political and evangelical accommodation to slavery made at the Constitutional Convention. In the late eighteenth century, most Americans believed that slavery, as institutionalized dependence, was neither good nor practical, and so would fade before the action of natural forces under the new, free political system.[14] In the new United States, what was good would prosper and what was evil would fail as Providence was given free reign to teach its moral lessons. Americans did not need a plan to end slavery or any other social problem. They merely had to remove the barriers to the American God's plan—whether they were centralized government interference, the international slave trade, or state monopolies—and then step back and let Providence and individuals' moral character work their magic. In 1790, as the North outlawed slavery, as southern slavery became less profitable with the decline in tobacco cultivation, and as southern Founding Fathers gradually emancipated their slaves and formed antislavery "colonization" societies, slavery appeared on its way to a natural death. An admitted "evil," slavery appeared rightfully doomed in the free land where the only king was God, and His providence ruled. Slavery was impractical. No further steps need be taken on the subject in the land where good was to succeed and evil to fail.

Intellectual developments and massive unforeseen events between the Revolution and the antebellum explosion of proslavery publications undermined Revolutionary-era arguments in both the North and South. The cotton gin's advent in 1793 and the massive boom economy, the rapid expansion of settlement over the Appalachian Mountains, the rapid growth of the white and black populations, and the growth of evangelical revivalism in the South after 1801 fundamentally changed the Revolutionary formulas and assumptions about southern slavery. Cultural and ideological changes between 1790 and 1831 influenced attitudes toward slavery just as profoundly. Nineteenth-century providentialism, for example, formalized the Revolutionary-era appeal to practicality. For the providentialist, social and economic advances were indications of divine will, and the resultant power was regarded as the fruit of proper moral organization. Necessity and evil were divorced.[15] America's rage for the emergent science of political economy in the late 1820s was due largely to this newly compelling vision of necessity. Free market economic laws were quickly evangelicalized by identification of them with God's inexorable purposes.[16]

In the South, political economist Thomas R. Dew (of William and Mary) was the central articulator and popularizer of these rapidly coalescing languages of economics and evangelicalism.[17] In 1832 he published a description of the economic and moral necessity of slavery. Other southerners saw in Dew's proslavery a confirmation of their certainty that southern slaveholders were "sanctioned by divine authority" and "the great *law* of necessity."[18] His "simple statistics" provided a powerful tool enabling a fleet of southern ministers to hear the voice of God in popular economic science. Hailing the economic course of Providence discovered by Dew, they defended slavery against a newly mature abolitionism.

Dew, immersed as he was in British economics, was a cogent interpreter of the economic and social life experienced by his generation of southerners. During the first thirty years of the century, the cotton economy, the slave population, and the evangelical movement had all grown at tremendous rates. Looking back on this prosperity from the 1830s, as Dew did, evangelical southerners saw new and incontrovertible evidence of divine pleasure. To their minds, evil practices were destined to reveal their true faces and fail, and were therefore impractical. Yet slaveholding had become more practical (profitable) after both the Revolutionary settlement and the close of the slave trade in 1808. Could it then be evil?[19] More important to evangelicals, after the Great Revival of 1801 they saw the most worldly and unchurched part of the country, home to genteel elitists and the deistic Jefferson who once said Unitarianism would be the regional creed, become a bastion of evangelical orthodoxy.[20] Whether these phenomena were viewed as practical results or providential miracles, southerners took them as vindications of slaveholding.

This comfortable position particularly affected evangelicals who had expressed doubts about slavery through their participation in the colonization movement, centered in the South before 1830.[21] Many proslavery spokesmen maintained that they had been converted to a defense of slavery from earlier uncertainty about it.[22] After the Revolution, many southern evangelicals and enlightened members of the slaveholding elite, Jefferson among them, had harbored strong reservations about slavery. These groups were not hostile to slaveholders themselves, nor were they promoters of emancipation. They did suspect, however, that slavery brought the corruptions of luxury and institutionalized power, and thereby the threat of socio-economic decay. And they knew for certain that slaveholding brought unwanted association with blacks. The colonization movement provided a popular refuge for such southerners. Dew's main feat in 1832 was his unmasking of the impotence and impracticality of this already fading program.[23] It was apparent to Dew that God was frustrating the antislavery movement at every turn while blessing the kingdom of cotton and evangelicalism, which was spreading across the land with an ease that had to be divinely inspired. He found the only parallels for such success in the rise of the nation of Israel from the slaveholder Abraham and in the story of his descendants who emerged from the wilderness to forge a slaveholding kingdom.[24]

Despite the South's enthusiastic defense of slavery and its own righteousness after 1832, southerners rarely justified slavery in the abstract or as a "positive good." A number of reactionary proslavery ministers, sociologists, and economists (though initially not Dew) did take historical and biblical arguments that favored the South as proof of not just the defensibility, but the necessity of the institution of slavery in a viable Christian society.[25] They argued that a just and practical society could not exist without slavery. At the time of the Revolution, these conservative advocates of slavery as a "positive good" and model of hierarchical social relations denounced Jeffersonian individualism and Revolutionary misgivings about southern slavery. In the antebellum period, their isolated reactionary intellectual progeny defended slavery as the necessary cornerstone of the Republic.[26] In the proslavery mainstream, however, evangelical and democratic optimism reigned. For the vast majority of white southerners, the status of slavery would be determined by the progress and judgment of a moralized free economy. Thomas R. Dew showed the way in 1832 by showing how God's law, modern progress, territorial expansion, evangelical expansion, individual liberty, and profit all favored southern slavery. Following Dew's lead, the evangelical proslavery mainstream would be optimistic and flexible about democratic institutions and the future of slavery. Slavery never constituted a "positive good," a superior or necessary basis for society, for Dew or southern evangelicals, but Dew showed in 1832 that, after two generations of change, the Revolutionary formulas and vague southern "antislavery" tradition no longer had much relevance.

While antebellum southerners usually rejected a "positive good" defense of slavery, southerners also rejected the Founding Fathers' so-called necessary evil compromise with slavery. Dew and the evangelicals rejected the terminology but retained most of the practical conclusions of Revolutionary formulas on slavery. Providentialism and evangelical ethics based on individual character gave southerners a way to attach evil to slavery and criticize it *in the abstract.* Providentialism enabled southerners to denounce the slave trade, non-southern slavery, and the abuses of slaveholding in the South as acts of evil men while maintaining that these sins did not reflect on the virtuous intentions, acts, and power of Christian slaveholders.[27] To the proslavery mainstream, the activity of individual southern slaveholders was positively good, and slavery was defended *in the particular*—as it was practiced in the South among evangelicals who understood the providential economy.

Evangelical moralism dominated proslavery after 1831, but southern spokesmen, following Dew's lead, incorporated traditional defenses of slavery into their contemporary arguments. The antebellum view of the question of the morality of slavery was informed by long-standing proslavery notions—biblical, racial, and philosophic. Evangelical ministers, in particular, blended some old arguments into the very different context of their moralism, regionalism, and emphasis on individual power. Defenses of slavery, when provided at all, had always been easiest to undertake in static, hierarchical societies with long-established legal structures and traditions of class deference—an ideal to which pre-Revolutionary southerners aspired, even if they did not realize it. The early literature of proslavery was written by persons for whom the virtues of such social arrangements were self-evident. Many of them felt their interests or emotional well-being threatened by democratic social change. Proslavery arguments were first published in the Boston area in 1701 and later issued elsewhere in the North—the center of education and publishing in colonial America. Puritans and the preachers of the eighteenth century's Great Awakening, like George Whitefield, took comfort in panacean visions in which masters beneficently guided their slaves out of heathenism. Writers in the North continued to defend slavery long after it was abolished there in the Revolutionary Era. The institutionalized privilege and social subordination inherent in slavery were attractive to wealthy, vocal minorities North and South, particularly after the Revolution. They found themselves in a society they did not entirely comprehend but in which they felt the status and ideals most regarded as their birthright might be taken away. Between 1790 and 1831, most of the published proslavery tracts in the United States came from this reactionary, threatened, and increasingly irrelevant elite (often members of the fading Federalist Party). The torrent of evangelical proslavery after 1831 would drown out the last trickles of this minor tradition.

The body of proslavery literature did not accumulate steadily from colonial times until the Civil War. Before and during the antebellum period, slaveholding was rarely questioned where it was economically viable, and therefore required no defense. Guilty consciences were rare. Proslavery publications were usually responses to criticism. Silence, however, was the norm. Proslavery declarations usually took the straightforward form of slaveholding. This proslavery argument, widespread and consistent over long periods, rarely included any apology for the practice.

Antebellum evangelicals, like the earliest American proslavery publicists in Puritan New England, were familiar with racist and biblical justifications for slaveholding that pervaded Western culture. Racist religious ideologies based on scripture, such as the so-called curse of Ham in Genesis 9, were used to justify enslavement of Africans before slavery was instituted in America.[28] Puritan minister Thomas Saffin's 1701 presentation of Bible passages inaugurated and typified the exegetical legitimations of slaveholding in America.[29] His scriptural references would be repeated ad nauseam by antebellum southern evangelicals. They repeatedly pointed out that the God of the Old Testament had sanctioned slaveholding. After all, his prophets, patriarchs, and chosen people all held slaves: Noah condemned Ham's descendants to slavery, two Decalogue commandments affirmed the master-slave relationship, and Leviticus 25 gave license to the holding of foreigners in perpetual bondage. Like all subsequent biblical proslavery writers, Saffin gave greatest emphasis to Pauline acknowledgments that slavery was consistent with Christianity (Ephesians 6), thus creating a New Testament link to the innumerable Old Testament passages.[30]

Two exegetical arguments that greatly impressed nineteenth-century proslavery apologists, however, were largely ignored by Saffin: although he preached in a slaveholding society, Jesus never condemned slavery; and Paul, in his letter to Philemon, sent a runaway slave back to his master. The Puritan writers, like Saffin and Cotton Mather, made scant use of these passages because they did not foresee the need to answer a critique of slavery by modern abolitionists who were Christian perfectionists. Nor did they recognize in Philemon a biblical parallel to the Constitution's fugitive slave law. Such exegesis awaited ministers attuned to the Bible as a primer for the design of a new society. Saffin and Mather, like their successors, emphasized passages pertinent to their age, the problems of which were of no concern to the evangelicals who later defended slavery.

The Puritans read Paul's analogy between man's body and the Church in 1 Corinthians 12 as a sanction of social organicism, ecclesiastical authority, and socio-political hierarchy. "God hath set," according to Saffin, "different Orders and Degrees of Men in the World, both in Church and Commonweal."[31]

The eighteenth-century brand of proslavery was doomed by the Great Awakening and the American Revolution, even if slavery was not.[32] Saffin's and Mather's proslavery writings were almost forgotten, and their isolated ideological descendants had to adapt traditional proslavery hierarchicalism to a critique of contemporary democratic impulses. In New England during and after the Revolution, the defense of slavery was taken up by occasional writers more interested in maintaining traditional social and intellectual hierarchies than in preserving slavery. Congregational and Episcopal ministers, for example, made a case for limits on Revolutionary dismantling of social distinctions (limits which would protect their own status) by playing on nascent fears about emancipation. In one of the few published debates of the 1770s containing a formal defense of slavery, Harvard graduate Theodore Parsons, wishing to demonstrate the consequences of overstepping conservative limits on the natural-rights philosophy of the rebellion, evoked the images of masses of freed blacks and of amalgamation. Manipulation of the slavery issue—hardly the issue itself—enabled Parsons to demonstrate that hierarchy and "degrees of authority and subordination" were essential to a properly ordered society.[33] Although the outcome of the Revolutionary War and the process of emancipation in the North undercut Parsons's traditional proslavery premises, diehard northern Federalists in the 1790s and after made similar appeals.[34]

Traditional proslavery dialectics resurfaced among northern clerical elites only after 1830. Like Federalists and conservative nationalists who favored slaveholding, antebellum northerners spoke out for it in order to protect and promote interests concomitant to slavery, namely biblical traditionalism, and social and theological authority. John Henry Hopkins, Episcopal Bishop of Vermont; John Hughes, Bishop of New York and leader of the Catholic hierarchy; and Old School theologians like Princeton's President Charles Hodge wistfully extolled the "grand system of ORDER and GRADATIONS and mutual dependence" found still in slavery but rare elsewhere in an era of national religious and democratic experimentation.[35]

Appeals to the fading strain of proslavery hierarchicalism and institutionalism continued to be heard through the Civil War, but there was little popular commitment to them.[36] The paucity of formal defenses of slavery between 1790 and 1820, and the decline among northern elites clinging to those that did appear, indicated that the tradition some had hoped would be the basis of a national proslavery ideology was losing authority. The history of proslavery publications before the antebellum period reveals an aspect of northern social conservativism. Southern proslavery during that period was expressed in the daily practice of race control and in modes of economic production that were time-honored elements of the region's Revolutionary Republicanism. A southern proslavery ideology was not articulated until nineteenth-century liberal doctrines were absorbed into the region. As long as the defense of slavery was associated with traditional social conservatism, few Americans made an overt commitment to the institution.

An isolated burst of proslavery writing in Charleston after the failure of the Denmark Vesey slave insurrection of 1822 revealed that while traditional proslavery ideas persisted, doubts about them had arisen during the protracted time of relative silence. When new voices broke that silence neither Revolutionary-era acceptance of slavery as a necessary evil nor patriarchal, hierarchical appeals to social order satisfied them. Among the first proslavery pamphleteers of the nineteenth-century South was Richard Furman (1755–1825). His *Exposition of the Views of Baptists* (1823) presented the most important proslavery statement to come out of Charleston in the 1820s. His work anticipates the new defense of slaveholding as moral that was to prevail in the Old South. The Baptist minister formulated the long implicit reconciliation of slavery with the Revolutionary heritage that would be perfected and popularized by Thomas R. Dew in Virginia after Nat Turner's slave revolt eight years later. Furman wrote in order to propagate his denomination's views and to reassure Charleston's leaders that Christians could be counted on to support slavery despite the religiously inspired Vesey plot. Evangelicals like Furman, a slaveholder and a central figure in the Baptist movement in the South, had much explaining to do.[37] The Baptist and Methodist churches had far more black communicants than any other group and so were more likely to be associated with the "*African* Christians" of the conspiracy. The pamphlet expounding Furman's views, solicited by Governor John L. Wilson, was widely distributed in the city.[38]

The peculiar and local Charleston circumstances that prompted Furman's *Exposition* guaranteed that his pamphlet—like other proslavery documents of the time and place—would not reach a wide audience and would address some concerns not reappearing in the later antebellum tidal wave of ministers writing proslavery. Tension between populist evangelicals and the governing elite had largely diminished in the South as a whole by 1823 and would dissolve altogether after the 1830s, but the old frictions still smoldered in Charleston when Furman issued his pamphlet. Sensitive to the sore spots of his dual audience, Furman occasionally subjugated issues of morality and policy to those of civil authority.[39] This move involved some hedging, as ever fewer southern evangelicals could agree that slavery was a purely civil concern. Evangelicals were increasingly reluctant to concede moral authority to the government as God's representative on earth or to maintain that the spirituality of the church removed political questions from the purview of church members or ministers. Standards of right conduct and social, political, and religious organization were increasingly judged by the degree to which they originated from and supported the actions of autonomous individuals. Furman's arguments for slavery mostly reflected this trend, which was the logical result of evangelical and Revolutionary accommodations to slaveholding.

Many of Furman's statements offer the first formal glimpse of the arguments that proslavery spokesmen would repeat and expand after 1830. The morality of slaveholding, for example, was a dominant concern of both Furman's work and that of the antebellum era generally.[40] He said he wrote to show that the "Providence of God" had saved Charleston from the slave revolt and needed to be "acknowledged for the future protection of the city," and to put forth "the moral and religious view" of slaveholding to "the satisfaction of scrupulous consciences."[41] The "necessary" evil defense was inadmissable on these terms. "To pious minds," Furman reported, "it has given pain to hear men, respectable for intelligence and morals, sometimes say that holding slaves is indeed indefensible, but that it is necessary and must be supported. . . . On this principle mere politicians, unmindful of morals may act."[42] Realizing that a less compromising ground was needed for scrupulous consciences, Furman was forthright in his insistence that a master might hold slaves "according to Christian principle" and that evil attached to slavery only through "the individual who abuses his authority."[43] This dissolution of the meaning of institutions into the discreet acts and circumstances of individuals became more pronounced in the rhetoric of antebellum proslavery.

The evolving argument took advantage of the moral code of the New Testament, which justified preoccupation with personal intent.[44] Therefore, while traditional biblical arguments focused on the sanction of slavery as a social arrangement, Furman paid more attention to duty under specific circumstances than to generalized roles. The difference between the two approaches was exemplified in his treatment of the Golden Rule. If the New Testament were to be interpreted in support of slavery, that doctrine had to be rendered equivocal. This was usually accomplished through insistence that the Golden Rule never applied to what Furman called "the order of things" or to assigned social status.[45] Under Furman's Golden Rule, a judge would not have to let a robber go free just because the judge would wish to go free if their positions were reversed. Likewise, a master was to do to slaves "what were he a slave [he] could consistently wish to be done to himself [as a slave]."[46] Such rhetorical shell games were traditional in the antebellum South.

Yet Furman's particular attention to the Golden Rule was new to proslavery. His essay demonstrated how, before its clash with perfectionist abolitionism, evangelical moral language required that the question of slavery must be worked out by southerners, especially by Christian slaveholders, within the framework of an individual ethic. Evangelicals saw slavery as a relation between morally responsible agents. "Though they are slaves," Furman wrote, "they are also men: and are with ourselves accountable."[47] This was no boon to slaves, regardless of its theoretical advance in recognition of their humanity, for to white minds it saddled slaves with the burden of moral responsibility within the institution. Furman's application of the Golden Rule was a case in point. He believed that "our desires do [should] not become a standard to us."[48] In other words, it might be generous for a master to free his slaves and natural for a slave to want freedom, just as felons, children, poor farmers, and even proslavery ministers would like others to make their lives easier, but such desires did not constitute a rule that placed obligation on others.[49] On the contrary, people were responsible for bearing their own burdens. They *should not* seek after "comfort or to mitigate the inconveniences of life" except when comfort came from curbing desire, facing responsibilities, and building moral character.[50]

Antebellum southern whites—even the nonreligious—did not acknowledge comforts and advantages as such. For them, what might appear to the envious and ignorant poor as the blessings of arbitrary fortunes were in fact the natural outcomes of virtue. The good man should no more revel in them than he would in the correct answer to a mathematical problem. Slaves and opponents of slavery would do well to stop bellyaching and work out their own salvations with the materials afforded them by Providence, which was all their masters had done. Furman and a host of antebellum southerners countered antislavery applications of the Golden Rule by saying in effect, "If I were a slave I would not expect my master to free me." In other words, "Do unto your neighbor as he would have done unto him if he knew what he should and might reasonably want done." In making this argument, southern evangelicals were not simply offering a cynical standard for Christian slaves but were stating the evangelical understanding of human action quite apart from the slavery issue. The evangelical project involved the denial of personal desire and the discernment of the divine will for every action. Evangelicals—ministers in particular—tried to convince themselves that this was the basis of all their conduct. They prayed, "Thy, not my, will be done."

Why should not slaves be expected to follow the same rule of life as did the ministers (and be faulted in so far as they did not)? It might be natural to assume that the ruling race stressed the rewards of renunciation of gain and acceptance of the rigors of labor only when they needed to justify keeping slaves in their place, but it should be said—in noting the deadly seriousness and commitment behind the seemingly most outrageous proslavery arguments—that evangelical spokesmen often took a similar approach to their own positions in the moral and political economy. Proslavery minister Basil Manly made a characteristic comment in his diary that it seemed "a prodigious slavery to be a pastor of a city church these days," and James Henley Thornwell made a similar comment in a private letter: "It [his divinity school job] is to me a dungeon, and I go to its duties like a slave whipped to his burden. Nothing keeps me there but the fact that God's Providence has put me there, and I am Afraid to leave without some marked intimation of the Divine will. Perhaps a day of greater usefulness may come; or perhaps the Almighty may open a way for my escape."[51] Not surprisingly, neither Thornwell nor Furman thought he was obligated to release his slaves.

Furman's *Exposition* gives some of the first signs that evangelicals were

forming an ideology of slavery consonant with their religious individualism and views of moral obligation. His ideas were unoriginal, but their
context and the energy of his exposition were new. Furman was working
toward the "moral and religious view" of the issue that would comple-
ment southern views on individualism and freedom. In two unique features of proslavery in the Old South, many defenders of slavery defined
the institution in contractual terms, and a majority thought slavery would
end naturally at some point.[52] Their arguments resulted from their definition of slavery as a relation between morally responsible beings and, as
such, a valid byproduct of democratic development.

Despite his unique situation, Furman anticipated these positions.
Furman, writing before abolitionist criticism and mostly for conservative
Charlestonians, was willing to appeal to traditional visions of slavery, and
of the plantation as a "little community." Yet the models of voluntary
society and abstract freedom of individuals were already appearing in
Furman's *Exposition*. According to Furman, slavery achieved what was
accomplished "in a free community, by taxes, benevolent institutions,
bettering houses, and penitentiaries." He granted that no one had a right
to enslave another man, but pointed out that a man may "be divested of
it [liberty] by his own consent, directly or indirectly given."[53] Furman's
definition of freedom made blacks responsible for their own condition:
"While men remain in the chains of ignorance, terror and under the
dominion of tyrant passions they cannot be free." His high-minded constructions, which would become rallying cries for antebellum evangelicals,
had the effect of making blacks, as accountable beings and potential owners of moral power, responsible for their own enslavement. If men had
put themselves into such a state, then they could take themselves out.
"When Africans in our country might be found qualified to enjoy freedom," Furman claimed he would be "happy in seeing them free."[54]

These banal apologetics departed from established proslavery logic.
Traditional hierarchical ideals were not critical to these newer formulations or to their appeal. The historical proslavery canon informed confident southern stances in a vague generalized way, and the very structure
of slavery forced some common conclusions, but antebellum proslavery
ideology had its roots outside the tradition. Furman had no coherent
ideological framework. He represented, rather, the development of a cluster
of ideas, attitudes, and events coalescing in the period of adjustment between 1790 and 1831. The explosion would come in 1831, and hundreds

of evangelical Furmans would quickly build a popular proslavery vision for the South.

The existence of dutiful Christian slaveholders was crucial to Richard Furman's reasoning. His arguments from this premise in 1823 were similar to those expressed in a private letter defending his own slaveholding to critics in his denomination in 1807.[55] The *Exposition* was in this context merely the first formal revelation of a process that evangelicals had been involved in for years: the conversion of slaveholding society. This process led to a new kind of proslavery. Two important groups in the South participated in the evolution of this evangelical proslavery. First were the southerners who owned slaves or who simply accepted it as an unquestioned social reality. In the process of their evangelization and conversion these southerners received a strong moral language with which to express their views, a powerful sense of self-affirmation, and often a sense that they were accepted—as slaveholders—by God.[56] Second were the evangelicals, including ministers from outside the South, who were converted to the possibility and potential of Christian slaveholding.[57]

Southern evangelicals in the mid-eighteenth century were largely outside the political and religious establishment, and so associated slavery with the worldly corruptions of the upper class. Their three denominations—Presbyterian, Baptist, and proto-Methodist—often opposed slavery during the period.[58] Classification of their position on slavery is a semantic matter: evangelicals were hostile to slavery insofar as they saw it as a bar to Christian profession. This last issue was the only pro or anti stance with which they were consistently concerned.[59] As the cultural barriers between them and slaveholders came down—as slaveholders and slaves displayed the signs of ecstatic conversion evangelicals revered, and as evangelicals gained social prominence[60]—denominational strictures and individual ministers' antislavery statements abated.

The Presbyterian General Assembly made the first overt recognition of slaveholder piety in 1797 when the session voted on the issue of slavery. As recorded by David Rice, a leading antislavery minister in Virginia and Kentucky, the Assembly voted as follows:

Is slavery a moral evil?
Yes.
Are all who hold slaves guilty of moral evil?
Negative.[61]

It is important to understand that this position on slavery was never really abandoned in the South. Proslavery emerged in the nineteenth century as the burden of argument, and the ideological and intellectual climate shifted to the second question—the status of individual slaveholders. Power was increasingly seen to flow from the moral organization of individuals. If slaveholding were not a moral evil in special circumstances, the first question—the status of the system and its power to corrupt individuals—lost much of its original (or potential) force. In subsequent discussions of slavery, the condemnation of the institution as a whole became an abstract concession not relevant to American "circumstances."

The evolution of the official Methodist Discipline on slavery followed the same lines.[62] It moved from an attempt at a general condemnation of the institution of slavery, with an accompanying rule of faith issued in 1784 that Methodists must not hold slaves (amended by a delay to study the "expedience" of this act), to the dissolution of the view of slavery as an institution *and* of the denomination's systematic approach to the question (and not coincidentally of the very power of the Methodist Conference itself) in the 1808 rule that let local bodies "form [their] own regulations."[63] Slavery and thought about slavery were decentralized. Individuals were conceded the power to determine and shape the meaning of the social system in which they were enmeshed. On a purely contextual and structural level, divorced from the specific issue, this shift between 1784 and 1808 harmonized with the general form of ideological and institutional adjustment growing out of the Revolution.

Of course, slavery was a very specific issue and the Methodist stance, like the clearer Presbyterian position, had the effect of lifting the onus of critiques of the institution by admitting there were cases—or, as the 1796 *Discipline* said, "circumstances"—in which Christians rightfully held slaves.[64] The moral status of the system of slavery supposedly had no standing in comparison with that of the a priori and formative one of moral individuals. The ultimate implications of this cognitive adjustment were expressed in Methodist parson William Brownlow's popular defense of slavery in the 1850s: "Bad men abuse negroes, good men do not and in all cases, the abuse arises from the character and disposition of the master; and not from the system."[65]

In the 1840s Presbyterian scholar and minister Nathan Rice's proslavery stance showed the same roots, and an even more explicit inability or refusal even to acknowledge the question of institutional power.

"It is common nowadays to declaim against 'the system of American slavery.' . . . I confess myself unable to understand precisely what is meant by this phrase. It is not at all clear to my mind that there is any such thing as a system of American slavery. . . . [It] relates exclusively to individuals."[66] Nathan Rice maintained he was teaching the same doctrine as his antislavery Kentucky forbear, David Rice. Nathan in the 1840s claimed that both the Synod of Kentucky and David Rice in his 1792 *Slavery Inconsistent with Justice and Good Policy* had criticized "what is called *the system of slavery*" and that he agreed with the critique in so far as any such thing existed.[67] Despite the evolution of ideas over two generations (and the chasm in spirit) that separated the two Rices, there was some practical truth in Nathan Rice's claim. David Rice's antislavery rhetoric had been aimed primarily at the state constitutional convention in 1792, urging them to do away with slavery because "slavery naturally tends to sap the foundations of moral and consequently political virtue . . . [and the] prosperity of a free people."[68] Disapproval of slavery at this abstract level had not induced Rice to free his own slaves, even in his will, executed in 1816. Rice accepted the 1797 General Assembly rule defending certain slaveholders and thus became an exemplar for later southerners for the holding of slaves on Christian principle.[69]

The gap between Revolutionary-era ministers and the defenders of slavery in the 1840s is easy to exaggerate when exceptional figures like David Rice make the basis of comparison. When even these men made an accommodation to American slavery, it is hardly surprising that a more widespread and less equivocal acceptance of slaveholding flourished in their own time, and also that modifications of the evangelicals' vague antislavery stances emerged during the first decades of the nineteenth century. It was hard for ministers who participated in the rapid evangelicalization of the South after 1801 to sustain Rice's fears that slavery would drain the foundations of moral virtue in the region. This was especially true when they could point to religious figures like Rice and politicians like Jefferson, who made such critiques in the abstract but did not think the holding of slaves would sap their own virtue. Apparently there was a right way to hold slaves and a kind of man with a fund of virtue that could not be sapped by threatening surroundings or social roles. Or so concluded a generation of ministers after 1801, many of whom, like Richard Furman and Nathan Rice, led the defense of slaveholders in the 1830s and after. But first another strain of contemporary argument would be added to Furman's biblicism and moralism by a Virginia academic responding to the twin southern nightmares of Nat Turner and William Lloyd Garrison.

There is no mystery in locating the emergence of proslavery ideology after 1831. Both Turner's revolt in Southampton, Virginia, and Garrison's launching of the *Liberator* and radical abolitionism took place in 1831. Following these events in the winter of 1831–1832 the Virginia Legislature debated and rejected several plans of emancipation and colonization. In 1832 Thomas R. Dew (1802–1846) wrote his influential proslavery *Review of the Debate in the Virginia Legislature*. Despite the inevitable linking of the watershed events of Garrison's publication and Turner's revolt, Garrison's work was completely unknown to both Turner and Dew. It was not until 1835, when abolitionists began a campaign to inundate the southern mails with antislavery literature, that proslavery publication took off.[70] Although Dew's arguments were crucial in confirming and theorizing southern accommodation to slavery and were representative of future ideological trends, the events of 1832 did not push the region toward proslavery. The South was already committed.

The year 1832 marked neither a reversal of southern opinion about slavery nor an opportunity for southerners to articulate a long-standing proslavery argument already imbedded in the South.[71] The 1830s brought, and Dew's writing signaled, the growth of the national obsession with the unity of moral and material progress, and of the ideological tools and activity necessary to propagate it in the South.[72] There was nothing inherently favorable or opposed to slavery in these cultural and intellectual developments. The spread and development of (1) evangelical visions of individual virtue and power, (2) the astonishing economic transformations of the times, and (3) ideologies of moral and economic sciences occurred in both the North and South before and through the slavery debate. They brought a new era of antislavery, or, more accurately in the case of abolitionists, a new urgency to antislavery sentiment.[73] It was also primarily the ideology of moral and material progress and not the threat of abolitionism that conditioned and fueled proslavery fires. By the 1830s, convincing and attractive formulations of the connection between moral and material progress had assumed the guise of imperatives in both regions. Dew was one of the first to present proslavery in these terms and to raise the stakes on commitment to the order of Providence in the South.

Dew fused the "moral and economic view" of the question of slavery, and did so with authority.[74] His main fields of study at William and Mary—political economy, history, and moral philosophy (Dew was one of the only nonclerics to teach moral philosophy in the South[75])—were ideally attuned to the project. Dew was also a slaveholder from an old Virginia family. Just recently returned from Europe (1824–1826) and just thirty, he was familiar with both American slavery and continental social and intellectual developments.

The dismal science (economics) and moral science as they were developing by the 1830s promulgated unequivocal and unforgiving laws of duty and development, of moral and material necessity. Now, plans for emancipation and colonization, and southern slavery itself, either fell within the purview of these laws, or they did not. Dew rendered verdicts on these questions in the uncompromising tone of the evangelical pulpit, under pain of sin. When dissecting emancipation, Dew found that "the evidence was not speculation in political economy—it was geometrical demonstration."[76] Plans in the Virginia legislature for colonization ran up against forces that "as sure as the moon in her transit" would render them ineffective.[77] It was "in both an economical and moral point of view," Dew held, "that we cannot upon any principle of right or expediency give it [emancipation] our sanction." Dew employed potent intellectual and theoretical, as well as rhetorical, developments to support his linking of material and moral arguments.

Dew preached laissez-faire and Malthusianism.[78] Legislative schemes for colonization and emancipation were dismissed on the grounds of both of these unequivocal theories. The very idea of deliberating on schemes for dismantling the economy constituted a conceit in Dew's eyes. Any such plan would involve the "government entering into the market with individuals" and tend to "destroy the great principle of responsibility" by interfering with property.[79] Colonization plans and the Colonization Society in particular were puffing up a "*little machinery* and grandly proposing it as an *engine*."[80] Attempts to buy slaves and transport them to Africa foundered on not only the tremendous cost (estimated at $100 million), but also the expanding slave population itself and the immutable "law of nature" that stood behind it. Malthus had shown the dangers of "tampering with the elastic and powerful spring of population."[81] The removal of a large number of slaves would only increase social space and the rate of expansion of the black population. The result would be a drain of money and resources (the total value of which Dew put at $206 million in Virginia) to colonize slaves but not necessarily decrease slave population. The laws of population "would operate like the blighting hand of Providence," if not respected.[82] The engine that mattered to Dew was "the great *law* of necessity . . . about which it is utterly useless to argue." Slaves would be "only gradually emancipated through the operation of *self-interest.*"[83]

At first this largely negative argument for slavery seems to represent only a dismal economic rather than a moral view. It was true that the first version of Dew's *Review,* titled "The Abolition of Negro Slavery," published in the *American Quarterly Review,* was heavily economic in emphasis. Dew, however, even in that essay, aligned his arguments with a biblical and ethical view. In the subsequent versions of his *Review,* those that reached the southern public, he added moralism and biblicism to help build proslavery optimism. This was crucial to the influence and appeal of the *Review.* Dew framed his political economics for popular sensibilities and reached a wide audience, as the earlier South Carolina economic proslavery publicists Whitemarsh Seabrook, Edward Brown, and Thomas Cooper had not. The laws of political economy were bleak and perhaps pointed to a social crisis as well as to the end of slavery, when immiserated free laborers would became a cheaper alternative to slaves.[84] Dew himself in his later academic writing would speculate on how enslaved laborers and a more permanent slave society might be the only bulwark against this brutal and socially disruptive process.[85] Yet in the 1830s and in his most publicly influential work, Dew did not take this ground. Theistic and moralistic viewpoints rescued the categories of the dismal science and southern slavery from a purely negative vindication and from predictions of a dire Malthusian future.

Laissez-faire homiletics took on different implications when supplemented by hints at God's purposes. Self-interest was neither the irreducible principle behind inexorable events nor the engine of future developments. Necessary and inevitable laws manifested the "God of nature."[86] Overwhelming economic barriers to colonization and emancipation followed the outline of God's hand. "Every principle," Dew interjected into his economic analysis of colonization, "when rightly understood, demonstrates the benevolence of the Deity even in this world."[87] Dew's statistics on slavery in Virginia were meant to awaken the Old Dominion (and the South) to the overwhelming reality of slavery's establishment. Despite putatively well-intentioned sentiments against it and schemes to wish it away, it had been and was "increasing and spreading—'growing with our growth, and strengthening with our strength.'"[88] Slavery, since it was inescapably a "*necessary result*" beyond the manipulations of legislatures or hopes of philanthropists, "marked some benevolent design . . . by our Creator."[89]

Dew saw two linked progressive benefits: the moral lessons of labor (and racial control) that slavery provided and the material advancement of the region. God was "impelling forward the civilization of mankind" through slavery as well as free labor. Virginia could rest assured that "the snail's pace at which she has hitherto been crawling is destined to be converted into the giant's stride and this very circumstance of itself will defeat all the gloomy predictions about the blacks. . . . Time and internal improvements will cure all our ills."[90] In the meantime, southerners should not again be so vain as to presume on the timing and outcome of God's plan. Slavery might well end, but this was for God to work out in his own way. Dew used the example of Israel's removing of itself from slavery in Egypt and colonizing of Canaan. He said, "Beware of imitation unless assisted by the constant presence of Jehovah."[91]

Dew likewise tamed Malthusianism and pessimism about Virginia's economic future with invocations of "moral power."[92] Malthusian laws had to be susceptible to moral modification in Dew's view. A benevolent God would not leave men in a biological and economic trap that foresight and will could not overcome. The slow growth of Virginia's population was blamed on the inefficiency of slave labor during the debates. Dew followed the lead of Malthus's second (and every subsequent) edition of *An Essay on the Principle of Population* (1803) and downplayed scarcity (or calamity) as the sole block to population growth. Dew thought that, like Scotland, Virginia could experience prosperity without population expansion: "the preventive checks [moral restraint] are in full operation in Virginia . . . they always mark a high degree of civilization—so that the slow progress of population in Virginia turns out to be her highest eulogy."[93] Dew, like proslavery ministers, would not accept that calamities and retributive collapses were unavoidably built into the divine economy. Where moral restraint and exertion were in place, cyclical calamities could be avoided and continuous growth could be achieved.

Free labor also had a less threatening aspect when conceived of not as a material force in itself but as an influence on "our moral and religious character."[94] A competitive labor market as a simple function of economic law implied an end to slavery. When the cost of free labor fell to near subsistence, slavery would become a poor and probably unviable economic choice. Dew, however, supported the "doctrine of the superior productiveness of free labor." He acknowledged, "We are, in the main, converts to this doctrine." He could have spoken for many proslavery ministers on this point (in so far as they understood the doctrine). Free labor was not attractive to southern spokesmen because of the market in labor it created. Rather, southerners celebrated the way free labor effectively taught individuals "the necessity of labor" and demanded that they build "character" by pursuing "constant exertions."[95] Where the free laborer was moral he remained productive, and only then did the system attain superiority.[96] Dew drew on Mill and Adam Smith to argue that the material and religious advantage of free labor was its removal of idleness as a matter of course.[97] Free labor, according to Dew, was not going to undermine slavery; slavery was accomplishing the same ends, "upon attendant circumstances."[98] Slavery achieved this same end under the historical conditions of the South, where there had been a "deterioration in character" among early white settlers in the tropics.[99]

Dew, with the vast majority of proslavery spokesmen, thought that the current character of the population had changed. They refused to defend slavery in the abstract because they thought it would have been easier if it had never been introduced.[100] God, however, was overcoming the "original sin of introduction" by using slavery for the "taming of man and rendering him fit for labor."[101] Slavery provided one way—and perhaps a temporary way—for this to be accomplished. Since southerners were inescapably obligated to participate in this divine process, Dew argued, they had nothing to fear. In the United States, slavery was more likely to end through becoming more like free labor (and, Dew hoped, perhaps bringing its industrial advances) than through a disastrous clash with it. Dew thought a calamitous crisis for slavery "will never in all probability occur."[102] The South could look forward to continued progress and "maintain its ground triumphantly against free labor" through "*steady perseverance* in the system now established."[103]

Dew's greater emphasis on moral and evangelical arguments and insertion of them into his popular work helped bolster his economic positions and his faith in southern progress. Materialist arguments from political economy that seemed to point to a crisis for slavery took on a new light when secular and sacred arguments merged and a single path to progress appeared. If the laws of material progress seemed to work against the South, moral progress in the region could counteract them. Dew in this vein relied on history to vindicate the South—both its social past and its future development. Like most evangelical defenders of slavery, Dew held that "with regard to the assertion that slavery is against the spirit of Christianity, we are ready to admit the *general* assertion."[104] Circumstances, as with the argument for the superiority of free labor, made the South— here and now—an exception. Besides the fact that according to Dew "there was no rule of conscience or revealed law of God which *can* condemn us," the South like Israel was a unique case.[105] The region was developing a special relation to God and a mission to preserve Christian order. Southerners in general shunned the "*selfishness* which withers and repels everything around it." Men of talent and virtue had become involved in slaveholding in the South, and Dew believed that a rule of conscience or duty against slaveholding would have the effect of "withdrawing the good and religious from society."[106] Dew, in other words, defended slavery not in general and in the abstract but in the particular economic circumstances of the South in his era. He, however, constructed such a defense on the basis of the most contemporary intellectual doctrines. So while he did not defend all slavery, slavery as a social system, or slavery as an ideal, he did provide southerners with a relatively logical and complete explanation for and defense of their social practices.

The minor moral and evangelical glosses Dew put on his arguments were insignificant compared to his arguments' additions to the southern and evangelical position on slavery.[107] Dew, by casting many of his arguments in these popular forms,[108] effectively linked the long-developing evangelical accommodation to slavery with the intellectual terms that made it coherent. Contemporary laissez-faire doctrines, especially as Dew presented them, were perfectly attuned to the theorizing of the southern evangelical position on slavery. Evangelicals had slowly left the issue to individuals and stopped directing their criticisms at the system as a whole. As early as the 1797 Presbyterian General Assembly, when this pattern had first emerged, evangelicals had resolved the apparent contradiction in their position (between an abstract condemnation of slavery and specific defense of slaveholders) by an affirmation: the issue was "of so much importance that the consideration of it [would] be put off til a future day."[109] This was in large part the Revolutionary settlement as well. By the 1830s, both Dew's theories and history could turn what might have been a sign of indecision or compromise into evidence of wisdom and a coherent, consistent course of action with a positive future.

Evangelicals had relied upon the drift of events, whose benevolent direction was assumed to be in God's hands.[110] Dew's approach consisted of an abstract justification of the evangelical decision to leave the issue to private judgments and to abandon systematic criticisms. The glory of Dew's classical economics was that it offered a systematic explanation of having no systematic approach to large-scale social questions. It provided both an imperative not to engage in systematic critique or in tampering with the process and a promise that individuals acting in their unified moral and material interest could ensure progress and stability. Consignment of the issue to individual principles and providential drift became a positive principle and general strategy of itself. Dew put theological and moral glosses on his laissez-faire doctrines, suggesting that the barriers to antislavery and the laws of necessity were laws of God. Ministers and future proslavery writers would make this an explicit argument. Where Dew had used cash figures produced by slavery to ask, "Do not these very simple statistics speak volumes on this subject?," fellow Virginian and best-selling proslavery minister Thornton Stringfellow thundered at the end of his examination of similar figures in his *Scriptural and Statistical Views:* "Is not this fact, like all those examined, *God's* Providential voice? and does not, in these facts, He speak a language we can *read and understand?*"[111] Dew's progressive economics provided a structure in which a variety of southerners could explain their stance on the issue and believe they shared a common ideal.

Even the delay and uncertainty of antebellum southerners with reservations about the institution, in fact the whole history of the southern Founding Fathers and founders of the evangelical movement, could be presented as part of a consistent approach to the issue and a sign of regional strength. It was right to have tested emancipation and antislavery, but Dew argued that the "experiment has been sufficiently tried."[112] The tradition of antislavery among the Virginia founders was not a contradiction of a proslavery stance. "Washington," a proslavery moralist said in expanding on Dew's argument, "emancipated them [his slaves] with the hope . . . [that they were] fitted for freedom or that they would be benefitted by their own self-control." In the historic context, such a stance could not be considered antislavery: "Washington therefore could not consistently oppose slavery as a wrong to the slave, nor conscientiously believe it to be wrong; because he would not oppose that which he could not overcome. It is against the prophetic character of Washington's mission ever crowned with success . . . to presume his hostility to slavery as a wrong or his opposition to it in a moral view when he knew, as we know, the emancipation of the slaves to be wrong itself; and impossible even if right."[113] Being a good antebellum moralist, this southern spokesman added that the last possibility could not be entertained because "right holds a just and heaven derived superiority over wrong."[114]

Dew popularized both the difficulty of emancipation and the condition of free blacks who had supposedly been part of this "experiment" as arguments that slavery had to be morally defensible. While Washington had not foreseen this outcome, God had (through the laws of Moses). "He foresaw that all efforts to eradicate these evils would be in vain," wrote a minister in 1837, and, "as became a wise lawgiver he adapted them into his system—adapted them to counteract their pernicious tendencies. Wonderful!" Men presumptively criticizing and attempting to dismantle slavery were not following God's plan. His will did not work in this way. Only by embracing the biblical directives of slaveholding might the system gradually progress, modernize, and perhaps disappear.[115] Matthew Estes, who wrote popular biblical defenses from Mississippi, maintained that Dew "opened the eyes of the South" to this potential of a slave economy and the "ground of abstract right" it provided. The message implanted in the Bible on slavery and the role of Israel that the South was re-enacting told stories of economic development. "Ancient slavery was a training ground," according to Estes, in which slaves were "trained to habits of industry." The Israelites had "settled the land of Canaan" where "forests had to be felled—cities, villages, and towns built up and improved." The "national wealth was increased" and "profitably directed" as a "division of labor emerged."[116]

Dew had demonstrated that market laws were in operation in slavery and could not easily be dismantled, even if this were desirable. Yet for Dew and certainly for evangelical defenders of slavery, the main point was that no one should presume to interfere with the purposes of God that must be working out through slavery. The moral training to industry (with its racist implications) was more important than the building of industry. Ministers assumed that attempts at eradicating slavery appeared to run up against insurmountable barriers because God had providential purposes for slavery. Presbyterian minister J.C. Mitchell thought even the

British antislavery forces would have to come to this conclusion: "They acknowledge their inability with all their wealth and power to extinguish slavery. They are beginning to recognize the fact, so patent to all who are not blinded by prejudice, that the finger of God is in this whole matter; that he will order and control the affairs of all nations in such a manner as to subserve the interests of his kingdom."[117] Dew and evangelical proslavery spokesmen after him, however, assumed that no choice had to be made between the purposes of Christendom and the best interest and prosperity of the South. This was not a new connection; "scripture and sound policy" had been vaguely linked in the earliest proslavery petitions to the Virginia Legislature after the Revolution.[118] Antislavery at the same time had made a similar speculative link. Dew noted Jefferson's famous objections to "*the moral effects*" of the institution, which undermined self-government in masters and slaves alike. Jefferson claimed to "tremble" for the country when he remembered "God was just" and would punish the country if this persisted. In 1832 Dew thought he was in a position "to boldly assert that the fact does not bear Mr. Jefferson out in his conclusion."[119] Where Jefferson could only conjecture, antebellum southerners thought that their new incontrovertible tools of analysis and evidence explained their past and future.

Methodist minister William Smith took Dew's correction of Jefferson further. Smith gave a more explicit application of both moral science and economic analysis. Jefferson's oversight according to Smith was his "assuming in this remark, that the providences as well as the attributes of the Deity are against the slaveholder."[120] Since "no people on the globe have shared more largely in the blessings of a bountiful Providence than those of the Southern States of this Union," slaveholders could not possibly be morally corrupt and unable to govern their passions. So it was not surprising that "in the progress of civilization and religion they have advanced more rapidly than any community in the country." Slavery had "daily for a long series of years become more and more practical." This would simply not have been possible "if those who oppose it [abolition] were really 'proslavery' men in the bad sense in which certain persons understand this phrase, that is, men who, on the subject of slavery wickedly do what they know and feel to be wrong. . . . It is not mere belief, nor is it mere honesty, that produces results in practice; but it is the *reception of truth in an honest heart,* which can never fail to result in practice." Southern slaveholders and proslavery men had achieved results in practice, so

Randolph-Macon's moral philosopher argued that this proved they had honest and morally unassailable hearts.[121]

Antislavery forces reasoned from the same heritage and the coalescing language of moral and material progress to very different conclusions. If slavery at the time of the Revolution was considered evil in the abstract and was expected to fade before the sunshine of evangelical truth and free institutions, its subsequent growth and spread were the growth and spread of an evil. This practical event was then evidence of the growth and spread of private vices and corrupted—not converted and honest—hearts in the South. Thus, the new sense of urgency and inflexible resolution among antislavery forces was directed against the very point upon which southerners had developed their most long-standing proslavery position: the moral standing of slaveholders. Dew had argued that the stakes had changed on the slavery issue; abolitionists showed the South that this was true. The intellectual trends Dew was immersed in and proselytizing were even more developed and widespread in the North. The path to progress and the social commandments of God seemed mysterious to fewer and fewer believers in both regions as the antebellum era unfolded. Neither God nor what abolitionist Wendell Phillips called "God's laws of political economy" laid down any rule that could be easily compromised.[122] Southern ministers rose to answer abolitionists in their own tones after 1835. The ensuing slavery debate revealed the growing sectional rift and the potential divisiveness of evangelical moralism.

3

Answering Abolitionists, Defending Slaveholders

The appearance of radical abolitionism and the subsequent growth of a moderate antislavery movement in the North after 1831 hastened and confirmed the transition already occurring in southern ideology.[1] Most movements do not become fully self-conscious until under assault. Abolitionist critiques confirmed growing southern self-righteousness. Innovative critiques of slaveholding had the effect of reinforcing long-standing patterns of religious identity in the South. In the slavery debate southern evangelicals reenacted familiar roles that had served them well in previous controversies. Although the parts were established, the script was still being perfected. The slavery debate brought more conscious applications of contemporary moral science and economic philosophy to regional myths and hopes. Both antislavery and proslavery evangelicals were learning to adopt the aggressive didacticism of the era in order to express their righteousness and to demand both recognition of their progressive mission and their material due.

The ministerial cliche of the 1850s, that the southern states were the true descendants of the Puritans and champions of "orthodox and evangelical religion," was a result of the stereotypes that arose as southerners compared their scriptural views to those of radical abolitionists in the 1830s and 1840s.[2] Part of the homogeneity—and occasional cooperation—among southern Protestants of different denominations was a product of their emphasis on the simple message of the Word over and against sophisticated theological speculation. In the slavery debate this became an argument for the superior social organization (and unity) of the South. Northern biblical and theological speculation was associated in southern minds with dangerous social experimentation. Both lines of danger seemed to be exposed in northerners' religiously inspired calls for the dismantling of southern racial controls. A number of abolitionist arguments denying the authority of certain biblical passages or explicitly advocating a higher law than the Bible received the same rapturous attention in the South as the scriptural passages acknowledging slaveholding. When acceptance of these scriptural proslavery passages then became a test of biblical fidelity, it was easy for southerners to say that all antislavery spokesmen deliberately corrupted or rejected the Bible in the manner of the radical abolitionists and European biblical scholars.

Alexander McCaine, a minister and southern delegate to the Methodist General Conference, perceived such a crisis for the faith looming behind abolitionist attacks on slaveholders as sinners. He accurately summarized the logic of these criticisms: "If slavery be 'a *great moral evil,*' no slaveholder has enjoyed or can enjoy, the grace and favor of God, as long as he owns slaves, and dying a slaveholder he is prevented from entering the kingdom." McCaine disagreed with the abolitionist argument because many southerners had observed or themselves experienced how "God communicates his grace and spirit to the slaveholder." McCaine asked, "Is their testimony to pass for nothing? Now this testimony is true or it is false." Had slaveholders experienced conversion as they said? If abolitionists continued to say such professions were false, McCaine believed that "religion itself receives a mortal stab and the infidel rejoices over the advocates of the cross. . . . If the testimony of the slaveholder can be thus easily set aside as being hypocritical, the testimony of the abolitionist can be set aside also." McCaine did not see this as an internal weakness of evangelical subjectivism and didactic moral science, but as betrayal by the abolitionists, who were undermining the evangelical movement. Worst of all, as McCaine said in his classic southern reaction to abolitionists, "They hate whom God loves."[3]

Presbyterian Nathan Rice came to the same point of dispute over conversion in his famous public debate with fellow Cincinnati Presbyterian Jonathan Blanchard, an antislavery minister and defender of abolitionism on biblical grounds. Rice constructed a proslavery argument on the basis of Lane Theological Seminary professor Calvin Stowe's (Harriet Beecher Stowe's husband) admission that "Christ does accept" slaveholders. Rice then argued against antislavery evangelicals: "There are Christian ministers who are involved in slaveholding, but who nevertheless are owned and blessed of God. Moreover it is a fact that many of the most efficient ministers in the free states were converted, if converted at all, in revivals in the slaveholding churches, and in answer to the prayers of those slaveholding Christians."[4] Rice thought there were only three possible explanations for this phenomenon: "God hears the prayers and blesses the labors of the most abominable criminals, or these revivals are all spurious and the converts are hypocrites, or abolitionism is false."[5] Reverend Blanchard, Rice's antislavery opponent, identified this attitude toward "revivals in slaveholding churches" as the source of southern proslavery arguments. Although he was willing to admit that there were "genuine conversions in them," he suspected not that abolitionism was in error but rather that "the slaveholders' hopes may be false."[6]

Baptist and Mercer professor Patrick Hues Mell articulated the southern answer to abolitionists' critiques of southern religion prior both to the sectional crisis and to schism in his denomination in 1845. Abolitionists, he noted, were "in the habit of making invidious comparisons between New England and southern Piety. We know we have little piety to boast ... we lay claim to no other character than to that of sinners; but we thank God, that a large and increasing number in our midst have 'a good hope' that *we are sinners* saved by *grace*."[7] In deference to his northern coreligionist Francis Wayland, Mell took a similar conciliatory approach to his moral and biblical defense of slaveholding: "There is no doubt that there are many cruel masters ... that there is much licentiousness in the slaveholding states cannot be denied, but I would that we had evidence that it is confined to this side of the Mason-Dixon Line."[8] B.F. Stringfellow, Missouri Baptist layman and organizer of proslavery "defense" forces in the region, writing in 1854 after more than a decade of further sectional dispute, saw no reason for conciliation and took the regional definition of true conversion and piety to its logical conclusion. "Modesty is no longer a virtue," Stringfellow announced, "slaveholders are more truly religious than the sons of Puritans." Righteous Puritans he pointed out had settled the North while the South was colonized by censurable "adventurers in search of fortune, by Chevaliers of Charles who in sheer hatred of the pious affected loose morals, a contempt for religion." Yet in the 1850s

Stringfellow found that "slaveholders" were "content with old-fashioned humble Christianity" while the sons of Puritans "'run after strange Gods.'" Stringfellow confessed, "We are more or less at a loss to comprehend such a revolution....What is it which has converted the indolent, thoughtless southerner into the humble, orthodox Christian?"[9]

The process of exchanging scriptural views with northerners added to the South's sense of its own special fidelity to the Bible and relation to God. Southerners thought abolitionists either did not understand the Bible or did not know God's will, and they suspected them of perverting both.[10] From the southern perspective the Bible offered an ideal source of vindication. If the Bible explicitly ordained slaveholding, as southern churchmen were sure it did, then to condemn slaveholding outright as a sin was to insult God's Word and betray His Will. Inasmuch as evangelical Protestantism was an experience, and scriptural quotation a method of discourse, shared with abolitionists, the Bible provided a perfect weapon for exposing abolitionist pretenses and winning allies for the South. Many strict exegetical proslavery writers had thought literal proofs from biblical quotation might "drive abolitionists to the wall and compel them to take an anti-Christian position and by so doing compel the whole Christianity of the North to array itself on our side."[11] Proslavery evangelicals found in this strategy several proofs of the strength and superiority of the South's biblical stand and faith, but few northern Christians were converted to the southern position.

The year 1835 was crucial for publication of both abolitionist and radical theological material. In that year, in which the antislavery postal campaign (and southern legal reaction against it) began, David Fiedrich Strauss's *Leben Jesus,* which demythologized Christ's biography, Wihelm Vatke's historicizing of ancient Judaic religion, and Christian Baur's hermeneutical and historical analysis of the early church letters *all* appeared. Like the coincident emergence of Garrison's *Liberator* and the Turner insurrection, these events had no real connection, and even their simultaneity was not noted at the time. Yet the symbolic link between the beginning of modern abolition and a bloody slave revolt had enormous popular (and paranoid) appeal, and a measure of logical plausibility. Gentlemen theologians made no less powerful a connection between the realization of their two worst fears: (1) the decline of scriptural and theological (as well as ministerial) authority, and (2) a popular movement that made such infidelity politically and socially relevant.

Frederick Ross was more pithy on this point, saying simply of the abolitionists' extremism, "God made them do it."[12] Much like Thomas R. Dew, Ross particularly welcomed their dismantling of the colonization movement and thought this to be God's way of showing that even that mild form of antislavery was "premature," impinging on the providential development of the southern economy. Ross was more enamored of later abolitionist arguments (in which Parker took a lead) about a "slave power conspiracy" because these even "more brought out, in the Providence of God, that *the slave power has been and is gaining ground in the United States. . . . This is the tone* of the past and present speech of Providence on the subject of slavery."[13] According to Ross, the national "moral soil needed . . . deep plowing," which the slavery debate had provided. The "moral agitation" had brought greater attention to the voice of Providence and insured that many "now read the Bible who never examined it before, with growing respect."[14] Looking back from the 1850s Ross saw how even the heresy of abolitionism had accomplished the purpose of spreading the true gospel.

Most ministers concluded that new respect for Scripture was confined to the South and needed no abolitionist agitation to bring it to fruition. By the time Ross achieved popularity in the 1850s southern ministers had long since simply stereotyped all northern religion on the basis of the biblical "errors" of radicals. In 1841, when Thornton Stringfellow sat down to write the best-selling proslavery tract in the Old South, he was, like other southerners, aware of the great apostasy to the North with which he had to contend.[15] "It is to be hoped that on a question of such vital importance as this to the peace and safety of our country, as well as to the welfare of the church, we shall be seen cleaving to the Bible, and taking all our decisions from its inspired pages. With men from the North, I have observed for many years a palpable ignorance of the divine will, in reference to the institution of slavery. I have seen but few of them who made the Bible their study that obtained knowledge of what it did reveal on this subject."[16] Scriptural proslavery arguments reinforced the southerners' sense of their region's being the redeemer nation's righteous remnant that still maintained fidelity to God's word and should receive His reward.

The waves of revivals across the South between 1801 and 1831 constituted a tacit argument in favor of slavery. Many southerners experienced consciousness of election through their conversion during religious revivals. The conversion experience—the moment of inner satisfaction that told a believer he was in direct communion with God—encouraged a strong regional identification since it was often fixed in time and place. It was this sense of power and elation in the grace of God that justified evangelicals and their worldly activities.[17] How could God do anything other than approve of slaveholding since southerners held slaves, believed in slavery, or were immersed in such a society when God signally blessed and saved them? "Thousands and tens of thousands of slaveholders have made profession of the religion of Jesus Christ at the very time they owned slaves," one minister pointed out, adding, "the slaveholder gives all the proof that scripture requires of the change in his heart."[18]

Many who experienced conversion and participated in revivals in the period of evangelization of the South were no more ready to doubt slavery than they were to doubt their own religious experience, especially when they could point to biblical parallels to their experience and conduct. "There are Christians and Christian churches in the slaveholding states," reported Presbyterians in the *Southern Christian Herald,* "and they sometimes enjoy seasons of religious reviving from the presence of the Lord. But it is Scripture truth, that God does not answer the prayers and bless the labors of men living in sin. He does hear and bless those involved in slaveholding."[19]

Before southerners came to defend slaveholding after 1831 as a condition "bestowed upon the virtuous," as one nonslaveholder described it, slaveholders had to be seen and to see themselves as sharing in evangelical virtues.[20] Often this presented no great difficulty, as ministers frequently held slaves. James Smylie, one of the first biblical proslavery spokesmen in the 1830s, estimated that 75 percent of his fellow Presbyterian pastors held slaves in the region.[21] He himself owned nearly thirty when he published his defense of slavery in 1836.[22] Smylie's estimate was high, but more accurate counts of Baptist ministers put slaveholders at over 40 percent, and most ministers reported at least occasionally hiring slaves for work on their home and church grounds.[23] They lived their proslavery arguments before they published them.

Ministers' views easily reached the public not only from pulpits but in the religious press, which experienced surging growth between 1820 and the Civil War. The Methodist *Christian Advocate* was the largest newspaper in the world in 1830. Proslavery ministers were often editors of the regional newspapers and periodicals that sprung up as the slavery issue divided the major evangelical denominations by 1846.[24] In isolated rural areas itinerant ministers often constituted the major source of information about the outside world, and the Bible was the source of the only abstract ideas many people in these areas encountered. It was a book with passages that recognized slavery, especially when reinforced by clerical interpretation.[25] Clergy were the most frequent defenders of slavery, their role as cultural leaders and controllers of education securing wide audiences for their views and giving them an unrivaled power to shape moral discourse.[26] Such men with day-to-day connections to slavery sufficed to guarantee the symbiosis of power and piety promulgated in proslavery.

In addition to clerical rhetoric, the general conversion of slaveholders was vital to ensuring broad moral support for slavery, especially in the period before 1831 when evangelicalism was spreading and slaveholding losing its association with worldly, genteel society. A more unified culture insured united support of slavery. Without such unity ministers and non-slaveholding evangelicals might have continued to see slavery as a threat or "slaveholders on Christian principle" as exceptions, and so have avoided publicly supporting slavery. Just as important, had there been no wave of revivals to penetrate the elites and bring evangelical culture and language to every level of southern society, the population of slaveholders and their supporters might not have expressed their commitment to slavery in such politically unthreatening terms. Many of the earliest and most vocal proslavery ministers did not hold slaves. Their suspicions of slavery were overcome by the presence of "Bible-worshiping" masters or master-worshiping Bible passages.[27] Fred Ross, who freed his slaves before the antebellum period, argued that because of revivals, "the master's *relation* to God and to his slave is now *wholly changed*," and he believed the South "stands *exactly* in that nick *of time and place,* in the course of Providence, where *wrong,* in the transmission of African slavery *ends,* and *right begins.*"[28]

Samuel Dunwoody, a non-slaveholding Methodist minister and one of the first of his denomination to publish a proslavery tract in the 1830s, also thought ill will in masters was being "generally melted down before the sunshine of evangelical truth." Dunwoody typically held to a "general view of slavery" as "an evil" and assumed "God would bring lasting Good out of present evils." He, however, considered it a "syllogism" that "God as he is infinitely wise, just and holy never could authorize the practice of moral evil. But God has authorized the practice of slavery, not only by bare permission of his Providence, but by the express provision of his Word."[29] This biblical and historical fact did not justify the system: "We are willing to give it up as altogether indefensible, but that Christians may lawfully hold slaves, in some particular cases." God authorized only "the right of a Christian to own a servant, whom he invariably treats with kindness."[30] Dunwoody added that "whenever we have followed this plain scriptural course, success has generally crowned our efforts."[31]

The successful scriptural course Dunwoody spoke about consisted of the denouncing of slavery in the abstract and the upholding of it in particular cases—increasingly the particular case of the entire South. This course had been successful because the adoption of a consistent stance on slavery in the evangelical denominations had followed a similar path. It was also considered the scriptural verdict. God chose Abraham and "blessed him while he held slaves."[32] In Luke 7, after curing the centurion's servant: "Our Savior commended a slaveholder as the best of men." In the spread of evangelical profession and conversion in the South, ministers thought they again saw the savior commending and blessing righteous men who held slaves. When Paul spoke of "believing masters" in Timothy 4, it was further confirmation that this constituted a special case.[33]

The South began to be a special case itself, as the model of the heretofore exceptional "chosen" master became the rule. Slavery was supposedly being remade by the power and principle of the new evangelical men filling the South. Slavery remained an evil in the abstract, but, since special individuals could participate in it without evil, the South as a whole could be, as proslavery minister Joshua Wilson wrote in 1834, "a derivation from all common examples." In all common examples a system of slavery was wrong; "American servitude," on the other hand, "was an anomaly."[34] It was a short step from this early evangelical position to later religious and economic arguments that a system of slavery per se did not exist in the South at all. In a religious formulation it was "a *peculiar* condition of servitude, regulated by law, having no parallel in profane history, instituted by God."[35] The peculiarity sprung—as in the circumstances and cases in denominational statements—from the perception of southerners that they were a peculiarly religious people, chosen and approved by God. This situation may not have had parallel in profane history; it did in the Bible.[36]

Southern evangelicals often described the scriptural sanction as a "discovery" of the 1830s. Although they and others perceived a shift in their arguments on these grounds,[37] this was the tail end of a process rather than a leap in logic or attitude.[38] Ministers, particularly non-slaveholding ones, had not appealed to a biblical sanction of slavery on a regional basis—on the basis of a peculiar people rather than persons—until they began to perceive a society of converts or a converted society after a generation of evangelical growth and emerging cultural dominance. As this occurred, ministers who would defend slavery after the 1830s were converted to and often converted by scriptural evidence and sanctions that now seemed to describe the society they perceived (or fervently hoped they were creating). The discovery of (or shift to) the biblical argument became possible as the Bible passages on slavery appeared in this new light.

Part of the discovery was rhetorical. The evolving approach to Bible reading and "searching the scriptures" adopted from the Scottish Common Sense school greatly emphasized the language of discovery as a whole.[39] Proslavery ministers insisted upon the objectivity with which they approached any moral question.[40] Long-standing biblical arguments were often known or available. Simple appeals to authority and tradition, however, were not morally or intellectually satisfying to the evangelical personality. Calm individual searches of scripture—with reception in the heart and communication to the conscience—were. It was requisite to describe the truths perceived as discoveries. As the Bible contained a moral law applicable in all personal and historic circumstances, there were always new applications to be found. Evangelical moral philosophy encouraged ministers to locate biblical facts and to match all the physical and social facts they experienced with them. The psychology of such scriptural arguments illuminates a fundamental aspect of the evangelical's personality as revealed in everyday situations. A non-slaveholding itinerant who defended slaveholders on biblical grounds once became hungry while traveling between two churches. He noticed some bees and discovered the appropriate sanction: "Industrious creatures—is it right to rob them? But I suppose they were made for the use of man? . . . Our Savior a honeycomb did eat. Let everything have a Bible warrant!"[41]

More important than the rhetorical and psychological needs expressed in the discovery of the biblical sanction were the evangelicals' readings of scriptural examples in new contexts. Southern proslavery minsters did not find general institutional sanctions of slavery as had defenders of slavery for hundreds of years. The paucity of written defenses of slavery on biblical grounds among evangelicals during the first fifty years of the

Republic was rooted in their rejection of this older abstract proslavery stance. Evangelicals in the period avoided appeals to scripture on the slavery issue and were occasionally hostile to biblical proslavery (or denied that the Bible supported slavery) because of its association with hierarchical positions they rejected in the ecclesiastical and social realms. In the 1830s, many evangelicals were still reluctant to invoke a biblical warrant, believing they had already rejected such an argument. When Presbyterian James Smylie of Mississippi published one of the first biblical arguments of the 1830s, he "gave great offense" to other ministers and to his congregation by appearing to trot out the old abstract vindication. Smylie's view of patriarchy and the master-slave relation as a characteristic social organization were fairly traditional. The support Smylie found for them in the Bible was, likewise, comparatively unqualified.[42] Most antebellum southerners were not ready to swallow this retrograde argument whole or in Smylie's updated form. The more populist evangelicals were discovering and framing a Bible argument that was another matter. It grew from the scriptural sanction of individual cases of Christian slaveholding that had often been presented as exceptions at the turn of the century in evangelicals' otherwise hostile statements and attitudes about the system of slavery. Over a generation these exceptions had been turned into rule, and Bible passages were being explained in this context, in tune with an emergent moral style. Ministers in the antebellum period could come to a defense of slavery through perception of new providential facts in the South, new institutionally innocent social ideologies, or examples of new readings of scripture. When the arguments were arranged to sanction the morally accountable actions of a peculiar people, rather than to justify an abstract social organization, biblical proslavery won many converts.

Evangelical defenders of slavery often gave just such a presentation of their move toward moral acceptance of slavery. Amasa Converse, born in Lyme, New Hampshire, moved South to become a leading editor of religious papers, such as the *Southern Religious Telegraph,* for Presbyterians. He prided himself on his "even temper and objectivity" and protection of "rights and liberties of the press."[43] Although his was an extreme case of a shift in views on slavery, it was not unlike those recorded by many southern evangelicals: "In my youth I believed slaveholding was a sin *per se*; such was my view of it when a student of theology [1817], and I endeavored—in debate—to maintain the right of the slave to commit murder to regain his freedom. Some years later an examination of what scriptures teach on the subject convinced me that the doctrine was false and pernicious. . . . The exercise of power becomes sinful only when abused in violation of the great law of love."[44] In their proslavery pamphlets southern defenders of slavery often provided more nebulous testimonies to the evolution of their views. Matthew Ewart remembered the time before 1830 in these terms: "I freely admit that I satisfactorily convinced myself, as to the fact that slavery is indeed and in truth a moral relation and humbly confess that I did not always think so; but searching scriptures brought me to a very different conclusion."[45] Southerners long committed to slavery could proclaim an ethical and exegetical version of their traditional attitudes and actions once these arguments and confessions were in circulation.

Before the evolution of the evangelicals' argument, politicians had constituted the only segment of the southern population to continue a tradition of defending slavery as a positive good. They often reframed their social and political proslavery rhetoric and provided it with religious glosses. President John Tyler was more honest than most in admitting the convenience of evangelical language of "moral character" and Providence for the non-evangelical advocates of slavery: "I sir, even I, do firmly, if not faithfully, intellectually, if not religiously, believe in a great and good over-ruling special Providence. . . . Which justifies slavery itself, in the abstract, and has made me wonder and adore a gracious special Providence."[46] Tyler's fellow politician and slaveholder Robert Barnwell Rhett Sr., father of the famous fire-eater Robert Barnwell Rhett Jr., was more typical in his claims to true conversion on the issue and his dropping of abstract categories for individual ones. He sent biblical proslavery pamphlets to his son and friends with this personal addendum to his conclusions after reading them[47] "If slavery is contrary to Christianity, undoubtedly it should be abolished. If it is a sin to hold slaves in bondage, undoubtedly they should be liberated. Reviewing the word of God in all reverence, *I* cannot but believe that I am sinless, so far as my slaves are concerned, serving in my moral and religious accountability."[48] This statement exemplifies the general and informal southern acceptance of slavery that had arrived by the 1830s. Fire-eater Barnwell Rhett's conversion to an evangelical and moral explanation for his long-established commitment to slavery may provide the regional model. The majority of Americans, with their positions on slavery and religious commitments less defined and their biblical ideas more vague than those of the abolitionists or proslavery ministers, easily arrived at similar conclusions by 1860. They could agree with T.W. Hoit, author of a very widely circulated proslavery tract: "If it [slavery] can be shown to be right, then it is expedient, if wrong, then it cannot be shown to be expedient."[49] Naturally, most Americans either denounced or defended slavery depending on whether it was personally expedient. There were, however, those in the South with true reservations about slavery and many more whose commitments to slavery were accompanied by reservations. New grounds for the scriptural and moral argument (based on a special personal and regional relation to God) and ubiquitous attention to it provided a justification of southern society that could be presented as consistent with the evangelicals' and others' previous convictions and reservations about slavery.

Baptist minister Jeremiah Jeter accurately linked his personal turning point on the issue of slavery with the regional one. Jeter was born and brought up in the midst of slavery in rural Virginia at the beginning of the century. "Of the *system* of slavery," he remembered in the 1840s, "my early impressions were not favorable." Although he "grew up with a determination never to own a slave, . . . whether slavery was right or wrong was a question which [he] did not consider." His views changed when he was engaged to marry "a lady who held slaves" and was faced with both a "practical question" and a moral dilemma. He found that none of the slaves wanted to go to Liberia and that he did not have the means to set them up in freedom. He also came across the popular biblical proslavery arguments of fellow Baptist minister and Virginian Thornton Stringfellow and found that the "scriptures were more favorable to slavery than I had been." He concluded that "slavery is not always right," but "under the circumstances" he had a "solemn obligation to hold and rule them for their interest and for my own."[50]

Jeter explained the evolution of the regional proslavery commitment in the same terms. At the turn of the century "prevalent opinion in Virginia was not that slavery was in all cases sinful, but that the *system* . . . was fraught with many evils, economical, social, political, and moral and should as soon as possible be abolished." Yet when individual and practical confrontations with the issue continually ran into "obstacles," the "more the matter was examined" over the first thirty years of the century, "the result was a marked change in public opinion."[51]

Although Jeter's Virginia was the site of Nat Turner's slave revolt and had an unusually strong antislavery tradition—both of which circumstances may have worked to make the shift in public opinion seem more marked, Jeter did not fix any date or event for the shift.[52] His own move to a more confident and self-conscious stance came in the 1840s. His views and those he reported as prevalent at the beginning of the century opposed the abstract system of slavery. He correctly noted that Virginians and other southerners stopped thinking about slavery and social power in institutional terms, but the exact time of this popular shift in emphasis—let alone when it became a conscious argument—is not possible to pinpoint. Between 1801 when the Great Revival swept the region and 1831 when the slavery debate began, southern evangelicals achieved cultural dominance in the region. Looking back over the first thirty years of the century, they concluded that God had converted and blessed their region. Clearly slavery did not bar a wave of righteousness. Many southern slaveholders and their supporters thus had a much more direct route to the sacralizing of slavery: evangelicals converted them and gave them a sense of their own righteousness while holding slaves or believing it to be right. As slaveholders seized the evangelical message, and antislavery ministers found that the institution did not bar the way to evangelical conversions, or as these ministers found themselves holding slaves, the evangelical rationale for criticism of slavery dissolved. The phasing out of antislavery sentiment happened gradually without comment, across the region prior to 1831. After 1832, southerners looked back at their personal histories and the history of their region over the first thirty years of the century and discovered that they had always been righteous.

As with the case of Jeremiah Jeter, ministers' own moves up the social ladder often played a key role in their view of slaveholding. Many northern-born ministers came South to new careers, missions, and congregations in the 1820s and 1830s. Those northern ministers who came South during the relatively quiescent period for proslavery between 1801 and 1831 arrived at conclusions similar to Jeremiah Jeter's.[53] Northern-born William Winans and Converse Amasa, as well as Massachusetts-born Presbyterians Theodore Clapp and Heman Packard (who wrote proslavery from their new churches in New Orleans), came to justify slavery after meeting "righteous" slaveholders, who often arranged and financed their career moves to the South. If their careers did not tie them to slaveholders, then, as with Jeter and countless other southern ministers, marriage often did. Ministers who made lucrative matrimonial alliances with planters' daughters were commonplace in the antebellum period, and this mode of initial involvement in slaveholding was important. Slaves, for these ministers, seemed to come to them in the natural course of things, as an outgrowth of the selfless acts of falling in love, successfully spreading the gospel, or gathering a flock. Whether ministers became slaveholders through marriage or inheritance, the occurrences reinforced their predilection to see material benefits as bestowed, not sought.[54] They then tended to qualify antislavery or to describe slaveholding in the South in these terms. Most defenders of slavery believed that God had "put" slaves into their hands. The Divine purpose, they thought, was that the master train slaves for "self-dependence and self-government."[55]

When Methodist itinerant William Winans had to explain his slaveholding to his family in Ohio in 1820, he provided a more rationalized explanation of this process than southern evangelicals for whom slaveholding often was a familiar act, even when they did not engage in—or even disapproved of—it. Winans's letters in response to his brother's disgust with his slaveholding correspond to the Presbyterian General Assembly's votes on the matter in 1797. Winans recorded an imaginary dialogue, presenting his brother's questions and his own answers:

> 1.) "Shall we make slaves of the Negro?"
>   "I would spill my blood in supporting the negative."
> 2.) "Shall we retain them in slavery when it is in our power to make them free?"
>   "No!"
>   "May a Christian hold them?"
>   I answer, "Why not?"

Winans explained that the Christian "does real service to those Negroes he purchases from unbelieving masters" and "may I believe keep a good conscience while he participates in this misfortune of our country."[56] Although Winans was an early and vocal opponent of abolitionism in the Methodist Conference, he was always a colonizationist rather than a proslavery publicist. He did think slavery was a curse, but much more clearly than Rice he was trying in 1820 to describe and defend an evangelical form of slaveholding.

Winans anticipated arguments to be applied more widely and fully by later proslavery southerners. This position concerning the modification of moral rules and duties by historical and individual "circumstances" was taken by almost every evangelical defender of slavery, including Old School Presbyterians like James Henley Thornwell.[57] Moral precepts not given in scripture—such as "men should not hold other men in slavery" or "parents should not strike their children"—were not moral imperatives. Depending on who was hitting a child or holding a slave or going to war and why, the act was not only justified but would have beneficial results. Thus Thornwell warned that "Good and evil it should never be forgotten are relative terms."[58] The character of the man involved determined how the rule or duty applied.[59] For men of inferior character in the seventeenth or eighteenth century, or for men who were "neither Protestants nor Americans," the abstract condemnation of slavery applied. Nineteenth-century Americans of foresight and moral sense, however, controlled themselves and thereby controlled their surroundings. The meanings and consequences of their actions were not dictated by forces outside themselves, to which they had to adjust or conform. Slaveholding in short would not corrupt them; in fact they had the power to determine what slavery would become, even though, in the abstract rule of right, slavery was an evil.

In this vein, Kentucky Baptist minister William Buck described in 1849 the origin of American slavery and the slave trade: "We can but think it is perfectly compatible with the purity and benevolence of God that from the beginning, he should have *intended it for good,* notwithstanding that wicked men have originated it and *intended it for evil.*" These were men "wholly uninfluenced by moral or religious impulses" and thus "selfish" and "justly chargeable with *moral wrong.* . . . God may and we believe will over-rule slavery, even in the hands of such moral monsters to his glory, in the social and moral elevation of the slaves." Such slaveholders and traders could in "no sense appeal to the example of scriptures for justification."[60] But the important point for Winans and Buck was "that there is another class of slaveholders": "Christians . . . who hope for the time when slaves in this country shall be so advanced in the arts, in sciences, and religion as to be perfectly capable of self-government." In 1849, the optimistic Kentucky Baptist Buck felt "confident that there are countless thousands of slaveholders in this country who hold slaves in fear of God."[61] Evangelicals, like Buck, had rhetorically transformed slavery from an economic and political system into a multitude of individual moral decisions. Slavery did not cause harm; bad slaveholders did. But evangelicals assumed that the bad slaveholders were few, and soon to be converted anyway. Besides, who was counting? All the good evangelical slaveholders would soon turn slavery to good by their moral power. *If* they were left alone.

Abolitionism attacked slavery on just this point. Slaveholding was sin and slaveholders should immediately give up their slaves. As with drinking or licentiousness, the sinners had the power to simply stop the offending act today, if they were righteous. Southerners had just spent a generation and a half building up a sense of their righteousness and becoming accustomed to speaking of themselves in the uncompromising and confident personal language of evangelical moralism. Abolitionism struck southerners exactly where they were least likely to listen or feel anyone else had authority to speak to them—in the realm of personal religious morality. The southern evangelical response to abolitionism was swift and certain. Abolitionism constituted a heresy. It also, however, offered an opportunity to express the South's position on a range of topics—the origins of slavery, the special relationship of the South to God, character, race, the future of slavery, and the possibility of emancipation. The chapter that follows examines how southern evangelicals built a proslavery vision of their region after they had dismissed abolitionism.

4

The Evangelical Vision of the South and Its Future

Ministers took up the battle against abolitionism with ferocious glee and quickly helped split the three evangelical churches into separate northern and southern wings. Religious secession and civil war followed instantly on the heels of the slavery debate. After they had split in spirit in 1835, the evangelical churches split in form in 1837 (the Presbyterians), 1844 (the Methodists), and 1845 (the Baptists). Proslavery then became even more popular after 1846, when evangelicals directed their messages to southerners from exclusively southern pulpits. Ministers had found a message that made them popular and relevant to events, and southern evangelicals published and preached an endless wave of proslavery that did not cease until 1865. The debate with the North never abated, but after 1845 at least, southerners denounced and dismissed abolitionism. There ceased to be any exchange of ideas with abolitionism. When northern and southern ministers met in debate, especially the three great public debates between Baptists Richard Fuller and Francis Wayland in 1846, Presbyterians Nathan Rice and Jonathan Blanchard in 1845, and Methodists William Brownlow and Abraham Pryne in 1857, moderate antislavery ministers—not perfectionist abolitionists—met southern ministers. Even these debates rarely constituted an exchange of ideas; they more resembled a contest of sectional champions, or a game of righteous, intellectual, and regional one-upsmanship. The combatants in these crucial debates were at least skilled and serious. Out of the national spotlight and without articulate opponents to share the stage, many southern evangelicals after 1835 turned the abolitionists and then the North into heretical bogeymen and fodder for scathing sermons. Evangelicals thereby built the cultural foundations for secession and civil war over the course of the generation prior to 1860. The innumerable proslavery documents produced in this generation give the most valuable window into the mind of the antebellum South. Southern ministers were preaching to the converted from southern pulpits and telling them what they wanted to hear. What they heard about the history and nature of slavery, the North, the nature of race, the possibility of emancipation, the economy, the future of the South, and the standards of conduct for ethical behavior would surprise most Americans in the twenty-first century. The surprise would be one of recognition, not just of the debunking of historical cliches. Slavery is now long dead, but the moral arguments used to support it have a familiar ring. Antebellum southern ideology had roots reaching deep into the enduring cultural foundations of the United States.

This chapter will examine southern evangelicals' role in church schisms, racism, southern nationalism, dreams of economic progress, and visions of the future of slavery (and emancipation). Southerners' positions on these issues were remarkably modern. They were based in "Christianized competitive individualism," which is a polite way of avoiding the term "capitalism." After the church schisms, southern evangelicals did not use their regional pulpits to denounce individualism, but to trumpet Victorian "force of character." Evangelical racism did not make its first principle biological and perpetual inferiority, but an ongoing competitive struggle for moral superiority. Evangelical southern nationalism did not imply political revolution, but a laissez-faire outlook. Evangelical economics did not appeal to fixed classes, scarcity, or providential disasters, but to fabulous technological, social, and material progress. Evangelical attitudes toward the future of slavery did not label slavery permanent, or emancipation anathema. The very flexibility of evangelical proslavery made its appeal stronger and its cultural legacy and damage more enduring. A static backward-looking proslavery, out of tune with the tenor of the times, would not have attached itself so permanently to the antebellum landscape or adjusted so well to the tumultuous events of the pre–Civil War era and its long aftermath.

The evangelical churches' organizational and annual conferences had long constituted the principal occasions for northerners and southerners to encounter each other in institutional settings. Participants in these meetings were well informed about developments outside their congregations and aware of the personalities and preoccupations of their counterparts from other regions. The inescapable course of sectional division within these churches was therefore apparent to leading proslavery ministers from the moment antislavery became a moral force. William Smith of Virginia was urging separation from the northern apostates in the General Conference of the Methodist Episcopal Church before 1836.[1] William Plumer of Richmond spoke for slavery at the 1837 General Synod Meeting that split the Presbyterian Church. Plumer was subsequently chosen moderator of the predominantly southern Old School wing.[2] Converse Amasa had been calling for a separate southern assembly even before this momentous meeting. Baptist William Brantley had announced before 1837 that southern Baptists were "a separate people" from their northern counterparts.[3] Smith, Plumer, Amasa, and Brantley were all either from the border states or among northern emigres to the South. Not coincidentally, all—Smith and Plumer in particular—were also well versed in the formulas of contemporary moral science and ready to transpose arguments about slavery into didactic exchanges on the unassailable religious orthodoxy of the South.

The division of the evangelical denominations preceded those of the political parties and the nation primarily because of the kind of men involved. Evangelical leaders were not politicians. As proslavery southern Baptist and colonizationist Richard Fuller commented, "Politics is a science of compromises, but religion allows no compromises with evil."[4] These religious and often intellectual leaders also made the first and most fervent commitments to the mid-nineteenth-century ideology of a formalistic faith in individual character (virtue-power) and a divine economy, which they helped popularize and politicize in the era. An important debate among historians involves the sincerity, and mix of moral and material motives, of proslavery ministers. Larry Tise, the leading historian of proslavery, made a powerful argument against the centrality of evangelical profession in these men's lives: "Although proslavery clergymen practiced evangelical religion, the diaries, journals, and personal correspondences hardly reflect these realities. Whereas proslavery clergymen endorsed religious forms and practices publicly from the pulpit, in their private lives they seemed concerned heavily with social and financial success. . . . They all had a will to power."[5] This analysis is exaggerated and in many ways inaccurate, but it does highlight a key reason for the rapid and acrimonious splits in the evangelical churches. Evangelical leaders who behaved in the manner described above were not being hypocritical or ignoring their beliefs; they also preached the "will to power," and it lay at the heart of evangelical morality. Moral virtue was exalted as the key to power, character as the key to virtue, and will as the key to character. These men did not believe in compromise and wanted to live the life of moral and material power that they preached. An assembly of leaders from a movement increasingly committed to didactic formulations of this moral ideal and to campaigns for encouraging social and individual conformity to the ideal, but with different interpretations of financial success, was not likely to find much common ground once those differences became clear.

Both the personalities and the purposes at these meetings exacerbated dissent. The denominational assemblies met to distribute funds and seats of leadership. Once the regional definitions of success became a moral issue, so did control of power and finances within the denominational structures. The sectional splits in both the Methodist and Baptist denominations—the two largest in the nation—clearly followed from this sequence.[6] The Presbyterian split of 1837 was not as clearly sectional nor as concerned with whether slaveholding represented moral success. (This, however, cannot be said of Presbyterianism's subsequent sectional splits in 1857, when the New School split into northern and southern wings, and in 1861, when the Old School similarly split after southern secession). The development of evangelical moralism itself, rather than its sectional applications, first set off alarms within Presbyterianism.

It was not surprising that the controversy over moralism came first and only in the denomination with the strictest emphasis on theology and education. By the early 1830s, Presbyterian moral reformers and Charles Finney's revivalism were celebrating individual efficacy and exposing the long-developing departure of Americans from the Westminster Confession (which Finney claimed never to have read) and Reformed tradition. Although the "New School" impulse to democratize theology, reform, and church government initiated controversy and division, slavery still played a crucial role in the southern repudiation of the departure from tradition. Many southern Presbyterians who were sympathetic to New School positions or to flexibility on these theological and other issues went with the Old School when it was clear that most antislavery forces were in the New School faction. Albert Barnes, the chief theological heretic on trial from the New School faction in 1837, was also a leading publisher of material on biblical antislavery. Presbyterian theological orientations also helped guarantee that the 1837 split would not be purely sectional, as all the subsequent antebellum evangelical schisms would be. Abolitionist theological heresies and the strength of traditional biblical sanctions for slaveholding held many northern Presbyterians to the predominantly southern Old School wing in the 1837 split.

The Methodist break in 1844 was more straightforwardly sectional and concerned with moral success and slavery. The controversy causing the split in the Methodist Conference centered around whether Bishop James Andrew could retain a position of power and leadership in Methodism after becoming a slaveholder. Although Andrew was willing to resign, his fellow southern ministers would not allow it because his was the perfect case for proving their point about slavery and the providential economy. Andrew, like so many southern ministers, had become a slaveholder through marriage. Southern Methodists could argue that his slaves had not been sought or bought but bestowed, as if from God's will and not Andrew's self-will. When it became clear that the Methodist Conference would not also bestow power on Andrew, the Conference agreed to a regional division "as brethren beloved in the Lord."[7] This facade crumbled four years later when the two sides contended in court over another measure of moral power: division of funds and territorial jurisdictions.[8]

The Baptists' less centralized organization split a year after the Methodists' over similar issues involving funds and leadership of missions. The mission and publishing boards controlling these areas functioned as the only national institutional connections among Baptists. Their sectional split had the ironic effect of more clearly defining and strengthening commitment to conference structures—particularly in the South. Reverend William Johnson commented at the first Southern Baptist Convention meeting in 1845 that ministers would now be free "to promote slavery as a Bible institution" within a stronger organization.[9] The ministers themselves realized a more immediate benefit. Southern Baptists would no longer have to meet in forums where, as Reverend Thornton Stringfellow put it, "our characters are traduced."[10]

The church schisms gave southern evangelicals both greater freedom to promote their vision of slaveholding and more powerful organizational and ideological tools with which to complete their capture of southern culture. The evangelical publishing empire, for example, was now fully under sectional direction. Proslavery arguments were increasingly directed toward other southerners rather than against the North. Evangelical proslavery teachings were ubiquitous in the South—indeed its major cultural product—and could appear almost anywhere, in any form.[11] The renewal of missionary work to the slaves in the 1830s was inseparable from religious proslavery, and the movement continued to grow as a forum for evangelical nostrums in the antebellum period.

Dissociation from northern evangelicals made it easier for many ministers to proselytize a Christian slaveholding ethic more aggressively. The slavery debate provided ministers with a ready-made verbal and political weapon with which to press their projects. Ministers in the newly independent sectional denominations adapted northern evangelicals' stereotypes of southern moral laxity and conduct to their own purposes. They easily employed such critiques to call for conformity to evangelical standards and professions in the South—thereby enhancing socio-political influence for evangelicals. Northern antislavery also provided a convenient threat against southerners who did not pay lip service to the regional predominance of evangelicalism and who thereby aided and abetted the enemy by embodying their stereotypes of impious, impulsive southerners. Ministers in effect held that their position in the biblical and moral debate on slavery *obligated* the South to display a front of evangelical orthodoxy and unity. As Presbyterian minister Robert Dabney commented, "To enjoy the advantages of the Bible argument in our favor slaveholders will have to pay the price."[12]

The price was not steep. The price that masters had to pay for their proslavery defense by ministers was that of attributing the economic behavior they were already engaged in to Christian motives.

Proslavery ministers were explicit about the practicality of their "reform" ideals in the debate over the morality of slavery with both abolitionists and evangelical antislavery forces and in their subsequent proslavery moralizing to southerners. In 1841 Methodist T.C. Thornton replied to abolitionist critiques that southerners treated their slaves well only out of self-interest: "Well be it so! Christ approved it [slavery] . . . for his master's interest. What objection can there be to all this?" That ameliorative acts and attitudes by antebellum slaveholders were interested and necessary proved they were natural and providential as well as biblical: "self-interest and self-preservation are powerful motives to human action. Man is a creature of motive—he cannot, he does not, and his God never commands him to act without motive.... He protects us *physically, morally, and politically* from all harm and all foes."[13]

Southern evangelicals, after the church schisms, directed their energies at stressing the formulas of character and conscience in publications aimed at fellow southerners rather than at replying to northern critics. Thereby they both answered northern criticisms and appropriated them as a spur for southerners who were not defining their conduct on the basis of evangelical standards. Georgia Baptist Iveson Brookes used his proslavery arguments "to exhort sister states" in the South to "with shameface confess that we have lived too much at our ease and have not exerted to the extent of our ability the opportunities afforded for the culture of genius and talents which God ... [has] given us." Brookes then ran through the typical antislavery list of southern shortcomings, agreeing that the South was "too exclusively agricultural" and that "proper levels of education and literature [were] not attained." Brookes, however, looked forward to the day when the South could "overwhelm them [northerners] with statistics" on "manufacturing, railroads, and canals in every quarter" of the South. The South needed further character-building, but Brookes rejected the antislavery criticism that the requisite moral and religious resources were not in place in the region: "We are represented as being now a posse of degenerate ignoramuses and heroes of the bowie knife ... is it true? ... degeneracy? If we look to the department of religion do Manleys, Fullers, and Howells indicate a degeneracy since Furmans, Mercers, and Brantleys?"[14] Brookes's list of his brother southern Baptists—and supporters of slavery—could have included Patrick Hues Mell, who took a similar view of critiques of southern character and violence. Mell admitted that "Christian masters" were "tempted to treat slaves harshly" but insisted that this made southerners superior moral athletes because "temptations themselves if resisted, do us no harm but the reverse." Slaveholders—according to southern evangelicals—had great opportunities to curb their desires and build habits of self-control and "individual character."[15]

Evangelicals also admitted and even celebrated the immorality and irreligion of the frontier in order to prove that conversion and character were sweeping them away.[16] Thornton Stringfellow pointed out that Texas, like colonial Virginia, had been settled by the "most lawless set of adventurers who ever lived," but "even out of these materials" evangelical "character" and slaveholding "could secure the highest results of human progress."[17]

The massive campaign for evangelical standards of respectability went on side by side, and often overlapped, with the torrent of proslavery moralizing coming from the pens of ministers involved in both projects. These proslavery ministers were frequently involved in the major project of formulating and fostering standards of childrearing. Proslavery evangelicals preached the values of internalized guilt and moral self-monitoring, common to contemporary British and northern religious awakenings. Southerners also obsessively linked conscience and character-building to domesticity. In response to abolitionist charges about "gross beastly licentiousness" in slaveholding areas, southerners often admitted such cases, pointed to northern urban prostitution as a similar failing, and then asserted that the major influence on southern mores lay elsewhere: "The restraining influences that oppose gratification of sensual desire are virtuous principles instilled by parents into children. . . . Have we not virtuous mothers to instill earnest principles in our youth?"[18]

The tendency of the regional moral debate to lapse into interpretations of economic statistics as the antebellum period progressed was particularly pronounced on this issue of domestic virtue. The census of 1850 was endlessly raked for providential proofs of character lapses in the opposing region. Prostitution was often directly tied to homelessness in the evangelical imagination, and southern ministers found in the census a tantalizing discrepancy between domiciles and population in New England, where "70,243 families [were] without a home." This statistic brought a typical antebellum hosanna from B.F. Stringfellow. He ascribed the low incidence of homelessness in his region to the influence of southern homes, with children "there to learn the lessons of virtue . . . rather than expose them to the corrupting influence of the public house: there is no mother who would not toil with aching bones to guard her daughter with the shield of the domestic hearth. At home virtue flourishes, abroad vice takes its seed . . . the earth of the cabin is the bed of man's integrity, of woman's purity." Antislavery forces hit back using southern statistics on lagging rates of literary production and manufacturing, and especially on the low numbers of educational (and reform) institutions. Many southern proslavery ministers were already involved in promoting reforms in these areas before the sectional debate reached a crescendo after 1850, and all conceded in their proslavery tracts that "we admire their [northern] efforts in the cause of education."[19]

Reform campaigns associated with conscience, character, domesticity, and childrearing were comparatively underdeveloped in the South; proslavery evangelicals admitted as much. They insisted (relatively accurately), however, that this was a case of material underdevelopment rather than of a paucity of adherents to evangelical profession and its rhetoric of respectability. Southerners believed they had laid the moral foundations for educational reform, so they did not doubt that the material progress would follow to rival the North's. Southerners were certain that they would catch up anyway, because the religious foundations under the North's schoolhouse were decaying. A Baptist proslavery tract lamented the deficiency of southern "intelligence," but mentioned that the author's state had attempted "to organize a system of common schools. Instruction failed, because of the sparseness of population.... Georgia was settled a century after Massachusetts. Who will say that she, a hundred years hence, will not have passed far beyond the position now occupied by Massachusetts?"[20] Further in the wilds of Texas and Alabama during the late 1830s and early 1840s, Presbyterian Daniel Baker conceded that "it is said, and I fear with too much truth, that we in the South are an impulsive people." Baker used this antislavery critique to discuss, not slaveholding, but the need for southerners to be more "systematic in organizing" and "foresighted" in their approaches to charity, reform, education, and childrearing.[21] A common school system was often out of reach, but organized households were not.

Advice to parents about forming unyielding evangelical characters and consciences was thus at the center of the enormous campaign for distribution of sermons and tracts in the South, as in the rest of the nation.[22] Baker himself was famous for children's sermons and pious literature, in which he gave typically horrific warnings about the effects of impulsive behavior. "Oh my dear little reader, *never* indulge in angry passions," he pleaded after graphically describing the body of a nine-year-old suicide victim who had allowed his thoughts to wander into violent channels.[23] The exercise of force of character against one's youthful instincts meant little without conscience to guide it, so Baker focused on giving younger children standards of self-reflection, foresight, and internalized guilt. In his popular *Daniel Baker's Talk to Little Children,* a six-year-old girl's proper response to the question "What is your soul?" was "*My think,*" to which Baker added for his pious young audience, "Don't you *think,* child? Well, see you do *think.*"[24] James Henry Thornwell once wrote to "congratulate" a friend on the death of his young son, assuring him the boy was in heaven, where the best of all possible things was happening to him: "his education was continuing."[25]

Baptist Richard Furman interlaced similar and even more demanding rhetoric about conscience among his sermons and tracts addressed to adults, in which he reminded them always to "look to the weight of *individual responsibility.*"[26] Furman's popular tract on *Human Accountability* shows the ubiquity not only of these models of personality but also of proslavery. This tract did not address the issue of slavery, but when Furman quoted the biblical injunction "to every servant the master says 'occupy til I come,'" he casually reminded southerners that since he was sure they knew slaves were to occupy themselves with heavenly thoughts, not material circumstances, whites were to do likewise. His vision of the constant self-reflection necessary to proper mental organization was arresting. Furman told his audience always to anticipate "an individual as well as a general judgment" at which "the daguerreotype of your whole life shall be held up before you."[27]

Strong consciences and characters were primarily advocated as necessities for proper parenting.[28] Tracts on childrearing stressed that "if parents do not govern themselves, they can never govern their children."[29] Such moral formulas were always cast in the terms of irrefutable physical laws of cause and effect. If individuals governed their instincts, they automatically affected and had control over their physical surroundings—even their children. Daniel Baker included the following story in his advice to parents. He had encountered the "best behaved" family of children he had ever seen amid the squalor of the town of Houston in 1840. When he asked the mother the secret of their remarkable behavior, she replied, "No secret sir, except I control myself."[30] Baker assumed that the instrumental connection between this internal act on the part of the mother and the resulting conduct of the children required no explanation—which it did not, given evangelical assumptions about "moral force."[31]

Similar lessons on the inevitable effects of *failing* to form character and proper habits of conscience often appeared in proslavery tracts. The evangelicals' strict character-based construction of self-identity encouraged unforgiving proscriptions against the acceptance of perceived disorder or deviance in others. Antebellum believers were anxious to perceive and preserve an automatic and absolute rule of punishment for the development of an improper personality. This was the flip-side of the rewards for (what southern evangelicals considered their own) self-control. Matthew Estes of Mississippi stressed that a single lapse into dishonesty or petty theft on the part of a young man would guarantee that he "will never recover his lost character . . . [and] will ever feel the scorn, contempt, and neglect of society."[32] The Reverend George Junkin, an educator in Virginia and Ohio, directly used such lapses to support slavery: "Some parents take no control over their children. They are too lenient, and have too little conscience to feel the obligation to rule their household." This gave children "freedom from all restraints; and of course they become pests of society, and, ultimately the inmates of penitentiaries and candidates for the gibbet. . . . So masters are bound to keep their servants in bondage until they are fitted to be free."[33] Changing patterns of white identity and social discipline clearly had implications for the prevalent forms of racism that supported slavery. Proslavery evangelicals' definition of slaves as school children being restrained and trained for self-government rather than as savages, sambos, or perpetual children simply ensured re-creation of the cycle of racial superiority and subordination in a new phase of slavery. Indeed the emphasis on character among evangelicals may have heightened the tensions implicit in the dynamics of racism.[34] Racism, like proslavery and the institution of slavery itself, was not a static, monolithic, or isolated phenomenon.

Whites had long used negative stereotypes of blacks to reinforce their own self-image and self-esteem.[35] The evangelical model of character constructed a new identity for nineteenth-century southerners, and so traditional racist images and dynamics were recast to perpetuate myths of white supremacy. From the time of the first English encounters with Africa during the period of exploration and colonization, religious moralism had been central to the dynamic of racism. Christian imagery of the realms of light and darkness, good and evil, easily translated into racial categories. Blacks became the locus of generalized debasement and enslavement even as English representatives of "Christian civilization" were supposed to control and repress their own "darker" selves. English proscriptions and battles against their "inner-blackness" and "animal-like passions" of dark instincts, particularly sexual ones, were associated with and projected onto Africans.[36] Next to the Bible, Mungo Park's *Travels, in the Interior of Africa,* filled with psycho-sexual myths about blacks and "ourangotangs," remained the work most often cited by defenders of slavery, including evangelical ministers.[37] Of course, stereotypes of blacks as savage and highly sexualized enabled whites to rationalize their own physical, economic, and sexual exploitation of them. Such distorted perceptions of black behavior, however, also had arisen—and were perpetuated—because they denied whites' own brutality and preserved their religious identity and sense of moral order. Projection of the categories of saved and damned, good Christians and heathens, onto racial differences assured white believers they had achieved a proper measure of moral and spiritual elevation over the general run of God's creatures.

The constructions of African heathenism, savagery, and outlandishness prevalent in the seventeenth and eighteenth centuries should have had little relevance to the racial views of proslavery ministers, whose congregations often included slaves. But racism has always had little to do with the objective behavior and beliefs of blacks and much to do with the cultural and psychological needs of whites. Given the traditional dynamic of racism in America, the fact that blacks were no longer "heathens" in the antebellum era mattered less than the fact that white southerners were no longer colonial Englishmen or nominal Anglicans. Evangelicals' obsessive self-monitoring introspection and stress on self-restraint preserved, when they did not heighten, the tensions implicit in the historical (and psycho-sexual) origins of American racism. Despite the biblical proslavery emphasis on the Christianizing of slaveholding and the conversion and uplifting of the slaves, the evangelical movement channeled white supremacy into contemporary modes of expression rather than narrowing the traditional gulf between the races.

Although the chasm between the races was not significantly modified by nineteenth-century evangelical concepts, the evangelical movement repudiated many earlier racist constructs and practices, as it had colonial religious and political ideals. Antebellum evangelicals, particularly educated ministers, rejected the traditional hierarchies of race, nature, and the heavens that placed blacks closer to higher animals and whites to the realm of angels, which had been formalized in the Great Chain of Being.[38] Evangelicals always pledged their allegiance to belief in the unity of races.[39] "There is no such thing as gradations from brute natures to that of human: for man stands alone being the image of God," pro-

nounced Josiah Priest in his *Bible Defense of Slavery*.[40] Priest's typical statement was an aside in his popular collection of an unbroken litany of
biblical and psycho-sexual attacks on blacks—all of which were amended
by his constant claim—echoed by D. W. Griffith at the start of *The Birth of
a Nation* and countless other racists—to "not have written a word out of
prejudice against blacks."[41] Priest, a former harness maker from New
York, was sadly representative of the evangelical's tendency to depart from
many of the racist arguments from creation or permanent curses, but to
recast brutal white supremacy in the framework of a competitive struggle
to build moral character.

The popular biblical argument from Genesis 9 was included in the
new rhetorical trend. Genesis 9 supposedly described how the black race
had descended through Noah's son Ham, whose offspring had been cursed
with enslavement. Antebellum abolitionists as well as proslavery southerners
accepted that blacks were "the children of Ham."[42] The story explained
the origins of racial differences, and southerners cited this divinely sanctioned institution of human bondage to prove that slavery could be acceptable to God. Although some proslavery spokesmen used this ancient
biblical tradition to argue that all blacks were forever relegated by God to
the status of slaves, most evangelical spokesmen stressed that Ham (and his
current descendants) "brought himself into his sad dilemma."[43] Sweeping racial dichotomies no longer stressed the ascendancy of civilized human over heathen beast, but of moral victors over vanquished—not in
competition with each other but, as ministers were forever sermonizing,
"with themselves."[44] Thornton Stringfellow provided the standard for-
mulation of character-based racism and competitive proslavery: "The slave
race is placed upon a common level with all other competitors for the
rewards of merit; but as the slaves are inferior in the qualities which give
success among competitors . . . [they find] poverty or die out by inches
degraded by vice and crime, unpitied by honest and virtuous men. Should
the time ever come, when emancipation in its consequences will com-
port with the moral, social, and political obligations of Christianity, then
Christian masters will invest their slaves with freedom, [masters] who
without any agency of their own, have been made in this land of liberty,
their providential guardians."[45] Under certain conditions such evangelical
constructions of the personality and of providential economy produced
even greater racist pressures and horrors than did traditional formulas alone.

The Christian prescription of character-building put whites' tenden-

cies both to associate blacks with the passions and to project their own
repressed instincts onto slaves into an ominous new context. Proslavery
Presbyterian Nathan Rice defined Christ's mission as "declaring a war of
extermination against all the guilty passions of this earth."[46] "*Extermination*" was a word that invariably appeared in moral defenses of slavery,
especially in reference to free blacks, "prematurely" emancipated slaves,
and Indians.[47] As in other aspects of southern proslavery, Thomas R. Dew
led the way in citing the travels of "Mungo Park" and describing how the
"decree of Providence had gone forth," promising "total extermination"
of those with weak character. Dew, like evangelical ministers, concluded
that slavery was "humane" because "there is nothing but slavery [to]
eradicate the character of improvidence" that would otherwise bring
extermination.

The vision of extermination offered by evangelicals was inevitably
providential—never a plan or action executed by the righteous but a
natural self-operating outcome of God's law and an individual's own failings. The development of force of character produced material benefits;
"inferiority of character" issued in punishment.[48] Dr. Matthew Estes, an
admirer of Dew, described how "ultimate extinction" of those who did
not make themselves "fit for freedom" was a result of the progressive and
utilitarian nature of Providence: "Ultimate extinction . . . why should we
lament such an event? . . . The extinction of a tribe, or even a whole
people, is not more to be lamented than the extinction of one generation
to make room for another. God cares nothing for the pride of man: he
executes his purposes regardless of the whims and caprices of men . . .
[and] does that which promotes the highest good of universal humanity."[49] Much of this language in southern proslavery applied to free blacks
and Africans; slavery was not considered an instrument of extinction.
Estes, for example, qualified his prediction about racial extermination by
noting that "the same race in the United States has made some advance
in civilization": "Protestant Christians constitute the only portion of the
globe in a progressive state. . . . The destiny of all the inferior grades of
mankind with the exception probably of the negroes is extinction—and
extinction, too, much earlier than most people imagine."[50] Most slaves
after all were Protestant Christians in 1843 when Estes made this argument, which fit the "reform" aspirations of evangelical proslavery. Such
claims were also a ready answer to the antislavery contention that slavery
corrupted black character.

Nonchalant contemplation of "utter extermination" in ministers' as well as other southern spokesmen's proslavery rhetoric often went hand in hand with praise for slaves' moral advancement.[51] Leading Baptist apologists Stringfellow and Iveson Brookes singled out the slaves' "dress and order" in church as proof that they were "daily improving" and "more elevated in character."[52] The evangelization of slaves was compatible with white supremacy because, as one biblical proslavery tract emphasized, "the moral superiority of the master over the slave . . . consists in a *greater* elevation of character."[53] This author added that "were it not for the restraints of [the slaves'] Christian religion," these "beings of impulse" would still be fit for "a blast from heaven as [the one that] ripped out Sodom and Gomorrah!"[54] Since white southerners had adopted stricter and more refined definitions of their characters, caricatures of mere looseness and inferiority of character in Christianized and "daily improving" slaves were enough to insure perceptions of a gulf between the races as great as that seen between seventeenth-century "Christian Englishmen" and "African savage heathens." Both nineteenth-century progressive providentialism and the evangelical emphasis on repression and eradication of the instincts and emotions associated with blacks encouraged virulent racial attitudes.

Discussions of religious exercises and gatherings present an exception to the general pattern of character-based racism in evangelical proslavery. Despite its overwhelming obsession with self-restraint and discipline in its followers' personal and social life (conduct in "the world"), the southern evangelical movement legitimated displays of emotional impulse in its religious services. Antebellum believers actually looked forward to the era's long church meetings and revivals because they offered a needed place of release. Even extreme racist proslavery ministers, like Iveson Brookes who took the minority view that slavery was perpetual, argued that character was lost in "any white person putting himself upon the level with a negro in anything other than religion."[55] Proslavery spokesmen who contemplated racial extermination had no qualms about praising the way slaves "possess great earnestness and zeal in their religious devotions . . . more earnestness and zeal than the whites themselves . . . infidelity among them is almost entirely unknown."[56] In religious practice alone white standards of emotional and instinctual restraint used to label and attack blacks were partially relaxed. Although southerners, once within the walls of evangelical—often biracial—churches, may have modified the intellectual and psychological construct fostering character-based racism, there were more definite historical and practical roots for this aspect of religious proslavery. Slaves had responded overwhelmingly to the evangelical message of Methodists and Baptists. Whether or not white worshipers in the decades before the Civil War treated slaves more nearly as equals in biracial congregations, there is ample evidence that evangelicals had done so at the turn of the century before they had achieved respectability and come to dominate the ranks of slaveholders.[57] This experience at least found echoes in the later proslavery sermons produced by evangelicals who were still ministering to and often actively promoting the mission to the slaves.[58]

Recognition of the religious morality of slaves naturally served a propagandistic function in the slavery debate and in several ways reinforced white supremacy. The Reverend Fred Ross condescendingly proclaimed that the slaves were the "most susceptible to social and religious love, of all the races of mankind."[59] This was little different from similar statements about women's religious propensity and moral elevation used to perpetuate subordination. Submission and slavery to Christ were prominent themes of evangelical sermonizing—as Old School Presbyterian James Sloan rhapsodized in his proslavery tract, "Christians do not belong to themselves."[60] This standard extended beyond the church walls to canonize slaves' and women's social roles, whereas it was not deemed appropriate to Christian manliness or the force of character men were expected to display in their social roles. A proslavery pamphlet by a Presbyterian minister's son recorded that "it is not degrading for a slave to submit to a blow—neither is it to a priest or woman."[61] The evangelical character ideal could be the basis for recasting traditional forms of racial subordination even as it dismantled their time-honored intellectual justifications and ameliorated some of their abuses.

The practice of moralizing on the theme of character formation was crucial to the racist justification of slavery and the development of an evangelical ethic of slaveholding and of labor discipline (to be discussed in the following chapter), but the wider socio-economic meaning and influence of this orientation was enormous. Southerners had already made claims to greater evangelical piety in their debate with abolitionists. In their arguments about the character ideal, they proceeded to establish an absolute and automatic relation between improper moral organization and failure on the one hand, and proper organization and the resultant "force of character" manifested in all relationships and actions on the other hand. Southern evangelicals then defined regional identity in terms of the rhetoric of character. The proslavery focus on the proving and building of regional character, therefore, demanded recognition of southerners' providential right to political and economic power, as well as their right to hold slaves. The evangelical ideal of character connected all of these positions. Louisiana Methodist T.C. Thornton explained the link in a classic evangelical passage: "As rights are most evidently conditional, the proper measure of them is to be found in the character of the man. . . . There is nothing of exaction in one man's possessing rights more extensive than another, for they are almost instinctively awarded to him."[62] Southern evangelicals who were spreading the doctrines of character and conscience in the region, therefore, understood Yankee claims to superior character and conscience as inextricably an assertion of national pre-eminence. In response, proslavery evangelicals were declaring that their standards of conduct were transforming households, children, and occasionally benighted frontier regions. "The Southern States," the Reverend William A. Smith asserted, "always great in the councils of the nation—are always and everywhere the *true friends* and invincible supporters of Protestant freedom, or the rights of conscience."[63]

Evangelical antislavery activists were busy not in disputing this doctrine of rights and freedom, but in establishing the opposite conclusion. Southerners lacked character, and their consciences were dead to their responsibilities toward slaves, so it inevitably followed that the region did not merit political and economic reward or control over new territory (or even the territory it already possessed). Georgia Methodist minister and educator A.B. Longstreet seized on the Wilmot Proviso of 1846 as the direct outcome of antislavery moralists' "undisguised purpose." The proposal would have denied any of the land won in the Mexican War to southern expansion. Longstreet, however, pointed out in his series of proslavery *Letters from Georgia to Massachusetts* that southerners had already attained the right to control over these areas through their development of evangelical personalities and will. Longstreet, quoting a citizen of Georgia who had written to the editor of the *Western Continent,* informed Massachusetts of the universal resolve in his region: the "sons [of the South] do not intend to be fibbed out of their character."[64]

Historians have long noted the vulgar features of the nineteenth-century character ideal, which trumpeted the self-made man and the nation's manifest destiny. Proslavery spokesmen boasted of their "individuality of character" and insisted that in the South "a man of real merit has a finer opportunity to demonstrate his character and realize distinction than anywhere in the world."[65] Enormous claims were made for the efficacy of individual will, and vast material rewards were promised for virtuous exertion.[66] The equally vital moral emphases of this mentality are not always explicated because they are highly irrational and contradictory.

American Protestants of the nineteenth century engaged in a simultaneous exaltation and denial of individual abilities through their emphasis on character. Antebellum ministers and parents attributed enormous powers to individual will but insisted that such exertions be directed only toward a limited set of moral goals and to internal acts of discipline. They also spoke of the innumerable spiritual and material "fruits" waiting to be plucked by those who strove against sin, while maintaining that the whole outcome was absolutely dependent on character formation and God's Providence.[67] "Do your duty," one proslavery minister instructed, "and leave the consequences to an over-ruling Providence."[68] A key to the ethical success preached by evangelicals as an explicit corollary to the character ideal was therefore that political or economic organization for the purpose of attaining wealth was unnecessary. In fact, to employ such techniques in order to seek or even analyze material power was insidiously atheistic.[69] In the 1850s southerners judged the Republican Party and especially Hinton Rowan Helper, the southern author of *The Impending Crisis* who supported the Republican criticism of slavery, to be guilty of these sins. These culprits betrayed a lack of faith in God's moral ordering of the universe by implying that lasting success was obtainable through mundane, demoralized means—such as the setting aside of territory for one group's benefit or the marshaling of cold statistics to prove equal opportunity a myth.

Men who did not allow individual character to find its reward betrayed the faith of the age. This constituted both the antislavery accusation against the South and the southern denunciation of antislavery. Southerners, according to antislavery activists, had built and maintained an artificial economic *"system"* allowing those who avoided labor to receive its rewards.[70] Unitarian abolitionist William E. Channing argued that slavery violated the sacred order of Nature because it blocked advancement when "a slave surpass[es] his master in intellect . . . or moral worth."[71] "It seems hard," argued antislavery evangelical Jonathan Blanchard, "that the hand made hard with toil should not feel the cash it earns."[72] *The New York Antislavery Standard* commented upon John Calhoun's death by saying that he "is only to be regarded as one who was a *systematic* robber of the poorest of God's children."[73] The slaveholder ate his bread by the sweat of another man's brow. In coercing and controlling the labor of other men, the slaveholder brought more than his own individual character to bear in economic competition. By building their own distorted moral system of desert and discipline, slaveholders thwarted the one based on character. Slaveholders, in other words, were assuming the role of God.

Worse, when northerners instructed slaveholders about their monumental heresy, southerners attempted to deny the sin. Antislavery ministers were sure this explained the proslavery evangelicals' "unwilling[ness] to discuss the right or wrong of slavery in the abstract—so that while *single exercises* of injustice may be condemned, *a system of injustice* may be vindicated."[74] Antislavery advocates argued that attempts by southerners to preserve the unnatural economic system both proved their prideful, evil intentions and guaranteed punishment and disaster from Providence. Horace Mann spoke in Congress in 1848, warning of the sweeping threat posed by this artificial economy: "Slavery diminishes the productive capacity of all operatives, bond and free, by cramping their minds and reducing them to mere machines. . . . Can Christian philanthropy, or enlightened patriotism, look without fear and horror upon the corruption of the old political faith?"[75] Although the Reverend Blanchard was more guarded in conceding that "careful distinction should be kept up between the sinfulness of slavery, in itself, and the personal wickedness of slaveholders," he concluded that the "system" itself constituted a "violation of the Kingdom of God on earth. . . . It must therefore be destroyed that the Kingdom of God may come."[76]

The most sophisticated version of the providential antislavery argument appeared in Edward Beecher's concept of "organic sin."[77] Beecher, like his father Lyman and sister Harriet, was immersed in the long tradition of Puritan (Congregational) theological speculation. The idea of organic sin grew from the tradition of covenant theology that assumed a national or community responsibility for the fulfillment of God's moral directives. The sin of an individual in the nation or community was not a solitary transgression against duty but a violation of the covenant—and therefore a threat to the entire body politic. New England abolitionists who were troubled in conscience about slavery saw its wrongs not simply as evil in themselves but as a reflection on (and direct threat to) their personal moral standing.

Beecher directly applied his theory of organic sin to the system of slavery. Sin was built into the institutional operations of slavery. This argument not only made the transgressions of evil slaveholders (which all the defenders of slavery acknowledged) reflect on the moral standing of everyone, but also made irrelevant the southern claim that "good Christians" redeemed the master-slave relation. Even these "good" slaveholders (whose existence most abolitionists conceded) were inevitably involved in sin by their participation in the system. Many radical abolitionists used this concept of sin as the rationale for attacking all slaveholders, but many more used it as an escape clause, which allowed them to be "charitable" to individual slaveholders but uncompromising on the issue of slavery. Antislavery gradualists were particularly attracted to such arguments about the "social wrong" or "social sin" of the South.[78] Such a monumental and unnatural organization of society would collapse of its own weight if the forces of Providence were left to their devices.

Few proslavery spokesmen would even consider the existence of a possibly evil "system" of slavery, let alone the concept of organic sin. Proslavery spokesmen protested that the antislavery charge "that *American* slavery is a system of spiritual despotism, is not true. . . . The charge therefore that the principle of slavery is a principle which aims at the usurpation of the rights of God over the human soul is as false as it is monstrous and impossible."[79] The antislavery argument that the sin was in the system was untenable because it implied that southerners had taken on God's role and so far had *compelled* Him to acquiesce in their sin. God had clearly not destroyed the system, so if it was a violation of His Kingdom on earth, abolitionists were accusing God of incompetence or of complicity in sin. If there were a "system" of slavery in the South, it was "a system of Providence."[80] This system arose from the southerners' alignment of their society—perfectly according to conservatives—with God's actions and commandments, and not from implementation or deliberate perpetuation of their own system.

Most southern minsters were simply baffled by the antislavery arguments based on the concept of social sin. In 1844 Southern Baptist Richard Fuller denied there was any social aspect to sin: "the Gospel operates gradually and indirectly . . . chiefly through Christian character in individuals . . . its direct business is never with masses but individuals."[81] Old School Presbyterian James Sloan—almost certainly drawing the argument from Fuller's proslavery debates—puzzled over Francis Wayland's arguments about the "social evil" of slavery and simply gave up. He concluded that this incoherence resulted from a lapse in intellect by "this usually clear and intelligent author."[82] At the Methodist General Conference in Baltimore in 1842, Alexander McCaine of South Carolina's Edgefield district puzzled over a moderate antislavery minister's statement that "the sin [of slavery] is in the system":

> Of all the strange and unintelligible things that were advanced in debate, nothing surprised me more than the above statement; because it was uttered by one of the most long-headed, clear-sighted, and discerning men in the church. How *he* came to adopt such a sentiment I know not, unless it was because he was unwilling to admit that slavery is *not* a moral evil. I hope he will allow me to suggest to him a review of his principles, on the following grounds: Is a "system" accountable? Can sin be in the "system," separate from the moral agent? Can a "system" be punished? . . . My brother I mean no disrespect when I attach a note on your hypothesis. You are involved in a labyrinth, and do what you will, you will never get clear of your difficulties until you take the Bible as your guide.[83]

The typical proslavery evangelical did not even bother to puzzle over this charge. Instead, like McCaine in the rest of his speech at the Methodist Conference, they attacked the way "abolitionists would disturb the settled order of Providence."[84] Proslavery spokesmen were sure that abolitionists were the ones subverting character and building up a "well-organized system" in violation of the natural plan of Providence.[85] Thornton Stringfellow strove to describe the basic social heresy of abolitionists: "they are *organized,*" he decided.[86] Conspiratorial terms were predicated of abolitionists as soon as they gained public notice. Southerners reviled their "premeditated designs" and "acts of systematic hostility," which were "prosecuted through the medium of the post office."[87]

Josiah Priest's popular paranoid proslavery tracts traced the source of the abolitionist conspiracy to the typical culprit: "It is a thing of British origins, of Lordly birth, aroused in that cradle of despotism [House of Lords]—as has been every opposing principle and plot against American republicanism."[88] The germ of abolitionism, according to A.B. Longstreet, had been transmitted to New England, where it found receptive carriers in the long degenerating tradition of Puritan theological speculation and "tricky" Federalist politics. Longstreet, looking back accusingly to England's role in the War of 1812, contrasted "France and England—the one a reformer; the other an intermeddler, and yet you [Massachusetts] took sides with the latter." Longstreet thought this anomaly could be traced to the difference between "*Hamilton your mentor in politics and Madison mine.*"[89] Longstreet more dramatically compared the dangerous religious spirit that Puritan abolitionism was fomenting in the North with the more farseeing piety of the South: "By your magic arts, a spirit has been waked up which baffles all description, and all philosophy. This—what shall I call it—I was going to say *hell-born* but it seems to have too much religion in it for that. *Enthusiasm?*—this Massachusetts, this satanic puritanism. There is but one expedient left, which is to hold up the mirror of the future before it."[90] Not surprisingly, Longstreet in 1846 predicted that abolitionists would soon disastrously attempt to usurp the roles of the U.S. government and of God. Both the implicit atheism and the governmental conspiracy of abolitionists were revealed in their fundamental sin. They were, as one proslavery spokesman succinctly put it, acting "as if they were the vice regents of Providence." Abolitionists wanted to determine what type of property could be held and who could hold it. If the legal or political system ever became their instrument, this would "destroy the operation of individual conscience" in the whole nation.[91]

Southerners were sure that such antislavery attitudes and activities hindered the unfolding of the Kingdom of God. Abolitionists not only threatened to bring social disruption but betrayed a corrupted pride in their own "abstract" reasoning and ability to manipulate nature and society.[92] The Reverend A. Campbell of Bethany College, Virginia, typically accused abolitionists of being "more in love with their own opinions than the rights of man."[93] The Reverend Nathan Lord argued in his proslavery tracts that "such Christian men [abolitionists] really, though unconsciously, counteract the better intentions and established course of Providence."[94] Iveson Brookes gave the more strictly biblical and evangelical judgment on abolitionists' speculative hubris: "It represents the very principle upon which sin entered the Garden."[95] In short, abolitionists, in trying to anticipate and outrun God's plan, were analyzing social questions conventionally and correctly left alone. Such conduct was not popular in either section of the nation. For southern evangelicals in particular it revealed a contradiction. If the South had set up a system contrary to the will of God, as abolitionists themselves asserted, it had to fail. Why then were abolitionists trying to destroy slavery by their own acts? Did they not trust God? One anti-abolitionist tract asked rhetorically: "Shall we adopt a plan of our own devising because from unbelief we doubt the efficacy of the Divine Plan?"[96] Another early proslavery argument similarly queried: "Who should question His *moral ability* to accomplish the benevolent object [ending slavery]?"[97] According to evangelicals, the true path of faith, character, and success was to act in a way that confirmed, as Reverend Benjamin Morgan Palmer put it, that "Providence must govern man, and not that man should control Providence."[98] Southerners thought that not just abolitionists, but antislavery forces and—as debate wore on to 1860 when Palmer made this statement—the entire North failed this test.[99]

William Smith also described how reform movements could not "force an entrance through" the "door of Providence." Such attempts were impractical as well as impious since there was "no power" that could stand before the "enlightened popular mind and will [which] must prevail."[100] Smith compared the liberating successes of Providence's "moral nature" to a "tariff" rather than "direct taxes" since "its results march forward without observation." Smith then found a more ministerial analogy, "or, more to the point it is like the 'Kingdom of heaven,' which comes without observation."[101] "But on the other hand," Smith cautioned, "if the movements in question are the work of only a few master spirits who have mistaken the actual condition of the masses, who have not yet risen to the moral condition of freedom, they will be found fighting against God." Smith drew a parallel between the failures of the Colonization Society, the Revolutions of Europe in 1848 (for which he had nourished hopes), and the future of antislavery: "a premature resistance in either case 'has its reward'—great suffering and a vast accumulation of guilt, but not success."[102]

Lack of results offered the clearest proof that antislavery activists were fighting Providence. "Is a single slave set free?" asked Leander Ker who ministered in Florida, "—not one. What is the *worth* . . . [of] vaporing?"[103] "What have we gained?" wondered a southern minister, "Has the way to relief been opened? Has Providence come forth from its darkness and provided means of delivery?" Jefferson Davis asked a similar question in the 1850 Congress after refusing to discuss the right or wrong of slavery "as an abstract proposition." Whatever the imperfections of slavery, Davis saw no use in discussion of them by the voices of antislavery: "Why not denounce criminal laws, declaim against disease, pain, or poverty as wrong?"[104] Proslavery writers in the 1840s had often been less politic about this aspect of antislavery. Antislavery activists were simply "improvident, "pampered stipendiaries," "idle dreamers," and "do nothings" who "must be discarded by this practical do something age."[105]

The only quality worse than the impracticality of the antislavery movement in southern eyes was its *practicality*—and the practical bent of mind of the entire North which it exposed. This seemingly schizophrenic accusation was not a product of southern insecurity or desperate proslavery propagandizing; it was a logical outgrowth of the evangelical mentality of the age. Antislavery forces leveled much the same charge against the South (about their calculated quest for power and concurrent frustration of their ambitions). Patrick Hues Mell was exasperated by the way antislavery forces with "one breath tell us [the South] we are self-interested and greedy, and the next that . . . [slavery] tends to make us regardless of money and ignorant of its value."[106] The surest way to bring personal or general economic and social ruin was to try to find or construct a means to secure self-interested ends. In the evangelical imagination a personality or society premised on deliberate self-interest was both impractical and dangerous. Southerners were thus also accusing the North of being too greedy to be successful; too rational to be sane. "The men of the North are a peculiarly 'calculating' people," B.F. Stringfellow noted. He was, therefore, not surprised to find statistical evidence of a greater incidence of insanity "among a people cold, calculating in temper [only] claiming to be particularly sober, temperate, practical."[107] Conservative proslavery intellectuals like James Henry Hammond often linked this failing to the North's "*artificial, money power system*" which was "cold, stern arithmetical . . . working up human lives with engines."[108] Thomas R. Dew in a more popular vein attributed northern economic heresies and social problems to personal greed: "That cold, contracted, calculating *selfishness*."[109] "*Self*," agreed Reverend Leander Ker, "is the source of it all."[110]

Proslavery evangelicals arrived at the most concise diagnosis of the general disease behind northern outbreaks of insanity and greed: "Isms."[111]

Abolitionism was simply the worst manifestation of this impious breed of "modern speculation," as James H. Thornwell labeled it in 1841.[112] The definitive list of "isms" in the 1850s usually included at least (in order of most frequent appearance) atheism, agrarianism, socialism, Fourierism, Mormonism, red republicanism, communism, and perfectionism. Thomas Smyth tried to abbreviate the list of northern offenders in 1860 and still came up with "atheists, infidels, communists, free lovers, Bible-haters, and anti-Christian levelers."[113]

"Isms" then was a necessary simplification. This label also indicated the characteristic of the North (and specific movements within it) that most offended southern evangelicals: a "devotion to artificial constructiveness," which "arraigns Providence and dictates its course of procedure."[114] "By the sphere of fervid and rigid economic systems," a proslavery minister warned, "the most salutary influence of human agency is destroyed."[115] Thornton Stringfellow similarly warned that the prime "design [of the] savior . . . is to impress strongly upon the human mind that *character* deficient in *correct moral feeling,* will prove fatal to human hopes in a coming day."[116] Character was a force of will and agency that southern evangelicals began to fear might be turned to purely secular ends. Antislavery activity and the development of northern society made this specter more threatening. Frederick Ross contemplated the debate over slavery and the emerging sectional schism in 1856, pronouncing on the real point of division: "The question is in a nutshell; it is this: *shall man submit to the revealed will of God, or to his own will."* If the choice were the second (as he believed the antislavery one to be) Ross wondered, "What is the progress and end of it? Some will suggest that all is the result of a fortuitous course of atoms. . . . Alas some, the Notts [followers of the southern biologist-phrenologist who advanced the theory of a separate and inferior creation/evolution of blacks], say man was *created* millions of years ago . . . while other some say man is the result of development from . . . monkey."[117] Some southern intellectuals anticipated a next step in the progression of Ross's thought. "They will then succeed to qualifying man, a being fit to govern the universe," forecasted Jonathan Fletcher after ruminating on the logical conclusion of northern theories of social development and antislavery.[118]

These were not the fears and accusations of isolated, romantic southerners out of tune with and refusing to accept the developments of the age. Most northern evangelicals rejected similar sins (and were nervous about modernizing trends), and the form of their sectional accusations against southerners was comparable. Central to the evangelical project, both North and South, was an attempt to embrace the expanding mental and material horizons of nineteenth-century Americans while containing them within morally and religiously prescribed bounds.[119] Therefore the proslavery and antislavery of evangelicals paradoxically included elements of both clarity (even prescience) and delusion.

Primarily because of the character ideal, each section better understood the material forces at work in (and determining the future of) the other's social system than those of its own. The self-interested motives and "self-will" the evangelicals were called on to repress and therefore would not acknowledge in their own actions, they quickly identified in others.[120] As shown, evangelical southerners who wrote biblically based defenses of slavery were often incapable of acknowledging slavery as a social system (institutional construct) at all. Likewise, antislavery evangelicals were usually incapable of discussing northern free labor as a system instituted by human agency: it resulted rather from the absence of any institutional manipulation and reflection. Abolitionists were exceptional in developing a moral vocabulary that demanded a systematic analysis of the social sources of power—at least in the South. They even tried to explain the South's "judicial blindness" both to social reality and to contradictions in its moral self-defense.[121] Through their arguments, some in the North were able to critique slavery and to recognize the brutal ethic and institutionalized greed at its core.[122] The mass of antislavery activists, however, skipped the analysis and simply attacked southerners as deliberate conspirators and hypocrites.

From the southern perspective the North was guilty of similar sins, because it covered self-interested motives with specious moralism in attacks on slaveholders. Southern evangelicals detected hypocrisy in the abolitionists' analysis of the southern social order.[123] Abolitionists' "abstract reasoning" on freedom and equality did not seem to apply to inequities in northern society. "This leveling system then is intended exclusively for southern men," T.C. Thornton complained.[124] Southern evangelicals suggested that northerners return Indian land or cut the hours of mill workers before they demand that the South dismantle slavery.[125] A general charge against northern hypocrites was also popular among the pious: "However they may condemn the relation of master and slave, they would not be so ready to dissolve the relation between themselves and their fortunes."[126] Northerners embodied the sin of Mammonism, the worship of money.

A few elite southerners—intellectual counterparts to abolitionist radicals—were able to criticize free labor systematically, as almost no one in the North or the rest of the world could.[127] Sociological, academic, and political doctrines, rather than reforming sensibility, informed these southerners' critiques. Yet, as with abolitionists' sensitivity to southern structural realities, these radical proslavery ideologues—George Fitzhugh and Henry Hughes outstanding among them—directed and demonstrated their analytic powers on northern institutions and trends of modernization. Fitzhugh's *Sociology for the South* would have been more appropriately titled "Sociology *of* the North," which was its alternate title. Fitzhugh detected an underlying pattern of consolidation "lurking in the system of free society."[128] The North had mere sociological patterns; the South had a society, which, at least in Fitzhugh's public work, was always assumed to be the embodiment of Christendom.[129] This bifurcation was easily accepted among less ideologically and intellectually self-conscious southern believers, who skipped the sociology but were well-prepared to embrace the conclusion. The North was a land of isms, schisms, and calculating Yankee materialists, while the South was a land of pure, unified religion, where the Kingdom was naturally unfolding free of impious intermeddling with its progress. As it is easier to see the thunderhead in the distance than the one overhead, it was easier to see an enormous, unnatural system of greed far to the North or South. Only in the other section (and economic order) dwelt a monster powerful enough to frustrate cherished (democratic and) evangelical values and visions of the future, and alien enough to be suspected of secretly intending such corruption.

As the debate over slavery progressed in the 1840s, the mutual attempts to identify those calculating power outcomes, those promoting a system for achieving these ends, and those thus interfering with Providence and threatening social disaster and divine retribution reached a crescendo. "This great battle with abolitionists, has not been fought in vain," declared James Henley Thornwell at the end of the 1840s, ". . . a real progress has been made in the practical solution of the problems which produced the collision. . . . The world is now the theatre of an extraordinary conflict of great principles—the foundations of society are about to be explored to their depths and the sources of social and political prosperity laid bare."The 1850s, a decade of crisis, would end with an extraordinary conflict between the free labor and slavery systems, but these were not the great principles to which evangelicals, like Thornwell, referred. Thornwell saw himself as the champion of natural providential development and prosperity against the challenge of conscious abolitionist manipulation of the economic order and of socialistic system-building.[130] Antislavery publicist O.B. Forthingham, writing two years after Thornwell, also saw the coming clash of principles entirely in moral and religious terms. He found that inequities and prosperity in the North "are providential" while "slavery on the other hand is an institution, which the conscious will of man has built up. . . . Pauperism involves no direct guilt. Slavery is essential guilt."[131] Who were "calculating"? Who were looking to expediency and self-interest? Who were planning and building "a piece of machinery" to deliver material rewards that reduced men themselves to mere machines or things? Who were organizing and consolidating an artificial system to guarantee their wealth and power? Who, thereby, were undermining values? Blocking the force and attainments of virtue and character? Blighting the flowering of an evangelical empire? The answer always lay on the other side of the Mason-Dixon line.

The general religious debate over the morality of slavery, which began in the 1830s and peaked in the 1840s with the sectional schisms in the evangelical denominations, accelerated contemporary developments in southern ideology. Southerners accused antislavery forces of dangerous hubris for their attempts to anticipate and affect the future course of Providence. This criticism was not rooted in Bible Belt fatalism; most southerners rejected not the theological project but its application against slavery. Proslavery spokesmen claimed that the South in its current social arrangements merely accepted and aligned itself with the course of Providence. During the abolition controversy, southern evangelicals began to emphasize not simply their faith in the Bible's message but the Bible's special fulfillment in the region. The South increasingly adopted the role of the chosen, and even "redeemer," segment of the nation. Such proper organization of course would bring appropriate rewards. Evangelical southerners did not eschew the northern search for God's single law of moral and material progress but made claims to superior knowledge of it. The slavery debate incubated this decisive ideological development in both regions. Its popular and political appeal and consequences extended far beyond the pulpit.

The proponents of evangelical proslavery made explicit appeals to visions of economic prosperity and progress that would follow from and confirm regional righteousness. Baptist Thornton Stringfellow, besides being the best-selling proslavery author, was the best exemplar of this project. He compiled economic and demographic statistics to support his biblical proslavery in order to describe the contemporary operation of Providence and "demonstrate the relative prosperity [of the South] . . . in religion / in morals / in the acquisition of wealth / in increase of native population."[132] For Stringfellow, a causal chain connected belief, to morality, to prosperity, to regional expansion. He accorded it the authority of science, and, given his view of southern religiosity, concluded axiomatically that "prosperity, unequaled in the annals of the world, has attended us."[133] Presbyterian Nathan Rice, noting in a public debate over slavery the insolvency of his abolitionist opponent's Cincinnati church, maintained that one clear proof of the morality of slavery was the evidence that "churches [in] Kentucky are quite as prosperous as those in Ohio."[134] This represented a pervasive attitude among evangelicals North and South. Historian Daniel Walker Howe has insightfully reminded modern readers of how blunt and unshamefaced such connections were in the era: "The people we are studying, not the subsequent historians, brought economics and religion together. Nineteenth-century people did not typically oppose Christianity and culture, or morality and self-interest, the way twentieth-century people have come to do."[135]

Before southern nationalists and political ideologues expanded their analysis of foreign markets into the deluded argument that the South controlled world commerce, made famous by the slogan "Cotton is King," the Christian economics embedded in evangelical proslavery fed more populist and general economic expectations. Presbyterian Fred Ross regaled his proslavery audiences with predictions of 1,250,000 people walking the streets of Charleston by 1953, and Virginia Baptist Jeremiah Jeter reported the common local belief that Lynchburg would rival London.[136] Although many proslavery evangelicals who made these arguments were unionists and Whigs, "King Cotton" southern nationalists made sure to draw on this fund of religious optimism when pitching their case for southern economic and political independence. Economic nationalist J.D.B. DeBow included biblical proslavery in his appeals to "the interests in slavery of the southern nonslaveholders" to assure them that through "honesty and industry" and "adhering to the simple faiths of the gospel" anyone in the region could expect to become a slaveholder in "the happiest and most prosperous and powerful nation on earth."[137] Often these appeals of southern nationalists in the 1850 were not so clearly manipulative of the region's religious culture. Spokesmen like E. N. Elliott, editor of the definitive prewar proslavery compilation *Cotton is King,* did not explicitly separate their regional propagandizing from their own (and their era's) biblical and Christian framework, language, and economics. Elliott, like Stringfellow, identified the South with "HE who ever favored those walking under the banner of truth and righteousness" and who "appointed the institution of slavery among his chosen and peculiar people [Israel], and under his divine goodness made it to that favored nation the great source of happiness and unexampled prosperity."[138]

As most defenders of slavery were not working for or assuming a separate southern nationality, they had to give particular attention to the moderate antislavery contention that "diminishing of *national* wealth be proof of variance from the ordinance of God."[139] Thomas R. Dew had inaugurated the era of mature proslavery with a similar argument demonstrating the converse. He argued that the applicability of current market theories to the circumstances of the southern economy and the profitability of slavery proved slavery to be of divine ordinance in that time and place. Moderate antislavery evangelicals like Francis Wayland altered the context of such southern apologetics by emphasizing the *progressive* trends of the *national* economy. Wayland framed debate by proposing, "Slavery whether in light of political economy, of philanthropy, or of Christianity . . . if it can be defended on either of these grounds its defense should be attempted. If it cannot be so defended, but on the contrary can be shown to be at variance both with virtue and self-interest, the sooner we are convinced of this the better." He then proved slavery was "a moral evil" because it was "ruinous [to] national prosperity."[140] In the 1850s Methodist minister and abolitionist Abram Pryne took Wayland's argument further, expressing the common belief that the sin of slavery was "*the* great incubus resting upon the material growth and progress of our country."[141] This position was used to dismiss arguments like Dew's by demanding a comparison of the southern economy to the best possible socio-economic arrangement—the one that had to be closest to the perfection of heaven and so bound to triumph in the end, whatever past prosperity or current conditions might seem to justify.

The intense focus in the antislavery camp on progress and a national comparative framework as tests of prosperity had parallels and even sources in proslavery. Thomas R. Dew had entertained appeals to future economic development as an escape clause from the contemporary weaknesses and evils of the slave economy, which he and other southerners acknowledged. While Dew had privately dropped this stance (and dropped dead) by the time the Wilmot Proviso (1846) made the direction of national economic expansion an obsession, similar invocations of progress by proslavery moralists flourished in the 1850s. W.D. Brown of Kentucky rehearsed the typical balancing act: "That there are evils growing out of the institution . . . all . . . admit. We go further, we admit that it is a moral and political evil of vast magnitude, as is proven by the low state of public morals in the South, and by comparison of the slave states with the free, in general improvement and prosperity."[142] Brown then ran through a standard statistical comparison of his Kentucky with Ohio, showing the former's lamentable "injudicious investment in capital."[143] If this premise resembled the logic of evangelical antislavery, the intrusion of a progressive perspective (and of superior southern providential prophetics) dispelled relative southern economic and moral failings: "Time is not far distant when these iron bands of commercial intercourse will traverse the sunny regions of the South, as well as the sterile plains of the North. . . . The telegraph . . . will be extended . . . mostly if not wholly upon slave territory." This development did not imply serious restructuring or reform in the South, but would come as a "natural result of the present existing state of things."[144]

Various arguments filled the gap between southern promise and performance—and the gap proslavery moralists presented was not always as wide or as honestly described as Brown's. One approach was similar to Dew's: because the South had a unique economic environment, its labor system and material lag were results of the best possible application of the same market laws at work in the rest of the nation. Misguided northern agitation and interference with this would have no positive effect and could only distort the natural development of the region. Matthew Estes insisted in his proslavery pronouncements that the division of labor operated in slavery and would "infinitely increase" wealth. "Destroy slavery," he bluntly told antislavery forces, "and you put a stop to all progress, and improvement at the South."[145] This implied that the purported goal of moderate antislavery was either self-defeating or a cover for just such a destructive project.

Even in the 1830s proslavery spokesmen did not rely solely on the negative appeals that "the North has retarded her [the South's] onward progress" or that "the South is more profitable than any scheme which northern abolitionists can devise," as one early pamphlet put it. The next step, as with W.D. Brown twenty years later, was to predict that the "South is destined to rival, perhaps outstrip, her more fortunate sisters in wealth and prosperity."[146] Proslavery advocates saw even the most glaring southern shortfalls in the war of statistical comparisons as portents of future prosperity and vindication. In 1854, B.F. Stringfellow of Missouri pointed out that the most obvious of northern abundances was a form of illusory wealth outside providential pathways: "The boasted increase of population in New England is not so much the result of natural increase as of foreign emigration. . . . Consider whether such increase be evidence of prosperity. . . . Providence in its wisdom does regulate the natural increase of population . . . population may by artificial means be increased far beyond its natural increase."[147] Southern evangelicals expected visible evidence of God's finger in material events equal to that in the Words of His revelation. Their obsession with economic statistics, prosperity, and future development reflected an attempt to fathom Providence and to ascertain that their society was a natural expression of virtuous evangelical individualism. The famous Tennessee Methodist divine and future governor William Brownlow insisted in 1858 that the slave economy would fulfill "*our* ends as well as the ends of Providence, which . . . are in *perfect* harmony."[148] Despite his virulent racism and proslavery, Parson Brownlow remained a staunch Unionist through the war and served as Tennessee governor during Reconstruction. Brownlow's combination of outspoken proslavery (and defense of southern interests before 1860) and distaste for southern secession were by no means unique. Sectionalism often sheltered threatened religious values and preserved a sense of moral order, before its use to proclaim economic, territorial, and political ascendancy.

Confrontations over emancipation, much like those over slavery's place in the future development of the nation, heightened consciousness of and solidified commitments to regional formulations of the divine economy. "Virtue is power" became an article of faith justifying the increasing focus on God's laws of political economy in both North and South. Northern arguments directed against slavery on the basis of these laws often had the unintended effect of drawing more attention to this ideology and solidifying it as the dominant species of social legitimation in the South. The issue of emancipation extended the ideological uses of providential economics to legitimate moral stances that went beyond appeals to regional prosperity. Although that strand of argument had the greatest popular appeal, pro and antislavery ministers also delved into the intellectual issues of conscience, rights, and freedom behind the mentality of the era.

Evangelicals assumed that material progress and market economics were just the superstructure of a moral order built on Christian individualism. Francis Wayland defined this religious base of nineteenth-century individualism at the beginning of his debate over the morality of slavery against fellow Baptist moderate Richard Fuller of South Carolina: "Every individual of our race was placed on earth to work out his own salvation ...surrounded by every temptation he must come off the conqueror over every moral enemy or else perish, under a most aggravated condemnation. . . . The Christian with these incentives and advantages, is left to apply for himself in each case the principles of the gospel. He is left to act at his own discretion, according to the dictates of his conscience, to cultivate a Christian disposition, and thus become a law unto himself."[149] This doctrine was not a point of debate between Fuller and Wayland, or between most northern and southern evangelicals. One need only realize how much of Social Darwinism was already implicit in the social vision of evangelicals to see that the justification of a brutal system of racial subordination was as natural a conclusion from these principles as a libertarian crusade. For this reason, Wayland's version of the antislavery argument had profound influence in the South. Wayland's and Fuller's oral debate at the 1840 Baptist conference in New York was one of the first and most highly publicized of such encounters. In combination with the exchange of letters both men sent through the *Christian Reflector,* collected and published in 1844, the debate inspired Thornton Stringfellow's popular biblical proslavery pamphlet, the influential published debates between Presbyterians David Rice and Jonathan Blanchard in 1845, and those of Methodists William Brownlow and Alexander Pryne in 1858. Wayland's antislavery was also, for example, the focus of the best-known proslavery works of Old School Presbyterians John Adger and James Sloan, of Baptist Patrick Hues Mell, and of Methodist W.A. Smith. Wayland's antislavery similarly received serious and extended treatment—never afforded to abolitionist arguments—in the work of proslavery intellectuals and moralists James Shannon, Albert Taylor Bledsoe, R.H. Rivers, and Jonathan Fletcher.

Wayland provided a moral and political vocabulary and point of reference that helped clarify and lend authority to the ideas and attitudes southern evangelicals employed in support of slavery. Both Richard Fuller and David Rice turned Wayland's definition of conscience to proslavery purposes. "My first argument," began Rice's proslavery, "is founded upon the admitted fact that the great principles of morality are written upon the human heart, and when presented do communicate themselves to the understanding and consciences of all men."[150] Richard Fuller showed specifically how southerners accepted slavery in conscience by imagining an attempt to have laws legalizing "piracy and adultery" passed in South Carolina (or attempts to describe a "Christian adulterer"): "These enactments are felt by all to be impossible, while no such emotions are excited by slavery; a truth in itself showing that, in the instinctive consciousness of mankind, slavery is not necessarily in the category of crimes."[151] Fuller's was only the first and most dramatic example of a southern spokesman's quoting directly from Wayland's *Moral Science* to establish the theoretical and theological bases of his proslavery.

It often took only a slight change in emphasis of antislavery arguments like Wayland's to frame a coherent explanation of the southern proslavery position. Wayland, for example, complained that "I never found one [proslavery spokesman] who would be willing to introduce slavery into this country, were it not established." He believed the South therefore had a duty to move against slavery: "The ground which is at present taken by the South in regard to the question of slavery seems to be of recent origin. At the time of the Constitution, I suppose it to have been very generally acknowledged throughout this country that slavery was an evil and a wrong and that it was, tacitly at least, understood to be the duty of those states in which it existed to remove it as soon as practicable."[152] This interpretation of the constitutional settlement was one of the main reasons that the slavery debate revolved around questions of what was "practical." Wayland's presentation of the constitutional compromise on slavery left southerners an escape clause very reminiscent of the denominational statements about emancipation issued at the end of the eighteenth century. If southerners had determined that the time had not yet come to dissolve slavery, the obligation described by Wayland was still as much a reason for doing nothing about slavery as for dismantling it. Southerners, therefore, saw no need to deny Wayland's account of proslavery (which was accurate on southern attitudes toward the introduction of slavery) or the traditional approach to slavery in America; they merely refuted the imputation by anti-slavery forces of novelty and of violation of the Founding compact. "This charge is unjust," E.N. Elliott wrote, and with most defenders of slavery he plausibly maintained that "earlier and later writers both stood on substantially the same ground."[153]

Moderates on the antislavery platform presented a version of the national tradition and standard of civil rights that was greeted with similar bewilderment by proslavery evangelicals. Southern evangelicals did not see that these adversaries' view of freedom and emancipation founded on the admixture of Christian morality and human rights was very different from their own proslavery position. The resemblance of evangelical antislavery philosophy to their own standards was simply further proof to southern believers that slavery was not necessarily a contradiction of democratic and Christian principles. Jonathan Blanchard used Wayland's definition of "human rights" to argue that the Declaration of Independence had been "running down for the last fifty years" in the South.[154] When Blanchard then proceeded to explain how democratic "governments may with just reason withhold civil rights without sin,"[155] his southern debating opponent Nathan Rice wondered why slaveholding was singled out as sin: "Surely the principles of the Declaration of Independence are running down with the gentleman himself. Will he please point us to the principle in the moral law, which permits us to deprive the colored people of certain important rights, but teaches that we shall not deprive them of certain other rights?"[156] Blanchard clarified his point by explaining that deprivations of civil rights ("voting," "intermarriage," "social rights") were only permissible so long as the sin of slaveholding was abolished: "I said that as ministers of Christ, when we have freed the slaves from their masters, abolitionists have done with them."[157] Blanchard, unlike the majority of northerners, was an abolitionist and so was willing to draw an uncompromising line that defined minimal rights.

Gradualist antislavery ministers' views of rights and emancipation left open clearer lines of argument through which southern evangelicals could easily and unapologetically pass slavery. Francis Wayland explicitly described the operation of the divine economy before, during, and after emancipation in the South (and the nation, since the two were still of a piece in 1843 when he wrote):

The soil will neither become diminished in quantity, nor inferior in fertility [by emancipation]. The number of laborers will be the same. The only difference I can perceive would be that the laborer would then work in conformity with the conditions God has appointed, whereas he now works at variance with them; in the one case we would be attempting to accumulate property under the blessing of God, whereas now we are attempting to do it under His peculiar malediction.

. . . I would gladly discuss this subject as a question of Political Economy.

. . . I have offered no suggestion as to the manner in which emancipation, whenever it occurs, shall be conducted.[158]

These last two statements about the end of slavery were inextricably linked in the dominant version of evangelical antislavery. If slavery were under a malediction of God and at variance with the laws of political economy, it would pass soon away. The only question concerned how southerners would choose to accept this reality. "I willingly leave it [the manner of emancipation]" to the South, Wayland concluded, adding that this was the "almost universal opinion of Christians of every denomination in the Northern States."[159] This laissez-faire attitude toward emancipation, if not toward antislavery commitment, was little different from southern evangelicals' tradition of accommodation to slavery.

It is not surprising, given this view of emancipation, that proslavery pamphlets inevitably offered political and religious formulations of the northern evangelical ideal. "This [slavery] is an evil," an early ministerial proslavery tract closed, "which under a free form of government will work out its own cure."[160] Twenty years later the Reverend W.A. Smith closed his proslavery tome of 1857 by noting that the slavery problem "will be found to solve itself."[161] Radical abolitionists may not have shared this political faith, but the majority of moderate antislavery forces in the North did. In fact, many northern evangelicals in the antebellum period retained a passive attitude toward the slavery question on this basis, as had most Americans prior to the 1830s.[162] Northern evangelicals who published proslavery tracts in the 1840s and 1850s were usually enamored of this approach. The Reverend Nathan Lord of Dartmouth asked Americans to leave slavery to "God's natural and moral Providence," which would "in due time" bring emancipation when Americans could "safely and usefully do without it, as the grown man puts away childish things."[163]

Some southern ministers expressed this providential ideal with less certainty about the time frame or about the likelihood of any transformation of the master-slave relationship. Old School Presbyterians were most likely to take these positions. John Adger was conservative in tone and left both questions open: "Are we then asked whether we believe slavery among us will be perpetual? We say, as far as Christianity is concerned, we do not see why it might not be perpetual, and yet we do not see reason to say that it will be so. It is a question for speculation or rather it is a question *not* for speculation, for how can we judge before hand what God intends to do? It is then more properly a question of Providence."[164] Bitter reactionary George Dodd Armstrong expected perpetual slavery and insisted Christians should not speak of "*when* Providence" would end slavery but "*if* Providence" will do so. The Reverend James Sloan of Mississippi was even less reticent in his reactionism: "And if preaching the pure and simple truths of the gospel tend to break down the system of domestic slavery, we say, let it go. But we have no fears on this point. The communication of spiritual truth never does work mischief."[165] Although such conservative providential doctrines still had a measure of influence (especially among Old School Presbyterians), their conclusions about the permanence of slavery were those of a small minority among proslavery evangelicals.

The proslavery-antislavery clash took place within a larger framework of socio-political and ethical agreement. Most proslavery evangelicals accepted the antislavery moral logic. As one southern minister commented in the 1850s, "If it is such an evil as you represent, Christianity must uproot it. So *you* say—so *we* say. . . . Trust Christianity to effect its divine work."[166] These visions of the end of slavery had almost nothing to do with any direct steps southerners might have planned to take to free their slaves. Slavery and other evils would pass away through and *by* the divine economy. Southern Methodist William Seat encouraged southerners to always look for a "gradually progressive" millennium as well as a change in slavery.

Proslavery moralizing was not changing southerners' image primarily of slaves or slavery, but of themselves. Evangelical ministers provided southerners with uniform terms of personal and regional identity and with a consistent way to express their interests and destiny. If the attribution of benevolence to slaveholders, the search for subtler and more internalized means of slave discipline (discussed in more detail in the following chapter), and the claims that southern slavery was increasingly characterized by such a "humane" regime relied mostly on rhetoric, the values behind the rhetoric were real. The evangelical movement was leading the South away from traditional physical penalties and social shaming as the means of self and social control. Southerners were beginning to embrace the attributes of mid-nineteenth-century modernity and the Victorian character ideal: strict self-discipline, internalized guilt, personal consistency, practical rationality. These trends appeared more clearly in the region's work ethic and market-oriented economic activity, handling of prisoners, education, and discipline of children in the home than they ever did in slaveholding. The genuine social content of these values, however, was strikingly apparent in the southern attempt to defend slavery on their basis.

5

Evangelical Proslavery, Free Labor, and Disunion, 1850–1861

During the sectional conflict of the 1850s, debate over the economic future of the country raged. A new enemy of southern evangelicals arose in the North: a self-consciously sectional movement based on the political and economic principle called "free labor." The free labor movement produced a moderate antislavery position, and by 1856 the Republican Party. Their criticisms of the South differed significantly from the abolitionist attacks of the 1830s. Southern evangelicals had to confront a new set of arguments in the 1850s in an atmosphere of political tension. Their ministers, however, had the luxury of preaching to already converted audiences, and no southern version of the free labor argument emerged until Hinton Rowan Helper published *The Impending Crisis* in 1857. Ministers instead answered free labor by producing a new genre of religious proslavery: the "Rights and Duties of Slavery" sermon or tract.

In these proslavery arguments many ministers tried to describe slaves as free laborers, and even in a few cases called for reforms of slaveholding laws and customs to give slaves more responsibilities and rights. The evangelical proslavery stance had always implied that slaves should be morally responsible individuals. In the 1850s more explicit and philosophical proslavery visions of southern society poured from the pens of ministers, politicians, and intellectuals alike. A great variety of proslavery philosophy, science, and sociology was produced, but ministers led the way again. Their subgenre of "Rights and Duties" was the most significant development of the final decade of proslavery writing.

Although some southern intellectuals constructed proslavery critiques of free labor in the 1850s and provided justifications of slavery in the abstract, the dominant proslavery position equated slavery and free labor. Ministers in particular sought to demonstrate that slaves had the same opportunities open to them as any moral agents. Proslavery spokesmen often tried to describe slaves as laborers with all the intrinsic rewards and opportunities of the work ethic open to them. Southerners professed that they honored the theory of the contractual and consensual nature of legitimate labor discipline. Ministers maintained that slaves labored voluntarily, and slaveholders were anxious to exact such statements from slaves.[1] James Henley Thornwell provided the most intellectually penetrating evangelical proslavery writing in the 1850s. He insisted that southern labor was "not involuntary servitude."[2] Thornwell elaborated on his dismissal of the northern definition of southern slavery as a unique form of "involuntary" labor: "If by voluntary be meant, however, that which results from hearty consent, and is accordingly rendered with cheerfulness, it is precisely the service which the law of God enjoins. Servants are exhorted to obey from considerations of duty . . . whether in point of fact, their service, in this sense shall be voluntary, will depend upon their moral character. But the same may be said of free labor."[3] Thornwell added that "the laborers in each case are equally moral, equally responsible, equally men," because southern slavery was merely "one of the conditions in which God is conducting the moral probation of man."[4] Fred Ross likewise defined slavery as "belonging to the same category as master and hireling . . . slavery as a system of labor, is *only one form* . . . [God uses] *to elevate* man."[5]

The definition of slaves as laborers was the starting point of all southern arguments that slavery did not contradict national standards of social discipline. Biblical proslavery tracts held that the South's "peculiar policy and institutions [were] in harmony with the genius of republicanism, and the true spirit of Christianity" in labor discipline as in all else.[6] Unitarian abolitionist William Channing popularized the northern counter-argument that slavery was properly defined by Bishop William Paley's phrase "obligation to labor without consent or contract."[7] Channing and the

North also adopted Paley's corollary that the slaves thereby lost human dignity by being reduced to a "thing" or object of another man's will.[8] Thornwell called this definition of slavery "ridiculous" because it degraded slaves from their "rank of responsible and voluntary agents."[9] Since proslavery spokesmen like Thornwell had defined slaves as laborers, they could then invoke the inherent dignity of work against the antislavery stance. Southerners argued that an attack on slavery constituted an assault on the sacred obligation to labor and the irrepressible moral nature of labor performed.[10] Baptist Patrick Mell stated "that in no part of this Union is labor held in more honorable estimation" than in the South.[11] T.W. Hoit echoed this boast and asserted that slavery could not be immoral because "labor degrades no man."[12] In 1857 Presbyterian James Sloan wondered how abolitionists could argue that slavery was a sin per se and asked rhetorically, "Is then labor sin *in* itself?"[13] Slaves were laborers, not chattels; therefore Thornwell argued that necessarily "ideas of personal rights and responsibilities pervade the whole system."[14]

The evangelical clash over the morality of slavery often focused on whether the institution undermined self-dependence—whether it taught or did not teach the lessons of self-discipline to slaves and slaveholders.[15] This question arose more from conflicting visions of labor discipline than from ideals of personal freedom and equality. Fundamental disagreement concerned *how* men were best situated to learn self-restraint. James Henley Thornwell acknowledged that the debate over slavery between northern and southern evangelicals turned solely on this point: "Moral responsibility . . . this question comprises . . . the whole moral difficulty of slavery." If slavery did not allow God's system of rewards and punishments for self-control to function, southern evangelicals, like their northern counterparts, thought it constituted a threat to the whole nation. All evangelicals held that the placement of men in a position to learn self-discipline produced moral order, freedom, material progress, and the growth of religious adherence.[16] The presence within the nation of a large body of people who were not being so schooled would inevitably retard progress toward true religion, true morality, and true wealth. Questions of equality and rights were ancillary. For Thornwell, as for most antislavery evangelicals, "the real question" was that of "whether it [slavery] is incompatible with the spiritual prosperity of individuals; or the general progress and education of society."[17]

Thornwell's idea of voluntary slavery was not his private fantasy. In the 1830s Theodore Clapp—a Louisiana Unitarian and ex-New England compatriot of Channing's—had taken a stance that anticipated Thornwell's and later southerners' veneration of labor and the inalienable power of the individual moral will. Clapp also discounted the possibility of chattel slavery and arrived at this position via a confrontation with Channing's use of Paley. "Others cannot enslave us," preached Clapp, "they cannot stop our thoughts. . . . He [the slave] enjoys the most precious attributes of man, who can turn his mind, by absolute effort of his will . . . from frivolous and vain to honorable and useful employments. All of this the slave is at liberty to do."[18] James Henley Thornwell made virtually the same point in the 1850s when he stated that slave labor expressed "voluntary homage to law."[19]

Other southerners insisted that they defended "voluntary slavery."[20] After proslavery advocates denied that slaves were chattels, they often came up with alternatives to the term "slavery" to describe southern labor. "Liberty labor" and "regulated liberty" were some favorites; several ministers used the oxymoronical designation "free-slave."[21] Joseph Wilson, Presbyterian minister and father of Woodrow Wilson, cited the King James Version of the Bible's use of the term "servant." He explained how this showed southern labor to be neither exceptional nor properly called slavery: "Servants, not in the rigid sense which slavery seems to imply, yet in a sense sufficiently obvious and strict . . . may be the voluntary or involuntary doers of offices which must fall to the lot of *someone* . . . even in those regions from which come the most heated denunciations of a slavery which, existing among us, differs at best from their own in degree."[22] The question of how blacks were supposed voluntarily to choose slavery when they did not have the right to legal self-ownership was circumvented by the evangelical belief that the Bible was the de facto law of the land (and irresistibly the "over-ruling" law anyway).[23]

Many of the most delusive and incredible elements in proslavery arose from the evangelicals' general and ongoing will to believe that objective conditions in their lives or regions meant less than biblical or providential realities. Thornwell looked not to southern slave laws but to the letters of Paul to discount chattel slavery, which "precluding as it does every idea of merit or demerit . . . never seems to have entered the head of the Apostle. He considered slavery as a social and political economy betwixt moral, intelligent, responsible beings, involving reciprocal rights and reciprocal obligations. . . . A moral character attaches to their work."[24] Baptist Richard Fuller simply used the idea of biblical injunction and moral duty to argue, "My own servants are placed under a contract, which no instrument of writing could make more sacred."[25] Methodist William Smith argued that slavery had to be voluntary because the Bible so described it when Romans 6:16 and Ephesians 6:5–7 commanded servants, "*Do the will of God with Good will.* We must certainly understand it was the duty of those [biblical] slaves to give both assent and consent to their condition."[26] Presbyterian James Mitchell gave a similar translation of 1 Corinthians, which he claimed instructed slaves to "care not for being slaves, but even if you can be free, prefer to remain as you are."[27] T.C. Thornton gave a more racist and popular explanation of the voluntary nature of slavery. The practice originated and was constantly reinitiated through slaves' own moral will rather than through a preexisting duty: "People may by their ignorance and vices not only prove, but actually render themselves unfit . . . they make themselves slaves. Yes! slaves of the most degraded character! Who will admit slavery, as a permanent institution of a country is right? Not one *perhaps.* For although slavery, from its great liability to abuse, may become the greatest evil that can befall a man, yet it is certain that it may be a voluntary, and indeed sometimes a necessary relation . . . for some people for a time."[28] Baptist William Buck gave a more technical version of this voluntary act: "Africans are made slaves by their own *implied consent.*"[29] Slave labor, southerners said, was "a training ground . . . improperly called slavery."[30]

If southern evangelicals supposed slaves to be laborers under a course of elevating discipline improperly called slavery, slaveholders could not properly be called owners or even masters. Bryan Tyson admitted bluntly in his proslavery apology that "the word master sounds badly to many [in North Carolina] even to me."[31] William Smith found a term more appropriate to the times by designating a slaveholder an employer or "*a chief director,* one who *governs or directs either men or business.*"[32] Patrick Mell aligned the slaveholder's role more directly with the work ethic: "9 out of 10 masters undergo as much physical labor in the field as their negroes do. . . . There are some few rich men here as well as in N.E., who unhappily, bring up their children in idleness. . . . Our sons and daughters yield to none in industry."[33] This evangelical construction of mastery differed significantly from the classic rationalization of slavery as the means of freeing a class of superior men for leisured pursuits.

Proslavery evangelicals would not admit that a system of unequal responsibility or privilege existed. They thought that taking credit for saving slaves from the responsibility of self-government was about as acceptable as taking the credit for converting slaves to Satan worshipers. Evangelicals usually deplored the proslavery argument that slaves obtained the benefits of "less labor" and "less accountability" because they were "beings for whose every act the master is held accountable."[34] In evangelical rationalizations, the slaves were responsible agents and the masters directors of labor, not of men. This idealized labor system presented opportunities not only for greater labor and accountability, but also for the compensations and inducements of meritorious exertion. Evangelicals built their proslavery fantasies on very different cultural and conceptual models than those of the elitist devotees of slavery as a positive good.

The definition of slaves as laborers was only the first step in the process of placing slavery under the sanctions of the work ethic. Evangelicals claimed that slaves received biblical "wages," much as they were under the protection of a biblical contract and guarantee of their self-ownership.[35] Thornton Stringfellow provided the typical statement on slaves' compensations: "God has ordained food and raiment, as wages for the sweat of the face. Christ has ordained that with these whether in slavery or freedom, his disciples shall be content. . . . I answer that ours are hired servants, too, and not slaves."[36] In addition to the Adamic obligation to labor, Ecclesiastes 6:7, Ephesians 6:1–13, Timothy 6, Titus 2, and especially Luke 10:7 ("the laborer is worth his hire") and Thessalonians 3:10 ("that if any would not work, neither should he eat") were standard fare in both proslavery justifications and free-labor explanations of the wage system. Antislavery spokesman Francis Wayland declared these biblical passages to be "everywhere appropriate at this moment; and just as appropriate to free laborers as slaves."[37] Wayland knew that proslavery apologists insisted that slaves received wages, so he used the biblical injunction that masters and employers "give that which is just and equal" (Ephesians 6) to prove that southern slavery violated its own code. His position was similar to that in an earlier critique of the South popularized by abolitionist William Goodell, among others. In *Slavery Tested by Its Own Code* (1835) Goodell explained why even those slaves who received sufficient food and clothing did not attain the standard of free laborers[38]: "Wages to be 'just and equal,' must be sufficient to the support of the laborer, not as a mere animal, but as an intelligent and moral being. Something which he can earn without consuming all his time, so as to leave no adequate space for rational improvement and social enjoyment."[39] Slavery, of course, did not pass the test.

Not surprisingly, proslavery forces were unwilling to concede this point. Introducing *Cotton is King* (1859), the massive and final compilation of proslavery arguments, E.N. Elliott noted that in Goodell's form of abolitionist argument the "idea here conveyed is that of compulsory and unrequited labor. Such is not our labor system."[40] In the 1830s Theodore Clapp had already sketched the relation of master to slave as "simply to enjoy the benefit of his labor during a term of years, for a fair and reasonable compensation."[41] These long-standing proslavery visions left an incomplete description of a moral and modernizing labor system. Benefits bestowed at the master's behest did not fully accord with labor's inherent dignity and ability to find its own level of reward.

Slave success stories—counterparts to proslavery tales of self-made slaves—filled out the evangelical's picture of southern labor in the 1840s and 1850s. Baptist Richard Fuller diagramed the evangelical myth of flexible plantation labor: "When that [work assigned] is performed, the slaves—to use a phrase common with them—are "their own master." You will find slaves tilling land for themselves and selling various articles of merchandise for themselves . . . they will speak of their rights and their property . . . as they could if free. To use another of their phrases—they do all this 'in their own time.'"[42] Conservative Baptist Iveson Brookes believed everyone had to prosper "if free to carry out their industrial pursuits"; slaves were in such a position, so the "more industrious part of them procure even the luxuries of life."[43] Thornton Stringfellow avoided the corrupt designation "luxuries" and instead emphasized how slaves worked their own property and acquired skills and advanced employments. Slaves "inherited portions of their masters' estates," became "tradesmen of every kind," and "nearly all have an income of their own."[44] Methodists T.C. Thornton and William Smith gave identical accounts of slaves' opportunities. "*Their own time,*" Smith lectured, "is usually employed by the more provident in cultivating a garden . . . or in various ways earning a few dollars."[45] Thornton used the examples of exceptionally provident slaves: "Among us are various mechanics and others, who have by industry and frugality, purchased housewares," and one by "his labor and industry [in his garden], buys 30 and 40 dollars worth of books at a time."[46] Other proslavery spokesmen collected testimony from masters about slaves who pursued the ultimate labor inducement and form of property hold-

ing—purchasing themselves: "No instance is known of the master's interfering with their little acquisitions; and it often happens, that they are
considerable enough to purchase themselves and family. . . . Other slaves
who are more provident, employ a portion of their holy days and eve-
nings in working for themselves. In this way, those who are at all industrious are enabled to appear as well dressed as any peasantry in the world. . . .
In each case, much depends on the industry and management of the
party." The industrious also naturally escaped the punishments of other
cases: "vicious idle servants are punished with stripes."[47]

The exceptional slave success stories provided the proslavery camp
with a rhetorical advantage. Overlooking of course the adage that exceptional cases make bad law, they proved that the vast majority of blacks
continued to render themselves slaves for life.[48] Evangelical plantation
legends also provided powerful ideological material because they were
not fictions. Slaves did acquire a variety of skills in different jobs, compensation systems, and labor conditions. A few bought their freedom and
became decently educated, and most slaves tended gardens to help keep
themselves fed.[49] Of course that such situations existed *in spite of* the labor
system and prevailing white attitudes never seems to have occurred to
southern apologists. When proslavery evangelicals did not take all the
credit for blacks' triumphs, they noted that blacks' chances for autonomous exertion vindicated southern respect for the natural operation of
the providential economy. Besides, proslavery forces believed that the
"slaveholder finds it in his interest to lift the more intelligent slave into
situations of higher responsibility."[50] Southern evangelicals' reaction to
the greatest moral phenomenon of the 1850s—*Uncle Tom's Cabin* (1852)—
often followed this pattern.

Although some evangelicals wrote dreadful proslavery novels in response, such as *Nellie Norton* (1861) and Mary Eastman's *Aunt Phillis's
Cabin* (1852), and many demanded that Harriet Beecher Stowe write a
similar exposé of the urban North or Britain, southern ministers also
employed examples from the novel in their rhetoric.[51] Presbyterian rabble-
rouser Frederick Ross told a proslavery crowd that "every incident in the
book occurs at the South" and urged them "to hunt down Simon Legree
who whipped Uncle Tom."[52] Methodist academic Albert Taylor Bledsoe
in his sophisticated proslavery work *Liberty and Slavery* (1856) found positive
confirmation of the southern view of slavery within Stowe's pages. The
whole nation would see that southern slavery produced "not brutes, but

a George Harris—or an Eliza—or an Uncle Tom. . . . We cannot possibly conceive, indeed, how Divine Providence could have placed them in a better school of correction."[53] Edward Pringle wrote one of the longest southern reviews of and replies to *Uncle Tom's Cabin*. In his conclusion, he assured southerners that if Stowe's view of slaves were right and slavery "disappears because of an increased energy and higher character in blacks, it will have had its day of usefulness."[54] White southerners could not be guilty, for they had left the way open for whatever good providence might draw from slavery.

Whether or not general emancipation waited at the end of the process of providential development, evangelicals wanted to demonstrate that individual slaves had the opportunity to prove their character and achieve upward mobility. William Smith worried in 1856 that abolitionism destroyed the "divinely sanctioned process" whereby the "voluntary principle was discriminating those in the moral condition of freedom."[55] Smith thought that the colonization movement had served as such a safety valve for slave achievement, but even with its demise slaves of merit would find their level: "Are they indeed fitted for political sovereignty? That . . . some among the slaves may be so, I think is more than probably true. . . . [It is] usually awarded them with great unanimity by southern people."[56] Other proslavery spokesmen were less circumspect, declaring simply that those who would make "provident citizens . . . generally become free."[57] Baptist William Buck, an ex-colonizationist like Smith, still hoped for a "rapidly approaching" removal of blacks from the South and identified the unfailing test for determining when slaves had worked their way toward emancipation.[58] According to Buck, many in the South "hope for the time when the slaves of this country shall be so advanced in the arts, in science and religion, as to be perfectly capable of self-government— *assured that when that is the case they will be useless as slaves,* [at] that [point] their owners will cheerfully surrender them."[59]

Emancipation could be pushed far into the future. This way southerners continued to exploit the peculiar institution without sacrificing the principles of the work ethic or their belief that the region had a flexible economy with competitive rewards for labor. Evangelicals easily cited biblical and divine sanctions for this comforting vision of southern society. The trick of sustaining the illusion of a labor order built on merit and equal opportunity lies in determining how recently and how often equality has to have been guaranteed. One biblical proslavery tract simply declared: "The races set out with equal opportunity, at the subsiding of the flood, but who has won the prize of power—of social and mental improvement?"[60] The more popular evangelical position extended the horizon of slaves' gradual schooling. "The Israelites were in bondage in Egypt," lectured T.C.Thornton, "[and a] second captivity in Babylon, could hardly prepare them for self-government."[61] A tract from the 1850s made the same biblical argument: "If indeed our fair and sunny South is the Egypt of this new Israel, can you not await the birth of its Moses and Exodus to the promised land?"[62] The flexibility and providential nature of the southern economic order, not a faith in advancing black character, inspired the majority of proslavery dreams about the end of the slave-labor system.

Most proslavery evangelicals were more concerned about the total welfare of the region than the peculiar destiny of the slaves. Matthew Estes responded to the question, "Shall slavery ever cease?": "I reply that it will."[63] Estes knew when and how the end would come: "The abolition of slavery can never be effected in any community, until Slavery has ceased to be beneficial to all parties; until it wears out ... [as it] fell into decay in our northern states."[64] Estes, with the majority of proslavery advocates, thought the point "when mechanical industry shall have partaken of the general progress" was far off, but others did not.[65] Howell Cobb in his *Scriptural Examination of the Constitution of Slavery in the United States* (1856) argued "that the time will not be a very long time" before population growth would bring a natural phasing out of slave labor: "There will be an extinction of slavery whenever the density of population of the United States shall be so great that free labor can be procured ... at a cheaper rate and under less onerous conditions."[66] The proslavery longing for the next stage in the development of the South's modernized and fully moralized meritocracy often combined with the longing to be rid of blacks.[67] As Methodist A.B. Longstreet wrote to Massachusetts about the slaves, ". . . most of [us] are just as sick of them as you are of their masters and their masters are of you."[68] Southerners often saw evils in slavery and felt it a burden even though they felt no personal responsibility (or guilt) about its existence. Fred Ross's proslavery vision of the imminent transition out of the slave economy and labor system combined the gamut of proslavery biblical, economic, and racial hopes. Black labor (the children of "Ham" to Ross) would be displaced by Chinese immigrants (the children of "Shem") who were "a law abiding people without castes, accustomed to rise by merit to highest distinctions. . . . Shem, then, can mingle with Japheth in America."[69] This would fulfill the biblical prophecy in Genesis 9 and insure the southern transition to a free-labor economy.

Antislavery forces despised the southern attempt to bring slavery under the aegis of freedom—actual or incipient.[70] Despite arguments such as Fred Ross's and William Buck's about emancipation and the eventual move to free labor in the South, most evangelical proslavery advocates proposed to demonstrate that slave labor already completely fulfilled the moral and religious standards of self-discipline. Francis Wayland recognized the southern tendency to admire free labor and attempt to describe slavery as "really identical." Wayland accurately described the proslavery southerners' claim that "in all respects slavery makes no difference between the slave and any other man." After noting that a slave's position was supposedly "precisely that of a freeman,"[71] Wayland sarcastically commented to a proslavery minister: "I am not certain dear brother that I clearly understand the nature of that domestic slavery which you defend."[72] Pennsylvanian Stephen Colwell also correctly pointed out that southerners "uphold slavery as a moral industrial institution."[73] Northerners willing to be moderate on the slavery question in the hope that the South would naturally make the transition to free labor were discouraged to hear in the 1850s that the South's current order had already passed this test.[74] A second aspect of the proslavery equation of the discipline of slave labor and the self-disciplining of free labor threatened popular northern sensibilities to a greater extent than the evangelical legend of the flexible possibilities of plantation life. This threat, of course, was the southern description of the northern labor system.[75]

No subject connected with the slavery debate has been misunderstood more than the issue of the southern critique of the northern wage labor system. First of all there was no uniform proslavery project concerning, or position on, this matter. There were a number of possible arguments and intellectual outcomes in the attempts to put the northern system on the defensive. For one, in the 1850s some proslavery scientists abandoned the biblical time line and the unity of races to argue that blacks were a product of a separate creation, and an inferior species rightly enslaved.[76] In another more widespread stance, proslavery economists and sociologists described slavery as the perfect labor system since it avoided the "cash nexus" and contradiction between capital and labor purportedly sweeping free society.[77]

Proslavery intellectuals who attacked the "free labor" of the North in the 1850s had often abandoned individualism and embraced the model of social hierarchy. Charlestonian novelist and poet William Gilmore Simms offers a particularly interesting case in point, because he had in the 1830s made proslavery arguments in line with evangelical formulas. He had, however, become crankier and less optimistic by the 1850s. Simms defended slavery "per se" on "higher ground," which included the Bible and a vision of the work ethic that sounded more aristocratic each year.[78] Simms came close to advocating slavery for everyone (regardless of race) but men like himself, who naturally drove themselves mercilessly and achieved perfect self-government. "Pity is," Simms commented in his proslavery stance of the 1850s, "that the lousy and lounging lazzaroni of Italy, cannot be made to labor in the fields, under the whip of a severe task master! They would then be much freer."[79] Simms extended this argument to Americans who "are singularly susceptible of the ridiculous."[80] He described the slavery debate in such terms: "The clamor about liberty and slavery is . . . the most arrant nonsense. License they mean when they cry liberty—and we may add . . . license they mean when they cry slavery. The right to govern themselves requires, first, a capacity for such government . . . the capacity requires long ages of preparation, of great trial, hardship, severe labor and perilous enterprise."[81] Much of the mainstream evangelical proslavery position and definition of freedom was implicit in this statement, but Simms said of the capacity for self-government, "*I will not even believe it to exist in the United States.*"[82] Such a conviction would have destroyed the entire evangelical moral project. Proslavery ideologues like Simms and James Henry Hammond—who like Henry Hughes and Josiah Nott were explicitly skeptical of revealed religion—were not really discussing the same formulas of success and self-government that evangelicals had in mind. The ideas of moral power and moral causation disappeared in Hammond's account of a natural aristocracy. These proslavery aristocrats were most often the advocates of "the primitive and patriarchal" as the "most sacred way."[83]

Criticisms of the cash-nexus and the alienation of labor from capital in free society became prevalent in a variety of proslavery publications in the 1850s. Yet these critiques of capitalism carried less weight than twentieth-century understandings of the issue would suggest. The arguments against competition were not accessible to the popular mind. More important, only a few ministers and intellectuals who made these points appreciated the economic winds that buffeted the nation, or intended these critiques to address the free-labor system as a whole. Fear about the cash-nexus and the competition between capital and labor were just as prevalent in the North.[84] James Henley Thornwell, Iveson Brookes, James Sloan, and William Smith, among other educated ministers, hailed the mutuality of labor relations in the South.[85] Yet abolitionists and paternalistic factory proprietors in the North maintained that the relationship between capitalists and wage-earners in the free states was one of mutual dependence.[86] Iveson Brookes, like many southerners, believed that the "nonslaveholding states contain in their social system the elements of their destruction."[87] Brookes, however, was primarily attacking the "excessive ill-gotten gain" of the region, not its rapidly emerging modern civilization or the cash-nexus at its center.[88] Many southerners lambasted New England "capitalists" for their greedy attempt to take advantage of the competitive labor market and to "purchase labor at the cheapest possible rates," without implying that this was an inevitable development of economic law.[89] Evangelicals generally demonstrated the superiority of their moral organization, not of their labor system.

Most southern evangelicals remained anxious to equate slavery and free labor, and their proslavery arguments often labeled northern labor "as involuntary as slave labor."[90] This was an insult to and assault on the North in antislavery eyes, and historians have too often assumed that it also constituted a serious southern attack on the ideals of free society and labor. Proslavery evangelicals were drawing no such dichotomy: they did not consider slavery particularly involuntary, nor a term of abuse. They sought to prove that the same moral law was in operation in both regions and had produced both forms of labor. Evangelicals quite openly admitted—unlike a number of other proslavery ideologues—that slavery was not the only, best, or even a necessary form that labor assumed under the rule of Providence.[91]

Many conservative evangelicals, however, pushed this argument close to the "positive good" view that slavery represented the economic wave of the future and that the rest of the nation's labor practices (and the world's as far as they did not already) would come to look more like the South's.[92] Was slavery a form of free labor or free labor a form of slavery? The line was not always clear in evangelical pronouncements using providential economics rather than economic philosophy as their basis. Conservative Presbyterian James Sloan exemplified the ambiguities in his absolute version of the evangelical equation of slavery with free labor: "Slavery may be properly defined to be *a certain relation which labor sustains to capital.* Wherever there is capital there will be servitude. You may call this relation *free* or *slave* labor—whichever you choose—but it is a matter of very small importance in a *practical* view whether the service rendered be *voluntary* or *involuntary.* . . . If this be the boasted liberty of the freedom-shriekers then the freeman is only so in *name,* while the reality is wanting."[93] Sloan clearly thought free labor a form of slavery, but he complained about the antislavery forces' fanciful demands for liberty for the slaves, not about the subordination in "free" labor. Sloan argued, "Christians do not belong to themselves," so "the real difference [between free and slave labor] is only in the mode of punishment" Providence designated for "idleness."[94] Sloan's fellow Old School Presbyterian James Henley Thornwell was considerably more open to the end of slavery and the growth of liberty within slavery. He also affirmed that northern society contained Christian liberty.[95] Thornwell, however, made statements similar to Sloan's in clarifying the involuntary aspect of free labor: "What is it that makes a man a slave? . . . We answer the obligation to labor for another, determined by the Providence of God, independently of the provisions of a contract. . . . God's command is often as stringent upon the free laborer, and determines, with as stern a mandate, what contracts he shall make. Neither can be said to select his employments."[96] The obligation to labor was involuntary in both regions.

Southern accounts of how free labor forced men into harsh employments most often described a practice southerners accepted. After all, "proslavery" ministers were unlikely to consider such assignments to labor as a denigration of northern society or of any other. The context of southern evangelicals' discussions of free labor in the 1850s resembled that of proslavery's use of women's (and Indians') position. Historians have hailed the brilliant widespread southern critique of free labor that emerged before the Civil War,[97] but no one has pointed to the similar denunciation of the degradation and enslavement of women (and the denunciation of the degradation of Indians and theft of their land) in proslavery.[98] That, of course, is because southerners intended no such thing and displayed no such sensitivity; they accepted the practices toward women. The same was usually true of those toward free laborers. In 1857 Fred Ross discussed women in the same terms used to discuss the restraint and unfreedom in northern labor: "The slave is held in *involun-*

tary service? So is the wife." He pointed out that when a woman made the decision to marry "for herself, how often and soon, does it become involuntary." Ross continued to support mock-feminist views, "I know how superior you are to your husbands. . . . Nay, I know you may surpass him in his own sphere [business]. . . . And you may wish to run away or kill him."[99] The reason for such discussion was obvious, and even more obvious in other proslavery tracts: "Females . . . they may be found of better faculties, and better qualified to exercise political privileges, and to attain the distinction of society than men. Yet who complains of the order of society by which they are excluded?"[100] The proslavery point usually was not that free laborers'—anymore than women's—positions constituted dangerous cases of injustice, but that slave labor was an equivalent case of divine justice. James Henley Thornwell tried to tell antislavery activists that the "arguments against slavery are not peculiar to slavery. They are incidents to poverty."[101] Thornwell knew that northerners thought poverty often called forth the exercise of denial and of other moral virtues, which produced achievement or drove men to labor. Southerners put slavery in the same category.

Most evangelicals did not run analogies to women's roles, poverty, or free labor to demonstrate the limits of their criticism of northern labor and defense of slave labor; they simply stated their views. Benjamin Morgan Palmer remains infamous as the Presbyterian divine who ignited much of the lower South with his biblical proslavery sermon in support of secession in the winter of 1860–1861. Yet even in this fire-breathing proslavery and southern nationalist tract meant for consumption in Dixie, Palmer caught his breath when it came to elevating the slave system above the free labor system: "[It is] not necessary here to inquire whether this is precisely the best relation in which the hewer of wood and drawer of water can stand to his employer. Still less are we required, dogmatically, to affirm that it will subsist through all time."[102] Albert Taylor Bledsoe in his 1854 *Liberty and Slavery* claimed to stand aghast that northerners thought proslavery meant a general advocacy of slave labor.[103] Bledsoe thought such an absurd argument as the proposal that northern laborers be enslaved to bring them under the benefits of southern practices was a product of antislavery propaganda. He, like many other educated and well-read Virginians, remained unaware that his contemporary George Fitzhugh had indeed suggested this. Bledsoe stuck to his typical Methodist phrasing of the justice of slavery: "It is not always and everywhere wrong." He, however, admitted that the slavery debate had pushed a few southerners to the "monstrous dogma that it is always and everywhere right!"[104]

Rather than reclarify the limits of their defense of slavery, many southern apologists foreswore any intent to denigrate free labor when describing slavery's similarities to northern labor or its unique benefits.[105] Although B.F. Stringfellow praised the ability of southern slavery to "identify the interests of labor and capital," he quickly added, "our purpose has not been to see motes in our brother's eye." This led to a discussion of the advantages of free labor and northern education.[106] T.C. Thornton insisted that evangelicals denounced cruel masters just as northerners did "lewdness in the treatment of *poor factory girls.*"[107] Thornton discussed the "14 hour days" in these factories in order to object not to factory labor but to criticism of the South. He provided northerners with a parable of the proper attitude toward labor subordination: if southerners suggested that "poor girls and boys in the factories should be worked 6 or 8 hours . . . what would Massachusetts say? Mind your own business."[108] When Matthew Estes argued that "in Great Britain, theoretical slavery does not exist; but practically it exists in its worst forms," and that in the North "laborers are driven to it [rough work] by necessity or authority," he criticized neither.[109] He added, "Slavery would be highly injurious to our northern brethren."[110] T.W. Hoit's proslavery pamphlet of 1860 enjoyed even wider circulation than Benjamin Morgan Palmer's sermon in New Orleans after Lincoln's election, partly because it was intended for a national audience that would preserve the union. He concluded, "Slavery is the left hand of our body politic. Free labor the right."[111] James Williams's proslavery plea of 1860 also followed an emerging southern pattern. "[There] can scarcely be said to be such a thing as free labor," lectured Williams, "*they must work or starve!* . . . I only refer to this state of things as a fact which none will deny. Not by way of complaint." Neither did he "deny the evils of slavery . . . nor the great benefits which have resulted to mankind from free labor."[112] Williams, like the Reverend Palmer, supported secession at the push because he "opposed [slavery] in abstract," but thought that "the slave states should have the benefit of that inexorable necessity which without any agency of their own, left them no alternative."[113]

Southern evangelicals very effectively blurred the line between freedom and slavery by obscuring the distinction between what was and what ought to be in the South. In the 1850s ministerial calls for the modernizing of slave discipline to the standards southerners had evoked in the slavery debate served to make a flexible and progressive picture of slave labor more realistic. Only a minority of proslavery ministers advocated actual reforms to help bring slavery into line with the standards of the Bible and the work ethic (as they were envisioned in proslavery sermons). Even these few reform-minded minsters, who were willing to press for changes in the slaveholding laws, believed that slavery could function like free labor. When one such reforming minister, Reverend A. Campbell of Bethany College, mentioned a flaw in southern slavery, he added, "Remedying it, will form a prominent feature of the New Economy."[114] Like southerners who understood the economic lag of their region yet believed in the potential for change and progress in (and ultimate vindication of) the Cotton South, many evangelicals claimed that they were already part of a movement afoot in the South to bring reality into line with the rhetoric of a proslavery work ethic. Few actually acted on this claim.

During the 1850s, southern evangelicals made more elaborate and explicit assertions about the character-building nature of slave labor in their private as well as their publicly propagandistic proclamations. Despite most southerners' uncritical professions about the intrinsic rewards and moral value of slave labor, many evangelicals presented the proslavery work ethic as a potential that the South needed to achieve, rather than a reality to be described. Within the South there arose a new form of proslavery pronouncement directed at masters and stressing the individual "Rights and Duties" embodied in a moral conception of slave labor and the master-slave relationship. Masters' main duty in this pietistical literature involved providing religious instruction for the slaves,[115] but evangelical advice also encompassed the subjects of labor discipline and economic rationality.[116] Much as in their flood of character-building advice to parents and children, evangelical proslavery spokesmen emphasized the need for Christian masters who would move slaves in moral paths through the inculcation of internal mechanisms of control. Ministers insisted that slaveholders take up the Bible, rather than the lash.[117] According to evangelicals, self-controlling Christian masters had the most effective control over their slaves and the most efficient plantations.[118]

Evangelicals extolled predictability and uniformity in masters in the certainty that such conduct best mirrored the providential scheme of punishments and rewards. In theory Christian masters (and, in some proslavery visions, a rationalized and Christianized legal system or government) would provide a dispassionate and predictable—swift and sure—scale of discipline and advancement for slaves. Evangelicals thought a clear system of rewards and punishments would thus facilitate slaves' internalization of plantation discipline and uplift their individual moral consciousness. Thornwell thought such a system of rules and rewards "would inspire a sense of personal responsibility—a certain degree of manliness and dignity of character . . . a security to the master, an immense blessing to the slave."[119] The suggested standard for whipping and punishment, however, was vague and contradictory: "Punishment should be *sure* and *certain* but always *just* and *merciful*," and "*Masters are required to govern their slaves with dignity and mildness but inflexible firmness.*[120] More specific was the advice on the minimal requirements ministers thought were outlined in scripture for food, shelter, clothing, and privacy. Advice on a system of rewards made up the bulk of this literature.[121]

In the 1850s, when mature free labor theory signaled a growing awareness that negative incentives were not the most effective or desirable motivations for hard work and self-discipline, evangelicals interested in modernizing southern slavery maintained that the lash was becoming obsolete in the South. The Southern Baptist Convention circulated essays by its ministers extolling a "system of rewards" for slaves as "an incentive to industry." Henry McTyeire gave the rationale for this campaign: "Whilst I would scorn the idea of bribing servants or children to do their duty, I would hold it not only as kind, but as a moral duty, to reward those who did well, and all in proportion as they did well."[122] Several ministers tried to find a scale for weighing which servants were "Christ's freemen" (Col. 4:1). Jesse Ferguson called for slaves who might be fit for freedom to be granted it after "their qualifications [were] submitted to a proper umpire"; others advocated a "mediator."[123] Tracts on *The Rights and Duties* involved in slavery invariably maintained that slavery was a relation between "rational, intelligent, responsible agents."[124] Slaves, it was argued, could be motivated both by the compensations and opportunities provided by masters, and by their proper understanding of the benefits of self-discipline and of themselves as moral agents.

The proslavery work ethic appeared in sermons directed at other southerners about the "Biblical rights" of virtuous slaveholding, rather than in sermons directed at slaves.[125] Slaveholders wanted to hear how slave workers should behave. They wanted to know the Christian standard for slave moral conduct and the master-slave relationship. Versions of the ethic were most often built on Ephesians 6: "Servants be obedient to them that are your masters according to the flesh, with fear and trembling, in singleness of heart, as unto Christ; not with eye service, as menpleasers; but as the servants of Christ, doing the will of God from the heart; with good will doing service as to the Lord, and not to men." If put into practice by a "reforming" Christian master, this vision could generate a new kind of nightmare for the slaves. Interpretations varied, but the implication in biblical proslavery was clear: slaves ought to work at all times and as if they chose it. Methodist William Hamilton believed that "an ungrateful, sullen, or idle servant is not a Christian." James Sloan similarly demanded that Christian slaves be the most obedient; he noted, "This is necessary that men see religion is not a mere form but a reality."[126] To many ministers this meant that slavery would inevitably take on elevating Christian attributes as all masters and slaves became Christians. Then slaves would work willingly—truly "free" labor—because they understood the moral nature of the work and its rewards. Presbyterian Joseph Wilson described the goals of the proslavery work ethic in these terms: "Masters are, for this end even required to guard their tempers— firm, consistent, orderly, paternal government, which will suitably mingle the mercy of punishment with the justice of reward. In short the master ... will find himself unequal to the task in all its length and breadth; unless he himself become a *Christian* [and] thus welcome down a world covered with righteousness—slavery freed from its stupid servility on one side and its excess of neglect or severity on the other, and appearing to all mankind to contain that [divine] scheme of politics and morals."[127] If this patently appeared not to be the case, it was only because the great society within which southern values and Christian civilization would prove themselves had not been completed.

Under the pressures of the war and the dissolution of slavery in the 1860s, this reforming rhetoric reached a new pitch and had some practical legal consequences.[128] It is, however, doubtful that the proslavery work ethic was often motivated by or produced widespread reforming zeal in the 1850s or before.[129] The self-critical and reforming potential of the proslavery work ethic did not emerge clearly until the possibility of southern defeat and the need for a proslavery theodicy to explain it (and keep the cause alive) became an overwhelming reality. Even in the tracts of antebellum ministers highly critical of the unbiblical aspects of southern slavery,[130] their calls for improvement were never very far removed from regional cheerleading and dreams of a perfected and powerful slaveholding South. Only as a desperate wartime measure, when both slavery and the southern cause began to expire in 1863, did some southern states institute reforms in slaves' education in literacy and access to reading the Bible, marriage, and minimal rights. Evangelicals hoped these moral reforms would win divine favor and boost the war effort as well as embody their ideal of slavery and the work ethic.

Mature proslavery in the 1850s reflected both a desperate, fervent hope and a sadistic, interested demand that slaves would internalize the work ethic and acquire an appreciation for the intrinsic value of their labor. Evangelicals in effect insisted that slaves, like free laborers, should work of their own initiative and as hard as if their own interests and advancement were at stake—as many evangelicals believed was the case. This brand of proslavery was an uneven mix of prescription and description aimed largely at fellow southerners rather than at slaves or the North. Evangelicals expressed a sometimes critical desire to modernize and improve southern slaveholding, while also offering an idealization of slavery as a labor practice that was already as morally unassailable and economically progressive as free labor. This last claim was not only implicit in the evangelical accommodation to slavery, but also necessitated by southern ministers' stance in the slavery debate. They had long argued that slavery rested on foundations of Christian individualism, much as did northern society. In the face of a hostile free-labor ideology some elite southerners abandoned faith in the possibility that an unfailing, fully moralized meritocracy was being achieved on this continent. Most southern evangelicals, however, were never prepared to abandon their optimistic faith in progress toward greater individual autonomy and in the end were willing to jettison the Union in order to keep their proslavery version of the dream intact.

The evangelical view that the South would come to look more like the rest of the nation in both its labor discipline and economic power provided a ready rationale for belligerent secession. Evangelicals believed that the South changed and grew as the character of its citizens carried it forward. Never static in institutions or ideology, the region had long been enthralled with the process of becoming something else. On the eve of secession southerners assumed that they possessed more than a God-given right—rather a God-given power—to take their region and labor system just as far as their individual character would lead. This was the way of

Providence. No one could interfere with it. Presbyterian minister Benjamin Morgan Palmer of New Orleans gave the most influential expression of these confident providential ideas on the eve of secession. In a sermon distributed all across the lower South after Lincoln's election in 1860 Palmer electrified the region with his insistence that the South needed regional independence in order to work out the problems of slavery "guided by nature and God, without intrusive interference."[131] Providence had to "have free scope for their solution" so that the slave economy could *go and take root wherever Providence and nature may carry.* He had no doubt that when southerners shed the "constraints" of the Union, Providence would "send forth its [the slave economy's] branches like the banyan tree." Palmer moved from metaphor to employing the explicit language of a free-market economy when he declared that there was no use in "setting bounds to what God only can regulate." Giving slavery "scope for its natural development . . . supports our material interests."[132]

The sectional debate leading up to the Civil War was simultaneously a debate about morality and economics and about political power because the evangelical success ethic was at the center both of the debate and of American culture. God bestowed his favor on the morally deserving, and governments and men were to stand aside and let His favor shower down on those who earned it. God guarded His material rewards and gave them to virtuous individuals who earned them. The reward that all antebellum Americans strove for was land. Land meant first survival, then independence, and perhaps wealth. Even small farmers were speculators in real estate and commodities. Land meant everything since it, not incidentally, also measured regional and national political power. In the 1850s the question of which region, slave or free, North or South, gained new states in the West determined future power in Washington. Most accounts of the causes of the Civil War focus minutely on the political crises after 1848 over this issue of the status of new territory in the West. But the land came from God. Who deserved it? Who had earned it, *morally* earned it? On whom was God trying to bestow that western land? This question had been raised by evangelicals in the 1830s and answered on a religious basis. The North and South gave two different answers, and all the evangelical churches split asunder by 1846. Northerners eventually concluded that God favored free labor, but the true revolution and the first revolution arose from the southern evangelical conclusion that God blessed southern slaveholders. Theirs was the moral and deserving personality type.

When this self-conscious and often belligerent southern evangelical message spread and hardened after 1831, northerners eventually reacted in kind with an elevation of free labor to the status of God's plan. They elected an administration and Congress from a new party that promised no new slave territories. No more rewards from God for the South. That was the newborn Republican Party's central platform. Born in 1854, the Republican Party captured all of the North and control of Washington by 1860. Evangelical proslavery had similarly captured the South twenty years earlier. Lincoln's election in 1860 signaled that each region had determined that the evangelical God intended to bestow upon it the reward He had delivered to the nation—the land West of the Mississippi. God had taken this territory from heathen natives and Mexican Catholics to bestow on his favored evangelicals. The western bounty opened before all southerners and northerners hungry for land. Lincoln and the Republicans offered none of the new territory to slaveholders. The southern response to Lincoln's election was typical, obvious, almost mathematical. No one can dictate God's distribution of His rewards! The North has tied God's hands and is stealing His bounty! An open society and economy must leave all in the hands of God and let deserving slaveholders take their property anywhere. Southerners marched off to defend God's freedom to bestow rewards without interference. No plans or "schemes" were necessary to insure that land or power went to the just. God took care of that. Not Washington and a Republican Party that apportioned all future success (land) to nonslaveholders.

Since evangelicals knew that God, or in their words "Providence," controlled the future and "knew" Him personally through an emotional and ongoing saving experience, they refused to admit the possibility of defeat for their moral position in the slavery debate. Evangelicals, North and South, refused to compromise, an attitude that was a hallmark of evangelical self-assurance as well as of the sectional crisis and bloody Civil War.

Of course the sectional crisis, secession, and the Civil War could not have occurred as they did if southerners in the 1830s had not accepted the morality of slavery and the nineteenth century's evangelical ideal of God. After 1831, southerners not only did this but went further and sacralized their entire society, driving out any dissenters on the issue of the morality of slaveholding and the prospect of an economy and future "open" to slavery and to further rewards from God for "good" slaveholding. The South went even beyond this in the 1830s and after. The evangelical South concluded that God especially blessed the South since it was loyal to the Bible, which defended slavery, loyal to the Constitution of the United States, which protected slavery, and loyal to its majority of nonslaveholding white citizens, whose opportunity to become self-made slaveholders was protected by an expanding empire of land and new states open to slaveholding. The evangelical God clearly intended an unfettered and expansive future for His chosen region. The South had earned it. The crucial moment was 1831. After that year southerners answered the questions of the morality of slaveholding and of God's intentions for their region. Evangelical ministers answered these questions, and their answers became the basis for a nearly monolithic regional ideology. Southerners might continue to disagree about the exact future of slavery, the region's politics, and the characteristic that made slavery and the South so wonderful, but public dissent on the wonderfulness of it all was rare and sharply punished.

The southern sanctification of slavery in the 1850s tells us a great deal about why a moral debate over slavery led to a national crisis. The moral debate produced a contest for moral supremacy, and morality was the language of economic and political status. In the debate on slavery the North and South declared themselves rivals for the same prize of economic and political power—as rightful heirs to the same tradition. Henry Ward Beecher, the greatest ministerial apologist for all things bourgeois and conventional in the North, realized that the main threat of the southern proslavery movement lay in its attempt to appropriate the national language of moral success. In the midst of secession in 1861 Beecher lectured about the South's attempt to equate the status of slavery and free labor—morally, politically, and economically:

> It is this that convulses the South. They wish to reap the fruits of liberty from the seed of slavery. They wish to have an institution which sets at naught the laws of God, and yet be as refined and prosperous and happy as we are who obey these laws; and since they cannot, they demand that we shall make up to them what they lack. The real gist of the controversy between the greatest number of the northern and southern states is simply this. The

South claims that the United States government is bound to make slavery as good as liberty for all the purposes of national life. That is the root of their philosophy. . . . They don't any longer talk of the evil of slavery. It is virtue, a religion. It is justice and divine economy![133]

Beecher's shock at hearing his sanctification of the northern order on the lips of slaveholders who justified southern aspirations highlights the ideological naivete of the era. A religiously inspired delusion operated at the heart of both evangelical proslavery dreams and northern free-labor moralism.

The overly optimistic antebellum expectations of individual success through moral discipline—of free labor republicanism as much as of proslavery nationalism—died on the battlefields of the Civil War. The former passed more slowly and silently, only because the latter succumbed so suddenly and spectacularly. When it came to preserving their formulas of moralism and expansive individualism, both sections lost the Civil War.[134] In many ways the Civil War itself was a product of the explosion of the era's uncompromising moral culture and its wildly expansive vision of success. Evangelicals in the slavery debate had always been speaking the language of competition. In 1849 the *Augusta Chronicle* declared: "Slaveholders must demonstrate in a large way, and by visible results, that slave labor is as profitable to you and as useful to the world as free labor is at the North or can be at the South—that it is not inimical to common schools, the improvement of the soil and the progress of manufactures. . . . We can only prove our view by obtaining prosperity."[135] Prosperity— economic statistics and power—constituted the reward, the very judgment of Providence. Evangelicals North and South longed for the coming of the glorious verdict of the Lord. How much more glorious; quicker; more biblical; more tied to death, judgment, and salvation; more powerful; more final were rupture and war than economics and debate? All heard the voice of Providence in the alarm bells and guns.

The crisis antislavery provoked in the nation, and the war itself, were glorious proof that to take a stand on moral principles was to produce direct physical results.[136] Ministers North and South gloried in the sectional explosion because it appeared to demonstrate the practical relevance of their stock in trade. A moral debate had led to a practical crisis: secession and civil war. Religious morality proved itself relevant—in fact it appeared to drive events. Ministers could claim to be at the center of national life. Soon many southern ministers could claim to be at the center of a new chosen nation and to be the special protectors of its holy cause.

By 1860 evangelical proslavery had popularized the South's unique fidelity to the Bible and the founding faith of the nation. The Bible supported slaveholding; God supported the South. The formula was clear. Right made might. The South had to triumph. The region constituted a righteous remnant that would receive the blessings of Providence as it alone carried the uncorrupted truths of pure religion and constitutional liberty into a glorious proslavery future. *DeBow's Review,* the leading commercial journal of the South, issued a paean to secession as the movement dawned: "Many causes will contribute to our happiness [as a separate nation], but pre-eminently in view stand two peculiar features: the one is a pure religion; the other is a perfect labor system. In religious sentiment the South stands as a unit. Its pure doctrines are linked inseparably, though not by legal constraint, with the laws of the land. No isms and schisms rankle our hearts. Christ is acknowledged as the common bond of union."[137] But of course the Confederacy would fall, and Providence would not issue the prescribed verdict.

6

The Proslavery Formula and the Test of War, 1860–1865

Evangelical morality and proslavery ideology constituted the heart of southern identity before the Confederacy existed. This identity encouraged a highly individualistic and future-oriented culture and ideology. Southern evangelical culture was *the* glue of secession and the war effort.[1] A fairly formalistic evangelical ideology winds its way through the southern religious culture before, during, and after the war. The collapse of the Confederacy and the end of slavery did not obliterate or even seriously challenge white southerners' views of their moral superiority or the justice of their cause. Indeed the war strengthened these convictions.

If southerners did not lose their proslavery self-righteousness after the war, they did lose much of their optimism and their faith in progress. God, it appeared, did not always distribute the earthly rewards to the just. God did not always give the just the power they needed to overcome earthly problems. After the Civil War, southerners looked more to heaven for their reward. This was a convenient and logical deduction from pre–Civil War providential formulas, just as proslavery and secession had been deductions from the dramatic rise of the cotton kingdom and of evangelical conversions and churches in the region after the post-Revolution settlement on slavery. Evangelicals' uncompromised faith in worldly success before the Civil War set them up for disappointment and a retreat to otherworldliness for almost four generations after 1865. But the drum beating from the pulpits in 1860 had not been so otherworldly.

The belligerence and assurance of success emanating from pulpits North and South during the crisis of secession and the outbreak of war, from November 1860 through the spring of 1861, were startlingly monotonous and have attained the status of an historical cliche.[2] Although less catalogued by history, the evangelical predictions and near assumptions of disunion and war offered in the slavery debate rehearsed the drum beating of 1860–1861. Ten years before secession Josiah Priest of Kentucky ventured to "foretell that the Union will be two distinct governments" and that "the North will be repelled by anger and violence."[3] Methodist minister Alexander McCaine and Baptist Iveson Brookes sounded nearly identical notes of destruction in the 1840s long before secession. "The course of the abolitionists," said McCaine, "must lead to their own destruction."[4] Brookes drew more explicit pictures: "Those who undertake to fight against the God of the Bible, must fall in fearful conflict."[5] He went on to predict that the "poisoned shaft" of abolition would hit the North, not the slaveholders, "because the curse of God must ever fall on any people who pervert His truth." Brookes prophesied that "the spirit of atheism was fast sweeping once Puritan New England" and that this apostasy "must throw its withering curse over the last remains of pilgrim puritanism."[6] Northerners had become infidels worthy of destruction long before the hysteria of secession and the propaganda of war.

Southern secession and war sermons connected the northern biblical "errors" made in criticizing slavery with fears of racial insurrection in the same way they had been linked in the pre-1860 rhetoric of proslavery. In 1845, when Alexander McCaine warned that "it is intended that the massacre in the slave states be conducted on a scale that, for grandeur and extent, shall eclipse everything that went before it,"[7] he was referring to the slave insurrection inspired by abolitionism rather than civil war. Civil war and race war melded into a single threat with the crisis of secession, especially as the crisis came on the heels of John Brown's Raid in 1859. James Henry Hammond, a leading elitist defender of slavery in the abstract and skeptic of evangelicalism, had predicted well prior to 1859 that the North would "consolidate a strong government" and "invade us with black troops."[8]

Evangelicals usually had more optimistic views of the coming conflict. Twelve years prior to secession Methodist A.B. Longstreet foresaw that the slavery debate would "produce a dissolution of the Union! This is inevitable . . . we shall hardly separate before we are involved in War."[9] Longstreet, however, believed that "the North will be divided" and defeated.[10] Fears of racial insurrection and chaos lurked in southern evangelicals' denunciation of the sins and schemes of Yankees, but their proslavery arguments committed them to an optimistic view of southern independence on two counts. First, separation from the North would create a southern nation with a pure religion and unleash the stifled "banyan tree" potential of the South's divine economy. Secession often sounded like the unleashing of God's providence and a fulfillment of plans as prophesied in evangelical sermons. Second, glorious visions of the pure and free southern economy were insured by the righteousness of biblical proslavery. God had to fight to vindicate the South and the Bible if the military crisis came. Confidence and optimism poured from the evangelical discussions of disunion.

There was no subtlety to the evangelical vision of southern economic and geographic expansion, nor to that of God's obligation to give the South victory—until the course of the Civil War dashed these hopes. In the spring of 1861, Tennessee Presbyterian William H. Vernor put it bluntly: "In all contests between nations God espouses the cause of the Righteous and makes it his own. . . . The institution of slavery according to the Bible is right. Therefore in the contest between North and South, He will espouse the cause of the South and make it His own."[11] Benjamin Morgan Palmer connected God's protection to a broader set of values than just the Bible's support of slavery. God's law gave power to independent people of moral character in the economic, political, and military realms. "A nation often has a character as well-defined and intense as that of an individual," Palmer lectured, and "this individuality of character alone" guarantees "progress" and "the particular trust assigned to such a people become[s] the pledge of divine protection, and their fidelity to it determines their fate."[12]

Before the war began and then in its first year, evangelical formulas and visions of the future exploded with the promises of prosperity, expansion, and power. Secession, and anticipated secession prior to 1860, represented a founding act—like the settling of the first Protestants in North America or the miraculous Revolution and birth of a free nation after 1776. Southerners expected staggering and rapid growth to flow from their founding act. The South of 1860 now appears deluded in the light of the sheer hyperbole and chutzpah of its citizens and the events of the subsequent five years. But the common religious conceits of the era and stunning improbability of the nation's history to that point as they understood it gave their predictions the weight of scientific axioms. Victorious revolt of the underdog followed by growth and transformation beyond the wildest dreams of progress had fueled stupendous optimism in both regions of the young realm. These events defined normalcy and had taken place in the life span of one man as if by alchemy. Southerners believed, with some plausibility by their lights, that they had inherited a tradition of providential, near miraculous blessing to their free Protestant government.[13] The South's prospects were bright in terms of objective advantages by comparison with those of the colonists in 1776. The example of their success enhanced southern confidence. In 1855 a biblical proslavery Missourian exulted over the lower South's chances for independence: "Thank Heaven, they [of the South] have *all the courage, more than twice the numbers and at least 20 times the resources* that our Revolutionary sires had. . . . It is therefore vain to imagine, suicidal to hope, that such a people will submit to a worse tyranny. God will defend the right!"[14] In the great 1858 formal debate between southern Methodist William Brownlow and northern Methodist Abraham Pryne, Brownlow indulged in expansive visions of proslavery morality that drew from the examples of Protestant settlement of America and the American Revolution (as well as the racial colonization movement): "Let us seize upon the vast territory of Africa, cultivate its rich soil, and force its millions of indolent, degraded, and starving natives, to labor, and thereby elevate themselves to the dignity of men made in the image of God! . . . opening up [*sic*] new *slave* States in Africa, where we may settle down, and compel the natives to labor thus causing civilization and Christianity to spread over a few millions of its population, and the moral effect would be irresistible!"[15] Dreams of providential proslavery expansion at the time of secession turned more often to the Amazon and Antilles, where the current population would "melt away like the Indians" before an advancing Protestant Confederacy.[16] Antislavery activist Abraham Pryne perceptively mocked Brownlow's and the proslavery southerners' expansionist and economic aspirations as well as their "providential" statistics: "We of the poor, sterile North, are impoverished by our freedom; and gentlemen come here from the South to teach us political economy. . . . But she has no trade, only a magnificent site for one, which she lacks the enterprise to build upon. But she is *going* to have a foreign trade! Her statesmen and political economists are *going* to do great things. . . . But her greatness is all in prospect."[17] Pryne catalogued the North's superior economic and demographic statistics and concluded not only that they had God's favor but that the South would have to subsist in a coming war on the only thing it actually produced in abundance. "When his [the southerner's] hog and hominy fail," Pryne predicted, "he can fill himself with proslavery texts."[18] Brownlow was unimpressed. He documented God's favor toward the South on biblical grounds and retorted, "I fear you not; nor all who commune with you, I mark your gathering hosts as calmly as I view the setting sun."[19]

Other evangelicals preached in the tones of secession and war before they became popular realities. Brownlow, however, did not support secession or the war. In the slavery debate southerners like him committed themselves to a language of natural development and progress that eschewed political machinations and deliberate "schemes." Such acts were the sins of plotting Yankee abolitionists who made plans rather than trusting in Providence. Southerners in the 1860–1861 crisis took care to portray secession as a natural, long-incubating development.[20] "Ours is not a revolution," Jefferson Davis claimed. Secession was the means "to save ourselves from revolution."[21] The Republican Party was "active and bristling with terrible designs."[22] Presbyterian minister Robert Lewis Dabney echoed this description of the cause of secession when he wrote in *A Defence of Virginia* that the war was "caused deliberately" when abolitionists with "calculated malice" forced the South to independence.[23] Abraham Lincoln, before his election in 1860, commented on the tendency of southerners to disclaim an active design, a willful plan of secession: "In the supposed event [his election] you [the South] say you will destroy the Union; and then, you say, the great crime of having destroyed it will be on us! That is cool. A highwayman holds a pistol to my ear, and mutters through his teeth, 'Stand and deliver or I shall kill you and then you will be a murderer.'"[24] Lincoln's addresses throughout the Civil War demonstrated his acute understanding of the nation's providential language. He always carefully ascribed an unnatural rupture of the course of divine and national events to the Confederate movement. In his Second Inaugural Address he returned to the refrain of willful acts in explicitly providential language when he framed the causes of the war: "One of them would *make* war rather than let the nation survive; and the other would *accept* war. . . ."[25] The white South radiated genuine confidence in the slavery debate and the Civil War, but the *act* of secession, since it was a deliberate political step of self-willing men, ran against the grain of many Americans' providentially based culture.[26] Lincoln knew this. Lincoln had to describe secession as a deliberate scheme of his opponents. He did so brilliantly and with a fine ear for the providential language of the era. In November of 1860, however, ministers in the South, led by Benjamin Morgan Palmer of New Orleans, had done an equally brilliant job of convincing southerners that Lincoln's election signaled a deliberate attempt to interfere with the natural development of God's plan. Several key proslavery evangelicals, chief among them Fred Ross and Parson Brownlow, remained unionist and criticized secession because it appeared to violate the laissez-faire evangelical approach to providential development. But Palmer's fiery description of Yankee heresies and vain attempts to legislate the future of the country more than carried the day. Evangelical proslavery had trained a generation of southerners to see southern expansion and power as natural and God-given, and to see northern "schemes" as grasping, interfering, and dangerously unbiblical. Palmer could have spoken to Lincoln, as Jefferson Davis did: "You, the North, make ungodly revolution. We, the South, accept separation to preserve our god-given destiny."

Ministerial hosannahs to the providential nature of secession, such as Benjamin Morgan Palmer's, contributed vital ideological work to the creation of the Confederacy. Such sermonizing language provided the appearance of a seamless bridge between proslavery and the revolution creating an independent nation. The apotheosis of the region, the scapegoating of the North, and the identification with the rebels of 1776 unified and motivated a new nation at war. Thirty years of proslavery rhetoric had helped train white southerners for combat. Palmer's sermon after Lincoln's election brilliantly dwelt on the natural growth of the South and reiterated the core value of individual "character" that stood above any political doctrine or action.[27] The moral principle of individual self-government spoke to southerners of all classes and denominations and made any act of independence appear as natural and irresistible as the setting of the sun.

The greatest and most revealing burst of proslavery propaganda came not with secession and the new nation's declaration of independence, but rather as the troops assembled to march to a war that had yet to be defined by providential events. The gusto with which religious leaders North and South proselytized their regions' war efforts bordered on righteous hysteria and unreflective sanctification of bloodshed. The advent of the war itself appeared to demonstrate the power of the ministry and of religious pronouncements. Providential moralism in many ways had been developed as a ministerial tactic that made religion and ministers powerful and relevant in a democratic milieu. Evangelical ministers had no temporal or ecclesiastical power in the nation or over local individuals; a minister in any traditional church-state setting did, including in Anglican and Puritan America before the Revolution. Post-Revolution ministers made a virtue of their lack of secular authority by persuading believers that religious professions and morality had vital practical consequences. They were the root of individual power. A war brought about by a struggle over religious morality, in which ministers took the lead, vindicated their role and that of religious belief in general.[28] The slavery debate had been conducted with the intensity of a revival and of a call for conversion; the Civil War would be preached with the fervor of the final judgment. Northern Methodist Granville Moody spoke in 1861 for the ministers of both regions: "We [ministers] are charged with having brought about this present contest. I believe it is true that we did bring it about, and I glory in it for it is a wreath of glory around our brow."[29] Southern ministers, in greater relative numbers than northern ones, not only proclaimed the glory of their role in creating the war but also went off to battle with the military in an attempt to add to their glory.[30] Ministers served as officers and line soldiers, as well as chaplains.[31]

Southern minsters speaking to the assembling troops of their region in 1861 both retraced the steps of the popular proslavery moralism that led to secession and projected its glorious future onto the blank slate of the aftermath of victory in a yet unfought war. Restrained tones scarcely appeared.[32] Methodist minster R.N. Sledd spoke to the Confederate Cadets of Petersburg, Virginia, on September 22, 1861, before they left for the war. Even at this early stage, before all the major battles save Bull Run, Sledd railed against the "infidel and fanatical foe" who resembled "the barbarity of an Atilla more than the civilization of the 19th century," whose actions would "disgrace the annals of the Middle Ages" with their show of "contempt for virtue and religion perfectly according to their savage purpose."[33] Sledd's sermon reflected the tone and content of most early Confederate proslavery pronouncements.[34] Sledd incorporated all the elements of presecession biblical proslavery ideology and confidently hailed the providential validation that secession and the war brought. Religious proslavery ideas unified southern identity and morale with a seamless set of causes and motivations for combat.[35]

Moral proslavery drew on most of the region's powerful cultural strains, many of which did not arise from slaveholding and its politics. These many causes—the aspiration for regional economic progress, the character ideal and virtues that promoted success, southerners' personal identities as moral and independent individuals, the sanctity of the Bible, the threat of servile insurrection and upset of the racial and gender "verdicts" of Providence, and the preservation of the evangelical value system—resonated with a diverse range of southerners.[36] The additional cause of the protection both of property in slaves and the political and social status they conferred on 25 percent of southerners neither contradicted nor divided southern nationalism. The belief that slavery was moral could be a cause in itself.[37] Religious proslavery had rehearsed a moral identity for the region and its inhabitants. Southerners, like Reverend Sledd, hailed their battle for "OUR GOD!"[38] As another 1861 proslavery sermon put it, the soldiers were marching into "the field of a great fight between good and evil."[39] Secession or the protection of slavery, which soldiers and civilians readily listed as their prime personal causes, or states' rights, which was rarely mentioned, paled before the causes of God's justice and the individual's view of right and wrong.[40] The quests for independence, wealth, and success, and for the region's safety (which so many Confederates acknowledged in their diaries and personal justifications of the war) often alluded directly to the protection of slave property, the protection of racial supremacy, the protection of political power, or the protection of ordered social status, but the entire tapestry of southern cultural values inspired individuals and motivated the cause.[41]

The worldview at stake in the slavery debate and Civil War could not be reduced to a single goal or ideological proposition.[42] Reverend Sledd ran through the gamut of values at work in the war. "The cause of equity and religion is at stake," he began. These were the tools as well as the goals of battle: "Oh be soldiers of Christ. Washington was never so great as when he was on his knees. . . . It is necessary that you keep a perpetual curb on . . . passions. Bid tumultuous passions all be still . . . and thus armed by a wholesome discipline . . . conscience . . . by reason and reli-

gious principle . . . we have access to His sympathy and exhaustless resources."[43] "Perfect submission to the disposal of God," Sledd intoned, is
the "surest way to secure the accomplishment of the end we seek."[44] The
evangelical ideal of character—with its constant battle to curb one's in-
stinct, to submit to God, and to contemplate death and judgment—not
only served to motivate the southern cause but was also a key to the
performance of soldiers in battle.[45] Despite the absence of military experience or military culture in America, antebellum young men made exceptional soldiers.[46] Antebellum citizens after all were steeped in the simple
evangelical pieties of discipline, brotherhood, submission, and death, all of
which transferred well into army life. (Independence and optimism perhaps did not serve as well in this war.)[47] Sledd's sermon to the troops
connected everyday values to the personal experience of war, and then to
the greater purposes motivating the conflict.

Sledd, in the pattern of countless regional tracts, climaxed his sermon
by reiterating the biblical defense of slavery. Many early Confederate
proslavery pronouncements admitted the root of "the contest of bitter-
ness . . . was to be found in a *peculiar institution* which is sanctioned by
God's Holy Word."[48] And although Sledd anticipated southerners' post-
war veneration of (mostly mythical) loyal slaves and asked the troops "to
pray for God to shield our faithful servants,"[49] the climactic purpose of
his recap of scriptural proslavery to the departing troops was not to inspire them to defend slavery. Sledd, instead, in a typical evangelical move,
reminded the soldiers of the biblical defense of slavery in order to inspire
them to defend the Bible and its author. "The God of Our Fathers,"
Sledd wailed, "His honor is assailed."[50] Sledd then launched into his per-
oration:

> Only yield to the idea of the fallibility of the Bible by admitting its
> error, or surrendering its teachings on this subject, and the way is
> open for the rejection of whatever it enjoins that comes into
> conflict with human opinions and passions.
>   . . . No, No! In God's name, give me the Bible, whatever it may
> cost and whatever it may enjoin! . . . And, oh, let me hand it down
> to my children, the charm unbroken, that they too may enjoy some
> of its sweetness and reap some of its blessed fruits! Nay, but the
> Ammonites are upon us with their strange gods. They would dispel
> the delusion. They would dissolve the charm. They would under-

mine the authority of my Bible. You go to contribute to the
salvation of your country from such a curse. You go to aid in the
glorious enterprise of rearing in our sunny south a temple to
constitutional liberty and Bible Christianity. You go to fight for
your people and for the cities of your God.[51]

Preaching before the departing troops only began the process of remind-
ing southerners, via evangelical proslavery, of who they were and why
they had come to fight. Sledd's words were echoed in combatants dairies
and memoirs and in regular revivals held among the troops near the front
during the war.[52]

Early in the Civil War the great instrument of the southern religious
press had yet to feel the pinch of deprivation and continued to dissemi-
nate innumerable newspapers and tracts. The same form of confidence
and of identification of the war with the totality of regional values appeared in the press as in the sermons.[53] The *Christian Observer* commented
that God had never destroyed a nation that had an evangelical church.[54]
"The Clergy of the South" (154 of them) in a collective letter, inspired
by a group of educated Presbyterian ministers and published in most
newspapers at the start of the Confederacy, issued a manifesto in which
they made "An Address to Christians throughout the World," declaring
slavery "a benevolent institution not incompatible with holy Christianity." The "Southern Clergy" also issued an alarm perfectly in tune with
the era's evangelical culture but containing an odd theological note akin
to the cosmic presumption of fighting "to protect God's Honor." The
southern clergy warned the world's Christians that the North was perpe-
trating a plot of "interference with the plans of Divine Providence."[55]
Although a Presbyterian and follower of Calvin's sovereign God, the editor of the *Southern Christian Advocate*, Amasa Converse, employed the same
fuzzy evangelical theology as Methodist R.N. Sledd and opined, "[The
South] cannot afford to fail. To lose our cause is to lose everything except
our souls."[56]

Southern evangelicals hailed the survival of the Confederacy into
1862 and the many southern victories that year as the expected providential validations of the cause that could not fail. An interest in actual
prophecy and attention to apocalyptics, as in the Book of Daniel and
Book of Revelation, wound their way into Confederate proslavery visions of the future in this climactic period of southern ideology. These

books of the Bible did not figure heavily in antebellum proslavery. At first southern evangelicals embraced apocalyptic biblical passages because they provided wonderful images and terms to describe an utterly corrupt, Satan-driven enemy. Apocalyptics were likewise bursting with images of the miraculous interventions of God into history in order to preserve his favored people.[57] These scriptural stories did not have the same allure in the antebellum period with its emphasis on the consistent system of moral law through which Providence acted, on steady economic progress, and on the near absolute autonomy and efficacy of individuals. But the collective, over-ruling, bloody, immediate, and miraculous judgments of apocalyptics characterized the lives of a new chosen people at war for their God.

The war drew everyone North and South toward harsher evangelical metaphors. The immensity of the event demanded them. Lincoln adopted starkly prophetic language to explain the conflict in his Second Inaugural Address. Proslavery wartime prophecies rarely had the artistic grandeur and humility of Lincoln's speech, partly because they reveal the evolving rigid and exaggerated apotheosis of the region brought about by success in prewar debates as well as in battle. Confederate official James Williams sounded the self-satisfied note typical of 1862: "No people ever had more unmistakable evidences that they were guided and directed by an over-ruling Providence than have the people of the south since the commencement of their great struggle."[58] The South could "readily convert" its economy "to the development of our great manufacturing."[59] The antebellum development of "electricity and steam" and the commerce that "nurtured slavery into giant manhood" served as examples for the wartime potential.[60] Politicians' dreams and visions were faint and placid next to ministers' increasingly prophetic productions. Jefferson Davis's frequent calls for days of prayer, fasting, and humiliation encouraged Catholic, Lutheran, and, particularly, Jewish religious leaders in key cities such as Richmond and Charleston to participate in pouring out familiar paeans to Confederate triumphs over the "infidel" and hailing God's vindication of southern life. Richmond's proslavery Rabbi Michael J. Michelbacher labeled the Yankees "philistines"[61] whom God in the coming days would "cause to fall into the pit of destruction."[62] Michelbacher wanted to publish a mainstream Confederate sermon in part to deflect criticisms of "speculation" and potential disloyalty directed at southern Jews, but he, like religious leaders of every denomination, had issued biblical proslavery tracts well before the war.[63]

Evangelical ministers' readings of Providence in 1862 attained a unique and often hysterical cosmic conceit.[64] Methodist minister William Seat of Texas wrote one of the great prophetic glorifications of the Confederacy. Seat's book was not only a wartime biblical proslavery tract and an interpretation of Providence's support of the war effort. It also gave ultimate expression to the modernizing desire at the heart of antebellum proslavery. Seat believed that "the United States constituted the first embodiment of the restored Israel of God"[65] spoken of in Revelation. It was a "Kingdom on Wheels" as prophesied in Isaiah, which Seat found "expressive of a moving, advancing, expanding nationality."[66] Then the main plot took off: "Lo! Suddenly and to the amazement of the world a mighty kingdom, even a final kingdom arose . . . [of] strictly providential Divine origin."[67] Drawing again from Isaiah and Hosea, Seat argued that the South was "the Stone Kingdom" by which "a remnant is reserved, as the kingdom that will never be moved . . . a sectional separation wide and permanent."[68] Seat went on for 250 pages of exegesis proving the "impossibility" of the defeat of the South.[69] Turning from Isaiah to the Books of Daniel and Revelation, Seat declared, "The One like the Son of Man has appeared in the rise of the Confederate States."[70] The war pointed toward the South's destiny and the spectacular import of its designation as the chosen:

> The amazing success at great Bethel, Bull Run, Manassas, and indeed throughout the War thus far, is a comment on this kindred prediction.
> . . . Never surely since the Wars of God's ancient people has there been such a remarkable and uniform success against tremendous odds. The explanation is found in the fact that the Lord goes forth to fight against the coercion by foes of his peculiar people. Thus it has been and thus it will be to the close of the War.[71]

With the Lord fighting for the South, not simply the nation but the world would be reorganized on the basis of the righteous southern remnant and "liberty and pure Christianity would go abroad on earth."[72] In the near future Confederate America would become involved "in the terrible convulsions of Europe" and "oppressed nationalities shall be liberated."[73] Seat worshiped the "gradually progressive" genius at the center of U.S. national existence.[74] The South would be a kingdom on "fiery wheels" of prosperity, liberty, and moral progress. Seat's eyes had seen the coming of the Lord in his fusion of the Book of Revelation and the South's divine economy: "The King with many crowns, or the Savior revealed in human civil government, will rule the nations with a 'Rod of iron,' which signifies, we believe, the commerce of the world. The newest nationality contains or surrounds the fountainhead of human commerce and possesses, as to outline at least, the highest ideal of human government."[75] Soon the "peaceful millennial reign would dawn" and the stone from the mountain—the South—would be glorified: "Then the stone cut out of the mountain shall become a great mountain and fill the earth. There shall be no more curse nor death nor sorrow nor crying. There shall be fullness of joy and pleasures for evermore. We solemnly believe that the great prophetic periods have closed: the mystery is finished and the vision of prophecy unsealed. The Final Kingdom has arisen, and the Divine Redeemer has come to reign."[76] Seat's ideas could be dismissed as the wartime ravings of a propagandist if such millennial conceits had not been common among evangelicals North and South before and during the war.[77] They even appeared on the lips of the brilliant, skeptical Union president. The South had preached and unified behind evangelicalism and prewar sectional rhetoric both before and more completely than the North. The experience of war also hit home more widely in the South and raised to a fever pitch southerners' prophetic beliefs about the future they had so long assumed they would control.

The fever, of course, broke, and serious defeats after 1862 forced the evangelical South to turn from prophecy to theodicy. Southerners had to explain how a just God could let Dixie suffer. The transition involved psychological as well as physical trials. The confidence and unity engendered during the slavery debate, and particularly during the early days of the Confederacy, exacerbated the difficulties of the transition from anticipation of the certain rewards of Providence to explanation of defeat and reconciliation to it.[78] The survival of the Confederate nation and certainly of its government may not have been essential goals of many southerners, but their autonomy was. Retaining the right to hold slaves may not have been a defining commitment (especially since a minority of southerners held slaves), but seeing their moral view of themselves and the proslavery Bible upheld was. The institution of slavery may not have had to endure—most southerners had accepted this possibility in their proslavery, but southerners' racial beliefs and habits did. Their own character and self-discipline may not have had to receive rewards of wealth and power, but the lazy or infidel invader should be punished, and character as the founding principle of society must remain. Confederates had a private, isolated religious world to walk away to when their national army and government expired. The white ex-Confederate South proved much more successful and clever in guarding this sacred realm in the struggle of 1865–1877 than in the conventional military one of 1861–1865.

Because they had to assure themselves that they had never given up anything essential to their cultural identity, white southerners during the war were slow to relinquish their traditional desires and commitments to boundless material and political power. They did so only after hard lessons and hard words. Stephen Elliot, an Episcopal bishop of Macon, Georgia, sharply articulated the dilemmas southerners had to face in a series of sermons starting in late 1863. The terms "error" and "delusion" appeared frequently in Elliot's sermons and in the enormous literature in which southerners began to explain the impossible.[79] "We cannot rule the world as we once conceived we could," Elliot lamented.[80] Despite southerners' continued hopes to avoid the loss of independence and the disappearance of slavery, by 1863 proslavery visions of economic progress and power had collapsed. When Confederates accepted this first failure, it gave them a model for confronting future disappointments. They began the process of imagining greater disappointments than loss of an expanding economy. The death of slavery and even defeat loomed. Since southern culture and Confederate aspirations were never compartmentalized, the economic decay of the slavery empire inevitably undermined a range of proslavery assumptions. Southern evangelicals had linked self-control, the justice of slavery, and economic growth. Therefore, declining fortunes in the power struggle and the search to reverse or explain them raised questions about slavery and proper moral organization. Stephen Elliot's sermons exemplify evangelicals' maneuvers on the issue of slavery and defeat. He was forced to return to the subjects repeatedly as 1863 turned to 1864 and Sherman's troops bore down on his Georgia home.[81] The drama of his position also helped promote the sermons' frequent printings and wide distribution.

Elliot's sermon *Vain is the Help of Man* in the days of defeat in Georgia in 1864 comforted southerners that nothing new had occurred. "This is to us no new phase in our affairs," Elliot said. "The odds against us were [always] too great, unless we believed that God was on our side."[82] Proslavery formulas would not be abandoned in defeat.[83] Elliot gloried in the lack of slave "insurrection," noting that "those who had studied this question most thoroughly and especially the Scriptures, did not fall into this error" of fearing servile insurrection. Slave "quiescence," he said, "vindicates us."[84] Further vindications *might* come if southerners could "diversify pursuits," since they would "never be a great and prosperous people til we change our [economic] policy."[85] Elliot, like other southern ministers in the midst of war, neither felt guilt about nor questioned the existence of slavery when he referred to the need for change and to the possibility of retribution for the "sins" of slavery.[86] The only change necessary was that of putting into more perfect practice the moral standards embodied in biblical slaveholding and evangelical mastery. God would reward such morality. Robert E. Lee, an Episcopal evangelical like Elliot, shared the same view of morality before and during the war. "God punishes us for our sins here as well as hereafter," he wrote his wife before the war.[87] Lee's wartime prayers compare well with Elliot's vision of the Confederates' "having sinned," since they were being punished.[88] Ministers found one explanation for the flagging southern fortunes in the failure to have implemented fully the standards of the proslavery work ethic that would allow slaves the autonomy to "work out [their] own deliverance, but to work it out in subjection to His will and in subservience to His purposes."[89] Many states reformed slave marriage laws and access to the Bible, expecting that God would return to fighting, as "visibly he fought for us" earlier in the war. "We can hereafter, with entire safety, and with most excellent results to ourselves, introduce [the slaves] gradually to a higher moral and religious life," preached Elliot. "When the war is over, we shall in token of their fidelity and good will, render their domestic relations more permanent and consult more closely their feelings and affections."[90] Tangible benefits would flow from the lessons of defeat for white southerners as well.[91]

Elliot reminded southerners that God tested his special people in order to improve them via "fresh infusion of virtue from the chastisements of God." For "without conflict and chastisement . . . effeminacy creeps in" and there would be less "scope for the nobler characteristics of self-denial and sacrifice."[92] No matter what, the retreating southerners must learn to see defeats as God's way of making his chosen people a special object of attention and discipline so they could be strengthened.

Stronger in faith, salvation, and spiritual (otherworldly) life, yes, but also *eventually*—and that was the key adjustment—receiving the rewards of His power on earth. The Second Coming might bring that moment of returned power, or Dixie could rise again, or the world or United States could embrace the faith and example of the righteous southern remnant. Then, right would make might again in worldly and public struggles as well as in private ones. The prophecies and apocalyptics appealed to during the Civil War offered southerners examples of how to defer and displace their hopes into the realm of the spirit and an uncertain future time of judgment.

Not many Confederates took the alternate ideological and theological road leading to the conclusion that slavery and the Cause had to be wrong because they lost. Slaves and northerners easily and often uncritically latched on to this conclusion, which they anticipated in their own evangelical beliefs when going into the Civil War. (One Union soldier, however, concluded bluntly, "We are the best killers . . . that establishes the righteousness of any cause.")[93] Southerners set themselves up for this conclusion as well by insisting that slavery could not fail, because if it could, then infidel propositions about the Bible would be correct. The many southern diarists, particularly Confederate women, who expressed anger at God or a loss of faith during the dark period of the war clearly toyed with abandoning their religious beliefs in order to maintain their faith in their own righteousness and that of the southern cause.[94] Methodist minister Stephen Caldwell, a Georgia compatriot of Elliot's, reached the other logical conclusion of retaining absolute faith in prewar theological formulas at the expense of support of slavery. Caldwell learned to his sadness after the war that he had also made this choice at the expense of acceptance by his congregation and ex-Confederate compatriots. By 1865 Caldwell made and announced the step few other southerners made, either in private records or openly: "If the institution of slavery had been right, God would not have suffered it to be overthrown."[95] He, in effect, lost his regional identity in order to maintain prior theological commitments. Much of Caldwell's congregation walked out on or openly criticized him for this sermon.[96] The war had made clear "this providential teaching: *God has* destroyed slavery."[97]

Despite his opinion about God's judgment of the South, Caldwell remained a proslavery evangelical and accepted the prewar arguments. He stated, "*The relation of master and slave is established in the Bible . . . the* relation itself does not necessarily involve moral evil." Caldwell concluded that it was "in the *practice*" that southerners had not only failed but sinned.[98] The sin was pride and the moral blindness it brought. Caldwell, having been an earlier practitioner of proslavery hubris, presciently identified the flaw of proslavery evangelicalism: "We have been accustomed to judge the character of our slaves more severely than our own."[99] In a "self-righteous" haze "we reproached our enemies for fighting against the God of Heaven"[100] and "from the grave which its own suicidal hand has dug *it [the South] never more can rise.*"[101] He climaxed his sermon with the plea, "I would reconcile you to events that are inevitable. . . . *GOD HAS SMITTEN US.*"[102] Caldwell's almost lone voice pleaded, but the evangelical South would not be reconciled. The best-selling proslavery minister Thornton Stringfellow passed his publications down in his will as sacred trusts for his children even though he died years after final emancipation.[103] After being chased by Union armies out of New Orleans in 1862 and Columbia, South Carolina, in 1865 and living into the next century, Benjamin Morgan Palmer did the same.[104] Proslavery ideology lived on in a world without slavery, much as the defense of the Confederate cause went on in a world without a Confederacy.[105]

The Civil War, however, was the theological turning point for southern culture. Evangelicals adjusted both to the failure of slavery to maintain itself as they thought it *had to* and to the failure of prosperity, independent power, and progress to rain down on the South as they had prophesied. The Civil War turned southerners toward apocalyptic and prophetic religion, which were not crucial in antebellum theology. The Civil War also heightened the emphasis already present in the region on a purely personal religion obsessed with human depravity and spiritual conversion. The optimism, free market ethics, and love of earthly power and success (and statistics documenting them) did not disappear from southern Protestantism; they were *postponed*. They were relocated in the prophetic and spiritual realms where they would not again be so directly tested and contradicted by events. Most southern evangelicals really gained no sense of defeat or self-critical insight from the Civil War experience, but it did force them into theological skepticism about the easy formulas of antebellum moral progress and all good deeds being rewarded on earth. If it had been that simple, southern evangelicals knew they would have won the war. After the war southern evangelicals preached about the fallen, corrupted nature of the world and mankind in tones not used

before 1860. These post–Civil War theological perspectives served southern Protestants well among the disasters of the twentieth century, which
made their skepticism about moral progress look prophetic. Southern
evangelicals did not forget how to crow when Providence threw them an
occasional gift or collapsed a house on the head of a Yankee. The slavery
debate and Civil War had given them too much practice in singing the
providential refrains of their religious heritage; the tone of the hymns,
however, had changed. For the South, the Civil War shattered the pieties
of the antebellum worldview that seamlessly identified God's moral law
with the practical world and economics. Darwin had a similar impact on
late-Victorian religion in other parts of the Protestant world. After Darwin, nature appeared driven more by blind, violent forces than by moral
forces. The Civil War had taught southern evangelicals this lesson. Right
did not make might in a world ruled by Yankees. The evangelical South
simply ignored and dismissed Darwin.[106] His ideas had no power to
shock a society already practiced at severing the link between religion
and the natural world. Southerners after the war expected little from
the corrupted world and expected even less from the knowledge of
corrupted men, especially men of science and power. The war brought
the South a theology, as well as a politics and economics, of diminished
expectations.

　　Calvin Wiley, the evangelical superintendent of North Carolina public schools, writing *God in History* in 1863 articulated, with brilliant analysis
and self-awareness if not balanced self-criticism, the southern religious
transformation at the height of the Civil War:

> God disrobes the veiled idol of the nineteenth century and sets it
> before the world in all it inherent vileness. . . . [And against] all the
> dialectics of philosophic theology and oppositions of science falsely
> so called . . . the world must now see that human skill has signally
> failed to heal the source of all human woes.[107] . . . Even among
> orthodox Christians there was [before the war] a strong disposition
> to put results before causes. Christianization and reformation of the
> world were made to depend on the progress of good government,
> commerce, arts and learning, while in fact these are themselves the
> product of gospel influences
> 　　. . . In these vast ruins [of war] a pernicious error has found its
> grave.[108]

This was as close as southern evangelicals could come to a self-critical perspective on their views. Wiley's genius lay in moral history and theology, not in objective social criticism. He repeated most of the popular pieties of antebellum and wartime proslavery, including the slight criticisms of southerners for failing to perfect slavery along lines of gospel duties and the work ethic. Wiley also assumed the northern armies were "the legions of hell" and that the South would lose only because "men are allowed to contend with [Satan], but they must not do it with his own devices."[109] The North had innumerable "devices" and "satanic legions," but the South in his eyes had a right to feel it had passed the special test of not turning to the tactics of Sherman (as if it had had that choice). Already in 1863 Wiley had encouraged the South, if need be, to "wear chains in a dungeon and lift up [its] serene and unconquered soul in proud defiance."[110] Hope waited ahead: "If we are teachable . . . this wilderness will lead us to our vineyards."[111]

The Civil War added the waiting and the "if" that had been missing in southern evangelicalism before defeat. But the war did not change proslavery sentiment or even end proslavery publication. The sanctification of horror and the confusion of morality and power implicit in American culture lived on in southern churches as elsewhere, but the region became more distinct and distanced from national pieties for generations. The Protestant North and West in the Gilded Age kept an unexamined and often vulgar faith that worldly success was bestowed by God on the virtuous. The North remained more this-worldly in its religion and made the transition to a more secular, interdependent, and competitive society. For southern religious culture the Civil War produced a greater discontinuity. Although the seeds of such developments had long been planted in the region, after the Civil War the South's religion became fatalistic, conservative, otherworldly, and backward-looking to a degree that would have been as unfamiliar to most evangelicals in the years before the war as it is to those evangelicals who now sacralize the satellite dish and corporate capitalism.[112]

Epilogue

During the Civil War abolitionist Charles Storey reflected on the future of the freed slaves. What would happen to them? What should the plan for them be? A simple solution was at hand, because in nineteenth-century America the natural operation of the moral law took care of everything. Storey said, "I have no fear that we can leave them [freed slaves] where the rest of us are, in the hands of God and subject to that great law which feeds the industrious and sometimes lets the idle starve."[1] The evangelicals who defended slavery could have and did echo these beliefs after the war, but they wondered why these ideals did not sanction forced labor as well as starvation. The antebellum defenders of slavery had embraced similar cultural formulas about God's laissez-faire moral order. The North's easy acquiescence in the brutal white supremacy and new forms of enslavement in the South via sharecropping, convict lease systems, lynching, and corrupt local politics after Reconstruction testifies to a fundamental cultural unity prior to the Civil War. The war had been a war of similar competitors wildly grasping at the same unrealistic prize—complete morality, independence, and economic prosperity. Their shared moral culture remained even after the war. This culture justified racial and labor subordination in both regions. The South, dominated as it was by evangelical principles, belongs in the mainstream of discussions of both antebellum culture and the subsequent national ideological development.

Before the Civil War, southern evangelicals rejected traditional justifications of social subordination, embraced individualism, espoused free-market philosophy, and celebrated moral, material, and technological progress. The defense of slavery after 1831 embodied modern rationalizations of racial and economic subordination. Late nineteenth-century economic and racial Social Darwinism and Anglo-Saxon Imperialism permeated antebellum southern religion. The sermons of the era raised hosannas to freedom and to a gloriously optimistic vision of future prosperity and morality, but they warned that this natural and rapid progress would continue only as long as the extermination or subjugation of those who stood in the way was accepted as a moral necessity. The justification for brutalizing blacks and Indians—who whites believed were not contributing to moral and economic progress in the antebellum period—and the justification for killing Yankees in the war sound eerily similar. The relatively modern and national roots of southern evangelical proslavery were also reflected in the post-Reconstruction triumph of, and national acquiescence in, segregation, lynching, imperialism, racial restrictions on immigration, and white supremacy. Proslavery ministers spoke a national language.

Cultural, ideological, religious, political, and economic developments in the last quarter of the twentieth century have encouraged historians to re-examine proslavery ideology and the modern elements in antebellum southern culture. The South has entered the national economy and since 1975 has achieved amazing political and cultural influence that has obliterated its regional isolation (and perhaps its regional identity). The South no longer looks like an aberration within or counterpoint to national patterns. The region establishes significant national patterns. Its religious and political traditions have been adopted throughout the nation. The post–World War II nationalization of the South and southernization of the nation have their roots in the antebellum United States. Prior to the Civil War, Americans both North and South built and shared religious traditions and cultural aspirations. Antebellum southerners' more unbridled individualism and more complete evangelical moral conformity often forestalled concerns about social reform and planning, and public education, that developed in parts of the North. But these were differences in the timing of historical development or in the application of principles, not in fundamental ideology. Despite the shock of defeat in the Civil War and seventy-five years of agricultural poverty and isolation, the evangelical South has reasserted its love of progress and laissez-faire capitalism in the last generation. The South's roots of modernity ran much deeper than the backward-looking pessimism often adopted in the region in the wake of the Civil War and too often stereotyped since. Antebellum evangelicals' discussions of "free" slaves and their voluntary labor system are much easier to take seriously in the twenty-first century when their contemporary descendants in all regions employ the same cultural ideals to espouse a color-blind society in which economic outcomes merely reflect "character" and "merit." Current inequities are not the equivalent of slavery, but the moral rhetoric now employed to justify them was developed in the antebellum slavery debate. If proslavery arguments are placed in the mainstream of U.S. national history and at the center of national culture prior to the Civil War, then the nation's subsequent moral debates and current ideological fault lines become much clearer.

Notes

Introduction

1. Levi-Strauss, *Savage Mind*, 94–95.

2. Potter, *Impending Crisis*, 472. See also Elkins, *Slavery*, 193.

3. David Brion Davis, et al., *The Great Republic* (Toronto: D.C. Heath and Co., 1985), 354.

4. Albert Bushnell Hart, *Slavery and Abolition, 1831–1841* (New York: Harper and Brothers, 1976); Mary R. and Charles A. Beard, *The Rise of American Civilization* (New York: Reprint Services Corp., 1927); Eaton, *Mind of the Old South*.

5. Robert Brown, *Modernization*; Taylor, *Cavalier and Yankee*; Degler, *Place over Time*; Grady McWhiney and Perry Jamieson, *Attack and Die: Civil War Military Tactics and Heritage* (Birmingham: Univ. of Alabama Press, 1982); Wyatt-Brown, *Southern Honor;* Bruce, *Violence and Culture*; Hindus, *Prison and Plantation;* Elliot J. Gorn, "'Gouge and Bite, Pull Hair and Scratch': The Social Significance of Fighting in the Southern Backcountry," *American Historical Review* 90 (February 1985), 18–43; Genovese, *The Political Economy of Slavery*; Genovese, *The World the Slaveholders Made;* Johnson, *Toward a Patriarchal Republic*.

6. Cash, *Mind of the South;* Phillips, *Life and Labor;* Ulrich Bonnel Phillips, "The Central Theme of Southern History," *American Historical Review* 24 (October 1928), 30–43.

7. O'Brien, *Rethinking the South;* O'Brien, *All Clever Men*; O'Brien, "The Nineteenth Century American South"; Pessen, "How Different Were the Antebellum North and South?"; Oakes, *The Ruling Race*; Glickstein, *Concepts of Free Labor.*

8. Priest, *Bible Defence of Slavery*, 385, also 388, 438–40. See also Ross, *Slavery Ordained of God*, 80; Smith, *Lectures*, 262; *Pro-slavery Argument*, 13; Clapp, *Autobiographical Sketches and Recollections*, 161; Hoit, *The Right of American Slavery*, 8.

9. Hill, *The North and South*, 46.

10. Hill, *The North and South*, 52.

11. Better historians than I, Eugene Genovese and Mark Smith in particular, have also rejected this argument and have been chronicling the complexity of religious proslavery for more than a decade. Genovese, *The Southern Tradition*; Genovese, *The Slaveholders' Dilemma*; Eugene Genovese, *A Consuming Fire*; Smith, *Debating Slavery.*

1. Freedom and Evangelical Culture in the South

1. This was possible because of the long history of adjustment to the problem of the modern self- and market-oriented social change, embodied in the Protestant theological message. See: Weber, *The Protestant Ethic;* Weber, *General Economic History.* The literature on the Weber thesis is almost endless, but the historiography of the Weber debate and modi-

fications to the thesis can be best followed in: Eisenstadt, ed., *The Protestant Ethic,* 302–22; Benjamin Nelson, "Weber's Protestant Ethic: Its Origins, Wanderings and Foreseeable Futures," in Glock and Hammonds, eds., *Beyond the Classics?,* 113–30; Green, ed., *Protestantism, Capitalism, and Social Science,* 191–200; and Poggi, *Calvinism and the Capitalist Spirit.*

2. Johnson, *A Shopkeeper's Millennium,* 3–15. Rogers, *The Call to Seriousness;* Fox and Lears, *The Culture of Consumption,* 8–9.

3. John B. Boles, "Evangelical Protestantism in the Old South: From Religious Dissent to Cultural Dominance," in Wilson, ed., *Religion in the Old South,* 13–34; Lewis, *The Pursuit of Happiness,* chapter two especially.

4. Hunter, *American Evangelicalism,* 7.

5. Smith, *Lectures,* 271.

6. Smith, *Lectures,* 95.

7. Boles, *The Great Revival.*

8. Jeter, *Recollections,* 38; Baker, *Life,* 66. See Boles, *Religion in Antebellum Kentucky,* 14–15.

9. Clapp, *Autobiographical Sketches,* 27.

10. Baker, *Life,* 163, 271.

11. Robert M. Calhoon, "Religion and Individualism in Early America," Robert E. Salhope, ed., *Individualism in the Early Republic* (Cambridge, Mass.: Harvard Univ. Press, 1991), 64; Boles, *The Great Revival,* 43; Boles, *Religion in Antebellum Kentucky,* 18–20.

12. Elliot, *Vain is the Help of Man,* 8.

13. Ward, *Andrew Jackson,* 150–75. See also Wylie, *The Self-Made Man in America.* For studies that emphasize an underlying ambivalence see in particular Meyers, *The Jacksonian Persuasion;* Remini, *The Revolutionary Age of Andrew Jackson.*

14. McKay, *Slavery,* 7. Clapp, *Autobiographical Sketches,* 154.

15. Boles, *Religion in Antebellum Kentucky,* 21. See also Boles, *The Great Revival.*

16. Thornwell, *Life and Letters,* 96–97, 584.

17. Lipscomb, *North and South,* from the *New York Daily Times,* 9.

18. Jeter, *Recollections,* 32.

19. Alexis De Tocqueville, *Democracy in America,* ed. Richard Heffner (New York: Signet Classic, 1984), 62–63. "It was never assumed in the United States that the citizen of a free country has the right to do whatever he pleases: on the contrary more social obligations were there imposed upon him than anywhere else. . . . subdues them compulsorily . . . it isolates them, and then influences them separately."

20. Patterson, *Freedom,* 3–5.

21. Charles G. Sellers, "The Travail of Slavery"; Freehling, *Prelude to the Civil War;* Freehling, "James Henley Thornwell's Mysterious Antislavery Moment"; Morrow, "The Proslavery Argument Revisited"; McPherson, "Slavery and Race"; Beringer, et al., *Why the South Lost the Civil War.*

22. Smith, *Lectures,* 48, 53, 265–66, 179, 279.

23. Patterson, *Freedom,* 321. See also his discussion of Paul, the birth of Christian individualism and conscience, and freedom in chapter nineteen, 325–44.

24. Thornwell, *Rights and Duties of Masters,* 36, 43–44. For the best discussion of Thornwell's philosophy and its social significance see Farmer, *The Metaphysical Confederacy.*

25. Smith, *Lectures,* 53; 27, 37, 51; Wayland, *Elements of Moral Science.*

26. Francis Wayland, *Sermons Delivered in the Chapel of Brown University* (Boston, 1849), 305, 316.

27. Fletcher, *Studies on Slavery,* 80. See also *Pro-slavery Argument,* 389; Richard Furman, *Exposition,* 14; Frederick Dalcho, *Practical Considerations,* 14; George Dodd Armstrong, *Conservative,* 9.

28. Catherine Beecher, *A Treatise on Domestic Economy* (1841), Kathryn Sklar, ed., (New York, 1977), 13. Sklar describes this "voluntary and self-initiated submission," 160.

29. Bercovitch, *American Jeremiad*, 12.

30. James Henley Thornwell, "Our Danger and Our Duty," reprinted in Thornwell, *Life and Letters*, 587.

31. Beverly Tucker in *Pro-slavery Argument*, 27; see also Dew, *Review of the Debate*, 300; Brownlow and Pryne, *Ought American Slavery*, 254; T.C. Hoit, *The Right of Slavery*, 49; Dalcho, *Remarks*, 27–28.

32. Smith, *Lectures*, 262.

33. James Henley Thornwell, "Our Danger and Our Duty," reprinted in Thornwell, *Life and Letters*, 588; see also 86, 94 on success and money.

34. Sledd, *A Sermon*, 17.

35. Sellers, *The Market Revolution*, 103.

36. Smith, *Lectures*, 259.

37. Wiley, *Scriptural Views*, 188, 195.

38. Clapp, *Autobiographical Sketches*, 96.

39. McTyeire, et al., *Duties of Masters to Servants*, 132.

40. Sledd, *A Sermon*, 12.

41. Oakes, *The Ruling Race*, 90–123; Loveland, *Southern Evangelicals and the Social Order*, 100–107; Matthews, *Religion in the Old South*, 125, 205–25.

42. James Henley Thornwell, *Discourse on Truth* (Charleston, 1856), 534.

43. The Papers of Rev. Daniel Baker (Montreat), Sermon Book. There are three versions of this sermon in his own hand. They were adapted from *Normand Smith or the Christian Serving God in his Business*. See also Smith, *Lectures*, 320, and Samuel Dunwoody, *A Sermon*, 12, for the same dual demand.

44. Wilson, *Relations and Duties of Servants and Masters*, 12. See also, W. Hamilton, *Duties of Masters and Slaves*, 8; McKay, *Slavery*, 1.

45. Jeter, *Recollections*, 41.

46. Furman, *Human Accountability*, 15. See also Hamilton, *Duties of Masters and Slaves*, 8.

47. Cobb, *A Scriptural Examination*, 10.

48. Cobb, *A Scriptural Examination*, 10.

49. Conkin, *Puritans and Pragmatists*, 48–53.

50. Thornwell, *Life and Letters*, 142–43. For the same definition of atheism see Palmer, *The South, Her Peril and Her Duty*, 11–12.

51. Smyth, *The Unity of Races*, xx. See also Farmer, *The Metaphysical Confederacy*, 135–37.

52. Jean Calvin, *The Institutes of Christian Religion*, translated by H. Beveridge (London, 1949), 47, 134.

53. Thornwell, *Rights and Duties of Masters*, 15. See also Thornwell, *Life and Letters*, 240, 265.

54. Baker, *Life*, 44.

55. Dehon, *A Sermon on the Death of Little Children*, 11, 4.

56. Elliot, *Vain is the Help of Man*, 8,9; Elliot, *Samson's Riddle*, 13. See also Thornwell, *Life and Letters*, 402, and Dunwoody, *A Sermon*, 8, on the natural aspects of miracles.

57. Fletcher, *Studies on Slavery*, 81. See Smith, *Lectures*, 23.

58. Buck, *The Slavery Question*, 8.

59. Fletcher, *Studies on Slavery*, 398–99.

60. Fletcher, *Studies on Slavery*, 80–81.

61. Smith, *Lectures*, 97.

62. Wiley, *Scriptural Views*, 18.

63.Thornwell, *Rights and Duties of Masters*, 15. See also Thornwell, *Life and Letters*, 87, for a critique of utilitarianism, and page 265 for a providential subsuming of its categories.

64. Fletcher, *Studies on Slavery*, 419.

65. Buck, *The Slavery Question*, 5. See similar statements in Hamilton, *Duties of Master and Slaves*, 17; [Hobby], *Remarks Upon Slavery*, 23; Clapp, *Autobiographical Sketches*, 162; Dew in *Pro-slavery Argument*, 325; McKay, *Slavery*, 6; Clapp, *Slavery: A Sermon*, 41–42; Priest, *Bible Defence of Slavery*, 255.

66. E.N. Elliott, ed., *Cotton is King and Proslavery Arguments*, x.

67. Elizabeth Fox-Genovese and Eugene Genovese, "The Religious Ideals of Southern Slave Society," *Georgia Historical Quarterly* 70 (spring 1986), 5, 7. See also Holifield, *Gentlemen Theologians*, 3–4, and passim.

68. Smyth, *The Unity of Races*, 120.

69. Smyth, *The Unity of Races*, 378. For other examples from a variety of denominations and education levels see Wiley, *Scriptural Views*, 17; Fletcher, *Studies on Slavery*, 393; Dunwoody, *A Sermon*, 21; Thornwell, *Rights and Duties of Masters*, 36; Mitchell, *A Bible Defence of Slavery*, 14.

70. Smith, *Lectures*, 63.

71. Fletcher, *Studies on Slavery*, 393. For comparison to a northern "radical" evangelical and abolitionist, see Albert Barnes, *An Inquiry*, 92–93: "The will of God may often be learned from the events of his providence. . . . when a certain course of conduct *always* tends to certain results, when there are laws in operation in the moral world as fixed as in the natural world . . . the revelation of the mind of God in such a case is not less clear than were the annunciations of his will on Sinai."

72. Wiley, *Scriptural Views*, 16; Fletcher, *Studies on Slavery*, 185; Dalcho, *Practical Considerations*, 14.

73. Thornwell, *Life and Letters*, 308, 329.

74. Buck, *The Slavery Question*, 6.

75. James Henley Thornwell, "The Christian Doctrine of Slavery," in John Adger and John Girardeau, eds., *The Collected Writings of James Henley Thornwell* (Richmond: Cogswell Press, 1875), 408, 407–14. See also Dew in *Pro-slavery Argument*, 389, and Smith, *Lectures*, 268–70.

76. Marty, *Righteous Empire*, 31–85.

77. Rhys Isaac, *The Transformation of Virginia*, 263. On Locke in America see Hartz, *The Liberal Tradition*; May, *The Enlightenment in America*. See also the controversy on Locke and "liberalism" in MacPherson, *Political Theory*, and critiques of his position in J.G.A. Pocock and Richard Ashcroft, *John Locke* (Los Angeles: Univ. of California-Los Angeles Press, 1980).

78. Smyth, *The Unity of Races*, 373, also 126, 312, 342. See also Smith, *Lectures*, 66; Thornwell, *Life and Letters*, 329; Mitchell, *A Bible Defence of Slavery*, 19; Brookes, *A Defence of the South*, 27.

79. Brookes, *A Defence of the South*, 29–30. Thornton Stringfellow, "Scriptural View," in Elliott, ed., *Cotton is King*, 503; Smith, *Lectures*, 66; Clapp, *Autobiographical Sketches*, 126; A Georgia Baptist (Mell), *Remarks Upon Slavery*, 20. See also Dew in *Pro-slavery Argument*, 454, for admiration of Rousseau and Jefferson by another conservative (also Thornwell, *Life and Letters*, 463). In their most public statements, these men were not critics of political liberalism (or the political mission of the French Revolution).

80. Elkins, *Slavery*, 34, 144, 167.

81. Smith, *Lectures*, 79.

82. Smith, *Lectures*, 265–66. See also Lipscomb, *North and South*, from the *New York Daily Times*, 31; [Hobby], *Remarks Upon Slavery*, 16.

83. John Adger, *Doctrine of Human Rights and Slavery,* 11, 14.

84. Dunwoody, *A Sermon,* 32.

85. Buck, *The Slavery Question,* 7. See also David Ewart, *A Scriptural View of the Moral Relations of African Slavery* (Charleston, 1849; revised 1859), 3; Smith, *Lectures,* 274; Brookes, *A Defence of the South,* 30; and [George Armstrong], *A Discussion of Slaveholding* (Philadelphia: Joseph Nilson, 1858), 45, for identical biblical support of republicanism traced to Moses. These biblical arguments had a Revolutionary heritage. See for example, Nicholas Street, *The American States Acting Over the Part of the Children of Israel in the Wilderness* (New Haven, 1777), in Reiner Smolinski, *The Kingdom, the Power, and the Glory: The Millenial Impulse in Early American Literature* (New York: Kendall Hunt Publishing, 1998); Samuel Langdon, *The Republic of the Israelites: An Example to the United States* (Exeter, N.H.: Lamson and Ranlet, 1788); Abiel Abbot, *Traits of Resemblance in the People of the United States of America to Ancient Israel* (Haverhill, Mass.: Moore and Stebbins, 1799).

86. Sledd, *A Sermon,* 6.

87. Boles, *The Great Revival,* chapter 2.

88. John Adger, "University Sermons," *Southern Presbyterian Review* 9 (March 1849); reprinted (Columbia, S.C., 1849), 23.

89. Smith, *Lectures,* 200, 221, 322; E.W. Warren, *Nellie Norton,* i; Wiley, *Scriptural Views,* 18.

90. See Sellers, *The Market Revolution,* especially chapters 3, 7, and 10.

91. Dorfman, *The Economic Mind in American Civilization,* vol. 2: 705–9.

92. Wiley, *Scriptural Views,* 18, 31.

93. Alexis De Tocqueville, *Democracy in America,* edited by Richard Heffner (New York, 1984), 213. Tocqueville used a perfect phrase for this impulse—"virtuous materialism"—which he held to be "a species of religious morality." See also Marsden, *Fundamentalism,* 13, on the uniformity of evangelical beliefs about political economy in the nineteenth century.

94. See examples in: McTyeire et al., *Duties of Masters to Servants,* 10, 66, 89; James Henley Thornwell, "The Principles of Political Economy," *Southern Presbyterian Review* 7 (1853–1854): 8–13; Thornwell, *Rights and Duties of Masters,* 21; Thornwell, *Life and Letters,* 51; Fletcher, *Studies on Slavery,* 21; [Patrick Hues Mell], *Slavery,* weekly numbers of the *Christian Index* under the signature "A Baptist Minister," 23.

95. Smith, *Lectures,* 236.

96. Smith, *Lectures,* 262 (my emphasis); also, 294, 295.

97. Holifield, *Gentlemen Theologians,* 127.

98. Lipscomb, *North and South,* from the *New York Daily Times,* 9. See also J.L. Wilson, *Relations and Duties* 30, 34; [Hobby], *Remarks Upon Slavery,* 19, 20.

99. Clapp, *Slavery: A Sermon,* 27.

100. Clapp, *Autobiographical Sketches,* 125.

101. Priest, *Bible Defence of Slavery,* 388; [Hobby], *Remarks Upon Slavery,* 3; Wiley, *Scriptural Views,* 31; Clapp, *Slavery: A Sermon,* 62; Clapp, *Autobiographical Sketches,* 126, 161; [Holland], *A Refutation,* 9; Hoit, *The Right of American Slavery,* 8; Cobb, *A Scriptural Examination,* 22; Smith, *Lecturers,* 259, 270, 277–78; Lipscomb, *North and South,* from the *New York Daily Times,* 22; Mitchell, *A Bible Defence of Slavery,* 14, 22; Thornwell, *Life and Letters,* 124, 286–88; Dew in *Pro-slavery Argument,* 300.

102. Rev. W.S. Brown, "Strictures on Abolitionism" as contained in Priest, *Bible Defence of Slavery,* 388–40.

103. Ross, *Slavery Ordained of God,* 80.

104. Jeter, *Recollections,* 83, 248. See also Ewart, *A Scriptural View,* 3–4; Furman, *Human Accountability,* 18; Smith, *Lectures,* 17, 287.

105. Wiley, *Scriptural Views*, 213.
106. Rev. W.S. Brown, *Strictures on Abolitionism* as contained in Priest, *Bible Defence of Slavery*, 439–40. Rev. Brown adapted this from the well-known speech of William Evans Arthur on 1776 (*Oration*, Covington Kentucky, July 4, 1850, 36): the work of "our fathers happily extends its surface, increases its destiny and exalts its summit. Onward! Onward!"
107. Jack P. Maddex, Jr., "'The Southern Apostasy' Revisited," 140; Tise, *Proslavery*, 3–45.
108. [Dalcho], *Practical Considerations*, 32–33.
109. Holifield, *Gentlemen Theologians*, 143.
110. May, *The Enlightenment in America*, 356.

2. The Post-1831 Birth of Evangelical Proslavery

1. Davis, *The Problem of Slavery in the Age of Revolution*, chapter 1; Davis, *The Problem of Slavery in Western Culture*, 3–23, and passim chapters 2–4; Morgan, *American Freedom, American Slavery*, 15–18; Tise, *Proslavery*, 10, 236.
2. Tise, *Proslavery*, 97–103, 122.
3. Faust, ed., *Ideology*, 4; Genovese, *The World the Slaveholders Made*, 97–101, 130–36. See also Elkins, *Slavery*, 60–65; Lewis Simpson, *The Dispossessed Garden* (Athens: Univ. of Georgia Press, 1975), 3–43; McCardell, *The Idea of a Southern Nation*, 52–61.
4. Eugene Genovese, "Larry Tise's *Proslavery*: An Appreciation and a Critique," *Georgia Historical Quarterly* 72 (1988), 679; Eugene Genovese and Elizabeth Fox-Genovese, "The Social Thought of the Antebellum Southern Divines," in *Looking South: Chapters in the Story of an American Region*, ed. Winfred Moore and Joseph Tripp (Westport, Conn.: Greenwood Publishing Group, 1989), 31–44; Genovese, "The Divine Sanction of the Social Order," 211–33; Faust, ed., *Ideology*, 8, 9.
5. Jenkins, *Proslavery*, 206.
6. Goen, *Broken Churches*, 105–7, and passim.
7. See for example Smith, *Lectures*, 24; Blanchard and Rice, *A Debate on Slavery*, 33; Fuller and Wayland, *Domestic Slavery*, 123; Wilson, *Relations and Duties*, 5; Adger, *Doctrine*, 13; Dunwoody, *A Sermon*, 3, 30; Thornton, *An Inquiry*, 56.
8. Loveland, *Southern Evangelicals*, 198–99; Kenneth Greenberg, *Masters and Statesmen: The Political Culture of American Slavery* (Baltimore: Johns Hopkins Univ. Press, 1985), 84–104; Matthews, *Religion in the Old South*, 152; Tise, *Proslavery*, 315.
9. Jordan, *White over Black*, 11–42, and passim; Fredrickson, *The Black Image*, 1971), 3–10.
10. Foner, *Free Soil*, chapter 5.
11. Larry Tise, "The Interregional Appeal of Proslavery Thought: An Ideological Profile of the Antebellum American Clergy," *Plantation Society* 1 (1979), 58–72; Rice, *American Catholic Opinion*, 88–109; Maddex, "'The Southern Apostasy' Revisited,"; Tise, *Proslavery*, 156–59, 163–64, 261–85; Morris Raphall, *Bible View of Slavery* (New York, 1861); Michelbacher, *A Sermon*.
12. Boles, *Religion in Antebellum Kentucky*, 106–10; Essig *Bonds of Wickedness*, 118; Matthews, *Religion in the Old South*, 74.
13. Tise, *Proslavery*, 36–37, 10, 76, 97; Loveland, *Southern Evangelicals*, 207, 198–99; Jenkins, *Proslavery*, 64–65. See for example *Southern Christian Advocate*, 14 April 1843, 172, and Oct. 1843, 71; *Christian Index*, 8 October 1840, 648–49; *Religious Herald*, 19 November 1840, 187; *Central Presbyterian Review*, 30 May 1857, 55; James Henry Hammond, in *Pro-slavery Argument*, 104; Thornton, *An Inquiry*, 56; Thornwell, *Rights and Duties*, 17 (Thornwell here comments that defenses of slavery "in their abstract forms can be characterized as little less than monstrous").

14. Gerteis, *Morality and Utility,* 3–4.

15. Smith, "Popular Objections to Christianity," in Ruffner, ed., *Lectures on the Evidences of Christianity,* 400.

16. Genovese, *The Slaveholders' Dilemma,* 33, 39; Tise, *Proslavery,* 108.

17. Genovese, *The Slaveholders' Dilemma,* 13–20, 55; Genovese, *The World the Slaveholders Made,* 129–30; Bruce, *The Rhetoric of Conservatism,* 179–88; McCardell, *The Idea of a Southern Nation,* 52–61; Faust, ed., *Ideology,* 8–9; Jenkins, *Proslavery,* 86–89; Peterson, *Ham and Japheth,* 34.

18. Thomas R. Dew, "Professor Dew on Slavery," in *Pro-slavery Argument,* 295, 316.

19. Beverly Tucker, *Southern Literary Messenger* 10 (1844), 329–34, 470–80.

20. John Boles, "Evangelical Protestantism in the Old South: From Religious Dissent to Cultural Dominance," in Wilson, ed., *Religion in the Old South,* 14–21; Boles, *The Great Revival.* See also Rhys Isaac, *The Transformation of Virginia,* chapters 8, 11, 13, for earlier roots of this cultural revolt.

21. Fuller, *Address Before the American Colonization Society,* 3–4.

22. Loveland, *Southern Evangelicals,* 188–92.

23. Tise, *Proslavery,* 70–74. Tise's emphasis on Dew's attack against colonization is the one important point in an otherwise flawed analysis of Dew's influence. For a more balanced account see Kenneth Stampp, "An Analysis of T.R. Dew's Review of the Debates in the Virginia Legislature," *Journal of Negro History* 27 (Oct. 1942), 380–87.

24. Peterson, *Ham and Japheth,* 34–38.

25. Armstrong, *Christian Doctrine,* 9; [Brookes], *A Defence of Southern Slavery,* 19, 44. See also the mature views of George Fitzhugh, Edmund Ruffin, James Henry Hammond, and Chancellor Harper in *Pro-slavery Argument;* Erik McKitrick, ed., *Slavery Defended: The Views of the Old South* (Englewood Cliffs, N.J.: Prentice Hall, 1963); Faust, ed., *Ideology.*

26. Tise, *Proslavery,* 347–62.

27. See for example, *Christian Advocate* 11 (1847), 113; *Christian Advocate* 14 (1850), 45; *Christian Advocate* 18 (1854): 24; *Southern Christian Advocate,* 5 Jan. 1838, 114; *Religious Herald,* 9 Aug. 1849, 126; *Baptist Advocate* 2 (1850), 112; *Baptist Banner* 11 (1849), 11, 18, 16; *Southern Presbyterian Review* 2 (Mar. 1849), 569–73. Adger, *Doctrine,* 9, 13; Wilson, *Relations and Duties,* 5, 30–33; McKay, *Slavery and the Obligations of Masters,* 2; Hamilton, *Duties of Masters and Slaves,* 5, 6; Dunwoody, *A Sermon,* 7, 11, 22.

28. H. Shelton Smith, *In His Image But . . . ,* 10, 19, 44; Peterson, *Ham and Japheth,* 2–9.

29. Jenkins, *Proslavery,* 200–207; Smith, *In His Image, But . . . ,* 129–36.

30. Reprinted in George H. Moore, *Notes on the History of Slavery in Massachusetts* (New York: D. Appleton and Co., 1866), 251–56.

31. Moore, 88.

32. Davis, *The Problem of Slavery in the Age of Revolution,* 257–342; MacLeod, *Slavery, Race, and the American Revolution,* 10–60.

33. [Parsons and Pearson], *A Forensic Dispute,* 8.

34. Tise, *Proslavery,* 41–56, 204–38.

35. Hopkins, *Scriptural,* 21, 23–24; Rice, *American Catholic Opinion,* 110–11, 120–21; Charles Hodge, "Reverend Hodge on Slavery," in Elliott, ed., *Cotton is King; Essays and Reviews Selected from the "Princeton Review"* (New York: Robert Carter, 1857). Nehemiah Adams, Simon Clough, Nathan Lord, Samuel How, and others who might have been added to this list were primarily anti-abolitionists and, except for Clough, not motivated by traditional conservative visions, and so will be cited in the subsequent chapter.

36. Genovese, *The Slaveholders' Dilemma,* 20.

37. Loveland, "Richard Furman's 'Questions on Slavery,'" Harvey Cook, ed., *A Biography of Richard Furman* (Greenville, S.C.: Baptist Courier Job Rooms, 1913), 2–11.

38. Furman, *Exposition,* 3, 17.

39. Furman, *Exposition,* 4, 10, 12, 19.

40. Tise, *Proslavery,* 115–19; Faust, ed., *Ideology,* 17.

41. Furman, *Exposition,* 7, 3–4.

42. Furman, *Exposition,* 13.

43. Furman, *Exposition,* 12.

44. Furman, *Exposition,* 8, 9.

45. Furman, *Exposition,* 9.

46. Furman, *Exposition,* 10.

47. Furman, *Exposition,* 16.

48. Furman, *Exposition,* 9.

49. See for example Estes, *Defence of Negro Slavery,* 46; weekly numbers of the *Christian Index* under the signature "A Baptist Minister," in [Mell], *Slavery,* 19; Priest, *Bible Defense of Slavery,* 398, 567; Ross, *Slavery Ordained of God,* 17, 160, 173; [Drayton], *The South Vindicated,* 98; [Patterson], *The Scripture Doctrine,* 8.

50. [James Henley Thornwell], "Report on Slavery," *Southern Presbyterian Review* 5 (Jan. 1852), 381–82; B.M. Palmer, *Formation of Character: Twelve Lectures* (New Orleans, 1889), 125–26. William Plumer, "Man Responsible for His Own Belief," 10; and Nathan Rice, "The Moral Effects of Christianity," 575, 585, 605, both collected in Ruffner, ed., *Lectures on the Evidences of Christianity.*

51. A.T. Robertson, ed., *Life and Letters of John Albert Broadus* (Philadelphia, 1901), 148; Thornwell, *Life and Letters,* 343.

52. Jenkins, *Proslavery,* 112, 113–19, 146, 216; Tise, *Proslavery,* 106; Genovese, *The Slaveholders' Dilemma,* 59.

53. Furman, *Exposition,* 11, 10.

54. Furman, *Exposition,* 14–15.

55. Loveland, "Richard Furman's 'Questions on Slavery,'" 177–79; Tise, *Proslavery,* 38–40.

56. Bailey, *Shadow on the Church,* 200, 202, 206.

57. Essig, *Bonds of Wickedness,* 134.

58. Boles, ed., "Introduction," *Masters and Slaves,* 1–18; Boles, *Religion in Antebellum Kentucky,* 100–102.

59. For two contrary views, see Bailey, *Shadow on the Church,* 22, 50, and Essig, *Bonds of Wickedness,* 5, 6–10.

60. See Allan Gallay, "Planters and Slaves in the Great Awakening," in Boles, ed., *Masters and Slaves,* 32, 31; and Bailey, *Shadow on the Church,* 126, 34–35.

61. William Sweet, ed., *Religion on the American Frontier,* vol. 2, *The Presbyterians, 1783–1840: A Collection of Their Source Material* (New York, 1936), 166–70.

62. Matthews, *Slavery and Methodism,* 20–25. Boles, *Antebellum Religion in Kentucky,* 108–10.

63. *Journals of the General Conference of the Methodist Episcopal Church* (New York, 1855), vol. 1: 19–23.

64. *Journals of the General Conference of the Methodist Episcopal Church* (New York, 1855), vol. 1: 22.

65. Brownlow and Pryne, *Ought American Slavery,* 94.

66. Blanchard and Rice, *A Debate on Slavery,* 31.

67. Blanchard and Rice, *A Debate on Slavery,* 130–32.

68. Rice, *Slavery Inconsistent,* 17.

69. Boles, *Religion in Antebellum Kentucky,* 107.

70. Faust, ed., *Ideology,* 8.

71. Nor did this year signal the South's articulation or appropriation of an intellectual tradition that supported slavery and that was derived from the North or older traditions. See such an argument in Tise, *Proslavery,* 7.

72. Genovese, *The Slaveholders' Dilemma,* 5, 21.

73. Gerteis, *Morality and Utility,* 21.

74. Thomas Dew, "The Abolition of Slavery," in Faust, ed., *Ideology,* 53.

75. Farmer, *Metaphysical Confederacy,* 162.

76. Thomas Dew, "The Abolition of Slavery," in Faust, ed., *Ideology,* 53.

77. Dew, "Review," in McKitrick, ed., *Slavery Defended,* 23.

78. See Allen Kaufman's *Capitalism, Slavery, and Republican Values* for a complete account of Dew's economic ideas. See also Alison Freehling's *Drift Toward Dissolution* for a differing interpretation.

79. Dew, "Review," in McKitrick, ed., *Slavery Defended,* 24, and Dew, "Review" in *Pro-slavery Argument,* 389.

80. Dew, "Review," in *Pro-slavery Argument,* 417.

81. Dew, "Review," in *Pro-slavery Argument,* 366.

82. Dew, "Review," in *Pro-slavery Argument,* 372.

83. Dew, "Review," in *Pro-slavery Argument,* 316, 380.

84. Cooper, *Lectures* (1826), 106–7. George Tucker embraced an even stronger version of this argument. See Genovese, *The Slaveholders' Dilemma,* 16.

85. Genovese, *Western Civilization.*

86. Dew, "Review," in *Pro-slavery Argument,* 325.

87. Dew, "Review," in *Pro-slavery Argument,* 325.

88. Dew, "Review," in *Pro-slavery Argument,* 287.

89. Dew, "Review," in *Pro-slavery Argument,* 326.

90. Dew, "Review," in *Pro-slavery Argument,* 480.

91. Dew, "Review," in *Pro-slavery Argument,* 412.

92. Dew, "Review," in *Pro-slavery Argument,* 341.

93. Dew, "Review," in *Pro-slavery Argument,* 488.

94. Thomas Dew, "The Abolition of Slavery," in Faust, ed., *Ideology,* 51.

95. Dew, "Review," in *Pro-slavery Argument,* 482; Thomas Dew, "The Abolition of Slavery," in Faust, ed., *Ideology,* 51.

96. Dew, "Review" in *Pro-slavery Argument,* 262.

97. Thomas Dew, "The Abolition of Slavery," in Faust, ed., *Ideology,* 51, 73, 74. See also [Hobby], *Remarks Upon Slavery,* 28; Fuller and Wayland, *Domestic Slavery,* 123.

98. Dew, "Review," in *Pro-slavery Argument,* 483.

99. Dew, "Review," in *Pro-slavery Argument,* 484.

100. Dew, "Review," in *Pro-slavery Argument,* 243, 451. See Adger, *Doctrine,* 13, for the best discussion of evangelicals' perspective on this issue. In the key section Adger maintains that "Comparing the present advantage of our white population with what might have been had not the negro been introduced, the Christian people of the South have never yet said that slavery is a positive blessing."

101. Dew, "Review," in *Pro-slavery Argument,* 451, 327.

102. Dew, "Review," in McKitrick, ed., 33.

103. Dew, "Review," in *Pro-slavery Argument,* 484; Thomas Dew, "The Abolition of Slavery," in Faust, ed., *Ideology,* 51.

104. Dew, "Review," in *Pro-slavery Argument,* 451 (my emphasis).

105. Dew, "Review," in *Pro-slavery Argument,* 451.

106. Dew, "Review," in *Pro-slavery Argument,* 454.

107. Shore, *Southern Capitalists,* 26.

108. Dew realized that "skepticism" on religious matters was no longer respectable. See Thomas Roderick Dew, *Southern Literary Messenger* 2 (Nov. 1836), 768.

109. William Sweet, ed., *Religion on the American Frontier,* vol. 2, *The Presbyterians, 1783–1840: A Collection of Their Source Material* (Chicago: Univ. of Chicago Press, 1936), 166–70.

110. Bertram Wyatt-Brown, "Modernizing Southern Slavery: The Proslavery Argument Reinterpreted," in Finkelman, ed., *Proslavery Thought,* 493.

111. Dew, "Review," in McKitrick, ed., 22; Thornton Stringfellow, *Scriptural and Statistical Views* (Richmond: J.W. Randolph, 1856), 149.

112. Dew, "Review," in McKitrick, ed., 30.

113. Hoit, *The Right of American Slavery,* 46.

114. Hoit, *The Right of American Slavery,* 49.

115. Clapp, *Slavery,* 16.

116. Matthew Estes, *Defence of Negro Slavery,* 23–27. See also Ewart, *A Scriptural View,* 3; and Priest, *Bible Defence of Slavery,* 144.

117. Mitchell, *A Bible Defence of Slavery,* 14.

118. Frederika Schmidt and Barbara Wilhelm, "Early Proslavery Petitions in Virginia," in Finkelman, ed., *Proslavery Thought,* 139 and passim.

119. Thomas Dew, "The Abolition of Slavery," in Faust, ed., *Ideology,* 63.

120. Smith, *Lectures,* 15.

121. Smith, *Lectures,* 23–25. See also Beverly Tucker, *Southern Literary Messenger* 10 (1844), 329–34, 470–80, on slavery's practical effects as evidence of moral righteousness.

122. Wendell Phillips, *Speeches, Lectures, and Letters* (Boston: Lee and Shepard, 1863).

3. Answering Abolitionists, Defending Slaveholders

1. Farmer, *The Metaphysical Confederacy,* 206.

2. Lipscomb, *North and South,* from the *New York Daily Times,* 23.

3. McCaine, *Slavery Defended from Scripture,* 20, 21.

4. Blanchard and Rice, *A Debate on Slavery,* 60, 85.

5. Blanchard and Rice, *A Debate on Slavery,* 7.

6. Blanchard and Rice, *A Debate on Slavery,* 162.

7. Mell, *Slavery,* 22.

8. Mell, *Slavery,* 26–27.

9. Stringfellow and Goodloe, *Information for the People,* 14–16.

10. Elliott, ed., *Cotton is King,* 847; Ross, *Slavery Ordained of God,* 84; Paskoff, ed., *The Cause of the South,* 227.

11. Robert L. Dabney, 15 January 1851, in Johnson, ed., *Life and Letters,* 32.

12. Ross, *Slavery Ordained of God,* 113. See a similar argument of James Henley Thornwell in John B. Adger, ed., *The Collected Writings of James Henley Thornwell* (Richmond: The Presbyterian Committee of Publications, 1871), 404.

13. Ross, *Slavery Ordained of God,* 113. He was referring to Theodore Parker's abolitionist tract *The Slave Power* (1852), rather than the Republican Party's political theories of a slave power conspiracy.

14. Ross, *Slavery Ordained of God,* 35, 33.

15. Thornton Stringfellow, Richmond *Religious Telegraph,* 25 Feb. 1841. See Faust, ed., *Ideology,* 136–38.

16. Stringfellow, *Scriptural and Statistical Views*, 6. Also in Elliott, ed., *Cotton is King* (1861), 461.

17. Boles, *The Great Revival*, 131–34 (on conversion experience), 9–26, 45–51, 88–9, and passim on its importance in the South.

18. McCaine, *Slavery Defended from Scripture*, 21–22.

19. "Report on Slavery," *Southern Presbyterian Review* 5 (1852), 370–85, quoted in Blanchard and Rice, *A Debate on Slavery*, 258.

20. [Capers], *Bondage*, 24, 39.

21. Smylie, *A Review of a Letter*, 6. Many fellow Presbyterian defenders of slavery disagreed with this figure and disapproved of Smylie's proslavery. See Blanchard and Rice, *A Debate on Slavery*, 43, 52.

22. Sparks, "Mississippi's Apostle of Slavery," 93. See also Randy Sparks, "A Mingled Yarn: Race and Religion in Mississippi, 1800–1876" (Ph.D. dissertation, Rice University, 1988).

23. Eugene Genovese, *Roll, Jordan, Roll* (New York: Pantheon, 1976), 202; Tise, *Proslavery*, 173; Larry Tise, "The Interregional Appeal of Proslavery Thought: An Ideological Profile of the Antebellum American Clergy," in Finkelman, ed., *Proslavery Thought*, 68; Hamilton, *Duties of Masters and Slaves*, 5.

24. Stroupe, *The Religious Press*, 11.

25. See Clapp, *Autobiographical Sketches*, 168, for a good description of this social phenomenon. Also, James Stirling, *Letters from the Slave States* (New York: H.H.W. Parker and Son, 1968 [1857]), 120; and Boles, *Religion in Antebellum Kentucky*, 87.

26. Goen, *Broken Churches*, 36–38; Jenkins, *Proslavery*, 206; Tise, *Proslavery*, xviii, 126, 127, 128–49; Genovese, *"Slavery Ordained of God,"* 7–9, 11.

27. Clapp, *Slavery*; Wilson, *Relations and Duties*; Thornton, *An Inquiry*; Dunwoody, *A Sermon*; [Capers], *Bondage*.

28. Ross, *Slavery Ordained of God*, 155, 157.

29. Dunwoody, *A Sermon*, 25, 4, 10.

30. Dunwoody, *A Sermon*, 12, 22.

31. Dunwoody, *A Sermon*, 25.

32. [Hobby], *Remarks Upon Slavery*, 7. Hobby was another of the early defenders of slavery raised in New England who could hammer back at abolitionists in their own terms of "moral law" and material progress.

33. [Drayton], *The South Vindicated*, 94; Mitchell, *A Bible Defence of Slavery*, 10, 11; Wilson, *Relations and Duties*, 11–12.

34. Wilson, *Relations and Duties*, 26, 28.

35. Cobb, *A Scriptural Examination*, 121.

36. Dunwoody, *A Sermon*, 4.

37. Loveland, *Southern Evangelicals*, 199–200.

38. Tise, *Proslavery*, 42; Elliott, ed., *Cotton is King*, viii, xiii, xx.

39. B.F. Stringfellow, "Negro Slavery, No Evil," *Information for the People: Two Tracts for the Times* (Boston: Alfred Mudge and Son, 1855), 9.

40. Joshua Wilson, *Relations and Duties*, 5; Dunwoody, *A Sermon*, 30. Ker, *Slavery Consistent with Christianity*, 3, 18.

41. Baker, *Life*, 322.

42. Sparks, "Mississippi's Apostle of Slavery," 98, 101–03.

43. Amasa Converse, *Autobiography*, in the Papers of Rev. Converse Amasa, Montreat, N.C., 120, 135.

44. Converse, *Autobiography*, 97–98.

45. Ewart, *A Scriptural View*, 11–12. See other examples in Ker, *Slavery Consistent with Christianity*, 3, 18–19; Priest, *Bible Defence of Slavery*, 424; Elliott, ed., *Cotton is King*, 20; Brookes, *A Defence of the South*, 31; Paulding, *Slavery in the United States*, 225; Warren, *Nellie Norton*, 8.

46. Quoted in Thornton, *An Inquiry*, 277, 341.

47. Rhett was himself one of the early defenders of slavery in the 1830s: see Rhett, *Address*. In this speech, Rhett did not give as much attention to the moral and biblical argument, which he confessed attachment to a few years later.

48. Rhett to Rhett, Jr., 1848, in Charles Colcock Jones, *Autograph Letters and Portraits of the Confederate States*, Duke University Manuscript Collection.

49. Hoit, *The Right of American Slavery*, 10.

50. Jeter, *Recollections of a Long Life*, 67–70 (my emphasis).

51. Jeter, *Recollections of a Long Life*, 69–70 (my emphasis).

52. Jeter, *Recollections of a Long Life*, 123. Jeter, like many evangelicals, was not particularly worried by the Turner Revolt, which he called a trifling thing. His main association with the event was that he "well remembered" the day vividly because, like Turner, he was impressed by the "green appearance" of the sun. See Jeter, *Recollections of a Long Life*, 17.

53. Farmer, *The Metaphysical Confederacy*, 200.

54. Tise (*Proslavery*, 177–78) determined that 60 percent of the ministers who defended slavery had originally become slaveholders in these fashions.

55. Loveland, *Southern Evangelicals*, 207. See also, Tise, *Proslavery*, 177–78; Holifield, *The Gentlemen Theologians*, chapter 1; Faust, "Evangelicalism and the Meaning of the Proslavery Argument," 3–17.

56. Holder, "On Slavery," 325–26.

57. See for example Thornwell, *Rights and Duties of Masters*, 33; *Pro-slavery Argument*, 451; Blanchard and Rice, *A Debate on Slavery*, 26, 259, 435; Farley, *Slavery*, 6; Clapp, *Slavery*, 5, 17; Wilson, *Relations and Duties*, 13; Hamilton, *The Duties of Masters and Slaves*, 16.

58. Thornwell, *Rights and Duties of Masters*, 32.

59. See a typical example in Hamilton, *The Duties of Masters and Slaves*, 14.

60. Buck, *The Slavery Question*, 11, 18.

61. Buck, *The Slavery Question*, 17, 22.

4. The Evangelical Vision of the South and Its Future

1. *Report of Delegates in the General Conference of the Methodist Episcopal Church* (New York, 1855), 144.

2. *Southern Religious Telegraph*, 8 Aug. 1837, 124.

3. William T. Brantley in *Southern Watchman and General Intelligencer*, 24 Nov. 1837, 187.

4. Fuller, *Address*, 8.

5. Tise, *Proslavery*, 177. For an account of similar attitudes among southern evangelical leaders, see Loveland, *Southern Evangelicals*, 3, 33, 58, 105–7.

6. Immigration made Catholicism the largest by the end of the 1840s.

7. Bishop Leonidas Hamline, quoted in Donald G. Matthews, *Slavery and Methodism*, 224. See also Robert A. West, ed., *Report of Debates in the General Conference of the Methodist Episcopal Church* (New York: Methodist General Conference, 1855), 90—"secession is preferable to schism."

8. Ahlstrom, *A Religious History*, 663.

9. *Southern Baptist Convention Annual* (1845), 19.

10. Elliott, ed., *Cotton is King,* 497.

11. Maddex, "'The Southern Apostasy' Revisited," 138.

12. Johnson, *Life and Letters,* 128–29.

13. Thornton, *An Inquiry,* 91, 89–90.

14. Brookes, *A Defence of the South,* 30–31.

15. [Mell], *Slavery,* 12.

16. *Pro-slavery Argument,* 162, 113–14.

17. Thornton Stringfellow, in Elliott, ed., *Cotton is King,* 522.

18. [Mell], *Slavery,* 27–28.

19. Stringfellow and Goodloe, *Information for the People,* 33.

20. [Mell], *Slavery,* 34.

21. Papers of Daniel Baker, Montreat, N.C., Letter from Tuscaloosa, Alabama, Feb. 1839.

22. See Censer, *North Carolina Planters;* William McLoughlin, "Evangelical Child-Rearing"; John B. Boles, "John Hersy: Dissenting Theologian of Abolitionism, Perfectionism, and Millennialism," *Methodist History* (July 1976), 225–31; Lewis, *The Pursuit of Happiness,* 37–67; Fliegelman, *Prodigals and Pilgrims.*

23. Baker, *Daniel Baker's Talk to Little Children,* 23; Papers of Daniel Baker, Tuscaloosa, Alabama, February 1839.

24. Baker, *Daniel Baker's Talk to Little Children,* 9.

25. Thornwell, *Life and Letters,* 342.

26. Furman, *Human Accountability,* 17.

27. Furman, *Human Accountability,* 18.

28. Greven, ed., *Child-Rearing Concepts;* Wishy, *The Child and the Republic.*

29. Baker, *Life,* 289.

30. Baker, *Life,* 249.

31. Justice, *The Slavery Question,* 10.

32. Estes, *Defence of Negro Slavery,* 138.

33. George Junkin, *Proposition* (1843), reprinted in Priest, *Bible Defence of Slavery,* 568.

34. Gertrude Himmelfarb, *Darwin and the Darwinian Revolution* (New York: W.W. Norton, 1959), 394.

35. Frederickson, *The Black Image,* 4–22.

36. Jordan, *White over Black,* 256–57, 567. These earlier terms often appeared verbatim in later proslavery literature. See, for example, [Drayton], *The South Vindicated,* 228; Priest, *Bible Defence of Slavery,* 178–80, 244, 301, 388; Sloan, *The Great Question Answered,* 49; *Pro-slavery Argument,* 14–15.

37. Mungo Park, *Travels, in the Interior of Africa* (London: William Bulmer and Co., 1816). See references in *Pro-slavery Argument,* 131, 375; [Mell], *Slavery,* 36; Paulding, *Slavery in the United States,* 270–71; Brookes, *A Defence of the South,* 20; Priest, *Bible Defence of Slavery,* 224; Stringfellow and Goodloe, *Information for the People,* 10; Ker, *Slavery Consistent with Christianity,* 6; Brownlow and Pryne, *Ought American Slavery,* 214–20.

38. This sixteenth-century racial construct (with ancient antecedents), however, was still used in almost unchanged form in proslavery justifications even on the eve of the Civil War. See Brownlow and Pryne, *Ought American Slavery,* 214, 264; also Sloan, *The Great Question Answered,* 49.

39. For the most educated—and often surprisingly unorthodox on racial doctrines—discussion of this issue, see Smyth, *The Unity of Human Races.* See also Mitchell, *A Bible Defence of Slavery.* For a less educated, more racist, and to modern readers utterly bizarre and incoherent version of this argument, see Baldwin, *Dominion.* Baldwin's works and their intricate exegetical and prophetic arguments were popular and accessible to ante-

bellum audiences. Both Mitchell and Smyth were part of the evangelical attack on what Mitchell called "the insidious appeal made to the prejudices of slaveholders, by some who deny the unity of the human race" (29). He was referring to the few biological arguments that appeared in the 1850s speculating that blacks were the product of a separate creation or biologically determined subspecies. Smyth in refuting this argument made arguments not usually associated with southern authors in the 1850s: "Where is the man that can prove he is a pure caucasian? There is not one" (45). Mitchell (24) made a similar argument. Smyth also identified Africa as the "center and origin of the human family" (45) and also, through the Egyptians who he speculated were black (55), the center and origin of much of Greek civilization (63). The point is not that these ministers challenged southern racism or slavery—they did not—but they do demonstrate the considerable intellectual latitude open to southerners behind the "Cotton Curtain."

40. Priest, *Bible Defence of Slavery*, 228.

41. Priest, *Bible Defence of Slavery*, 424.

42. Peterson, *Ham and Japheth*, 14.

43. Ker, *Slavery Consistent with Christianity*, 9.

44. Ross, *Slavery Ordained of God*, 123.

45. Elliott, ed., *Cotton is King*, 520–21.

46. Blanchard and Rice, *A Debate on Slavery*, 14.

47. Sloan, *The Great Question Answered*, 78. For identical examples see Porter, *Our Danger and Our Duty*, 6; Longstreet, *A Voice from the South*, 17; Mitchell, *A Bible Defence of Slavery*, 7, 32; Ferguson, *Address*, 11; Tyson, *The Institution*, 37; [Drayton], *The South Vindicated*, 227; Priest, *Bible Defence of Slavery*, 102; Brookes, *A Defence of the South*, 20.

48. [Drayton], *The South Vindicated*, 92.

49. Estes, *Defence of Negro Slavery*, 243, 251.

50. Estes, *Defence of Negro Slavery*, 104, 183. See also Mitchell, *A Bible Defence of Slavery*, 7, 11; Porter, *Our Danger and Our Duty*, 6.

51. *Pro-slavery Argument*, 222. James Stirling, an antislavery traveler and acute observer in the South, was amazed at antebellum southerners' mania for the phrase "utter extermination." He perceptively noted: "It is not difficult to guess which race they propose to exterminate; but the extermination of four millions of people is no such simple matter, though passionate editors talk so glibly of it." Stirling, *Letters from the Slave States*, 52.

52. Brookes, *A Defence of the South*, 17; Elliott, ed., *Cotton is King*, 491.

53. Priest, *Bible Defence of Slavery*, 299 (my emphasis). See also Elliott, ed., *Cotton is King*, 599, 719.

54. Priest, *Bible Defence of Slavery*, 197, 247, 301.

55. Brookes, *A Defense of the South*, 33.

56. Estes, *Defence of Negro Slavery*, 99, 260.

57. Boles, ed., *Masters and Slaves*, 8–10, 37–39.

58. [Mell], *Slavery*, 39.

59. Ross, *Slavery Ordained of God*, 68.

60. Sloan, *The Great Question Answered*, 207.

61. Elliott, ed., *Cotton is King*, 598. See also [Drayton}, *The South Vindicated*, 94; Baker, *Life*, 244; Priest, *Bible Defence of Slavery*, 57; Estes, *Defence of Negro Slavery*, 136–37, 251.

62. Thornton, *An Inquiry*, 65. See also Smith, *Lectures*, 37.

63. Smith, *Lectures*, 275 (my emphasis).

64. Longstreet, *A Voice from the South* (1st edition), 7.

65. Estes, *Defence of Negro Slavery*, 132; Lipscomb, *North and South*, from the *New York Daily Times*, 25.

66. Bender, ed., *The Antislavery Debate*, 252–59.

67. See Beverly Tucker's address to students in *Pro-slavery Argument*, 27: "Personal purity of character, individual integrity of purpose ... never sacrifice it to be expedient ... even to attain power. Be assured its ripening fruit awaits to reward the votary of virtue."

68. Justice, *The Slavery Question*, 20.

69. For sophisticated descriptions of the interaction of religious and economic factors in Jacksonian politics and ideology, see Watson, *Liberty and Power*, 172–75, 185–86; Howe, *Political Culture*; William Shade, *Banks or No Banks: The Money Issue in Western Politics, 1832–1865* (Detroit: Wayne State Univ. Press, 1972); Brock, *Parties and Political Conscience*.

70. Fuller and Wayland, *Domestic Slavery*, 119, 234, 308.

71. William Channing, *The Works of William E. Channing*, vol. 2 (Boston: American Unitarian Association, 1886), 20–22.

72. Blanchard and Rice, *A Debate on Slavery*, 46.

73. Quoted in Priest, *Bible Defence of Slavery*, 481 (my emphasis).

74. Smectymnuus, *Slavery and the Church*, 7–8, 40.

75. Quoted in Brookes, *A Defence of the South*, 25.

76. Blanchard and Rice, *A Debate on Slavery*, 170, 308, 168–69.

77. Edward Beecher, *Antislavery Record* (Boston: Stearns, 1845). Also see *Emancipator*, 19 November 1845; *AFAS Reporter*, October 1845, 65–66; Robert Meredith, *The Politics of the Universe*, 106–12.

78. Fuller and Wayland, *Domestic Slavery*, 32; Blanchard and Rice, *A Debate on Slavery*, 208.

79. Priest, *Bible Defence of Slavery*, 345–46.

80. Paulding, *Slavery*, 12.

81. Fuller and Wayland, *Domestic Slavery*, 208–9.

82. Sloan, *The Great Question Answered*, 167, 169.

83. McCaine, *Slavery Defended*, 19.

84. McCaine, *Slavery Defended*, 14.

85. Priest, *Bible Defence of Slavery*, 450, 466, 350, 267.

86. Elliott, ed., *Cotton is King*, 505.

87. Thornton, *An Inquiry*, 135, 138; [Drayton], *The South Vindicated*, 313, 174.

88. Priest, *Bible Defence of Slavery*, 422.

89. Longstreet, *A Voice from the South*, 12.

90. Longstreet, *A Voice from the South*, 26.

91. *Pro-slavery Argument*, 24.

92. Estes, *Defence of Negro Slavery*, 187. Lipscomb, *North and South*, from the *New York Daily Times*, 19.

93. Reprinted in Priest, *Bible Defence of Slavery*, 521.

94. Lord, *A Letter of Inquiry*, 23.

95. Brookes, *A Defence of the South*, 34.

96. Graham, *The Contrast*, 47–48.

97. [Capers], *Bondage*, 16.

98. Palmer, *The South*, 12.

99. See Thomas Haskell, "Conventions," in Bender, ed., *The Antislavery Debate*, 7, 230; Highham, *From Boundlessness to Consolidation*; Fredrickson, *The Inner Civil War*.

100. Smith, *Lectures*, 251.

101. Smith, *Lectures*, 242.

102. Smith, *Lectures*, 251.

103. Ker, *Slavery Consistent with Christianity,* 28.

104. Davis, *Speech,* 17.

105. Thornton, *An Inquiry,* 176; W.D. Brown, "Strictures on Abolitionism," in Priest, *Bible Defence of Slavery,* 442; Beverly Tucker in *Pro-slavery Argument,* 13.

106. [Mell], *Slavery,* 30.

107. Stringfellow and Goodloe, *Information for the People,* 10, 22.

108. *Pro-slavery Argument,* 163.

109. *Pro-slavery Argument,* 453.

110. Ker, *Slavery Consistent with Christianity,* 18.

111. Jenkins, *Proslavery,* 207–38. See, for example, *New York Weekly Observer,* "Our Paper," January 3, 1856; McCaine, *Slavery Defended,* 24; Estes, *Defence of Negro Slavery,* 109, 148; Brookes, *A Defense of the South,* 22, 35.

112. Thornwell, "The Relation of the Church and Society" (New York: Mission Society, 1851), 19; *The Collected Writings of James Thornwell,* 4 vols. (Richmond, Presbyterian Committee of Publications), 4:393.

113. Thomas Smyth, "The Sin and the Curse: Or the Union and the True Source of Dominion," (1860) *Complete Works of Thomas Smyth,* 10 vols. (Columbia: R.L. Bryan Company, 1910), 7:543, 545. See also "North and South," *Southern Presbyterian Review* 3 (January, 1850), 344.

114. Lipscomb, *North and South,* from the *New York Daily Times,* 19.

115. Lipscomb, *North and South,* from the *New York Daily Times,* 9.

116. Elliott, ed., *Cotton is King,* 506.

117. Ross, *Slavery Ordained of God,* 81.

118. Fletcher, *Studies on Slavery,* 94.

119. Harriet Beecher Stowe, *Uncle Tom's Cabin* (New York, 1981), 200–202.

120. For a discussion of these issues in Jacksonian political culture see: Kohl, *Politics of Individualism,* 22, 27, 50, 60.

121. See for example, Brownlow and Pryne, *Ought American Slavery,* 223, 311; Blanchard and Rice, *A Debate on Slavery,* 117, 132; Stirling, *Letters from the Slave States,* 147.

122. Thomas Haskell, "Capitalism and the Origins of the Humanitarian Sensibility," in Bender, ed., *The Antislavery Debate,* 155–56.

123. Jenkins, *Proslavery,* 222.

124. Thornton, *An Inquiry,* 15.

125. Thornton, *An Inquiry,* 227, 86; Blanchard and Rice, *A Debate on Slavery,* 189–92.

126. Blanchard and Rice, *A Debate on Slavery,* 191.

127. George Fitzhugh, *Sociology for the South,* in McKitrick, ed., *Slavery Defended,* 23–45, 67–75, 122, passim.

128. Henry Wish, ed., *Antebellum: Writing of George Fitzhugh and Hinton Rowan Helper on Slavery* (New York, 1960), 45; George Fitzhugh, *Sociology for the South,* in McKitrick, ed., *Slavery Defended,* 35.

129. George Fitzhugh, *Sociology for the South,* in McKitrick, ed., *Slavery Defended,* 46; George Fitzhugh, "Southern Thought" and "Southern Thought Again," *DeBow's Review* 23 (1857), 338–50, 449–62, in Faust, ed., *Ideology,* 274–76; Harvey Wish, *George Fitzhugh, Propagandist of the Old South* (Gloucester, Mass.: P. Smith, 1962), 111.

130. Thornwell, *Rights and Duties of Masters,* 13, 14–16.

131. O.B. Forthingham, *Liberty Bell* 13 (Boston: American Antislavery Society, 1853), 167–70.

132. Elliott, ed., *Cotton is King,* 523.

133. Elliott, ed., *Cotton is King,* 544.

134. Blanchard and Rice, *Debate on Slavery*, 316.

135. Daniel Walker Howe, "Evangelical Movement," 1225.

136. Ross, *Slavery Ordained of God*, 25; Jeter, *Recollections of a Long Life*, 81.

137. J.D.B. DeBow, *The Interest in Slavery of the Southern Non-slaveholder: and the Right of Slavery and Peaceful Secession in the Bible* (Charleston: Evans and Cogswell, 1860), 8–12; Rev. Van Dyke of Brooklyn, "Bible View," *DeBow's Review* 30 (January 1861); Rev. Van Dyke of Brooklyn, "The Origin, Progress and Prospects of Slavery," *Review* 9 (July 1850); Rev. Van Dyke of Brooklyn, "Harper's Memoir on Slavery," *Review* 8 (March 1850); Paskoff, *The Cause of the South*, 1.

138. Elliott, ed., *Cotton is King*, 25, 31.

139. Fletcher, *Studies on Slavery*, 24.

140. Fuller and Wayland, *Domestic Slavery*, 19.

141. Brownlow and Pryne, *Ought American Slavery*, 139.

142. W.D. Brown, "Strictures on Abolitionism," in Priest, *Bible Defence of Slavery*, 422.

143. W.D. Brown, "Strictures on Abolitionism," in Priest, *Bible Defence of Slavery*, 482–83.

144. W.D. Brown, "Strictures on Abolitionism," in Priest, *Bible Defence of Slavery*, 484.

145. Estes, *Defence of Negro Slavery*, 182–83.

146. [Drayton], *The South Vindicated*, 119, 121.

147. Stringfellow and Goodloe, *Information for the People*, 31.

148. Brownlow and Pryne, *Ought American Slavery*, 254.

149. Fuller and Wayland, *Domestic Slavery*, 91–95.

150. Blanchard and Rice, *A Debate on Slavery*, 36.

151. Fuller and Wayland, *Debate*, 145.

152. Fuller and Wayland, 123, 15.

153. Elliott, ed., *Cotton is King*, viii, xiii; Ewart, *Scriptural View*, 8; Blanchard and Rice, *A Debate on Slavery*, 109.

154. Blanchard and Rice, *A Debate on Slavery*, 14, 19.

155. Blanchard and Rice, *A Debate on Slavery*, 90.

156. Blanchard and Rice, *A Debate on Slavery*, 53.

157. Blanchard and Rice, *A Debate on Slavery*, 372.

158. Fuller and Wayland, *Domestic Slavery*, 119–121.

159. Fuller and Wayland, *Domestic Slavery*, 122.

160. Clapp, *Slavery*, 28. See also *Christian Index*, August 13, 1840, 525; Cobb, *A Scriptural Examination*, 22; Smith, *Lectures*, 252, 227; Buck, *The Slavery Question*, 18; Wilson, *Relations and Duties*, 34; [Capers], *Bondage*, 16; Hamilton, *Duties of Masters and Slaves*, 17.

161. Smith, *Lectures*, 227.

162. Walters, *The Antislavery Appeal*, 37–53; Scott, *From Office to Profession*, chapter 6.

163. Lord, *A Letter of Inquiry*, 8. See also Taylor, *Essay on Slavery*, 268–69; George Junkin, *Proposition* (1843), in Priest, *Bible Defence of Slavery*, 523.

164. Adger, *Doctrine*, 18.

165. Sloan, *The Great Question*, 237.

166. Lipscomb, *North and South*, from the *New York Daily Times*, 32, 20, 22.

5. Evangelical Proslavery, Free Labor, and Disunion, 1850–1861

1. Fletcher, *Studies on Slavery*, 59.

2. Thornwell, *Rights and Duties of Masters*, 27.

3. Thornwell, *Rights and Duties of Masters*, 27–28.

4. Thornwell, *Rights and Duties of Masters*, 24, 43.

5. Ross, *Slavery Ordained of God*, 94.

6. Priest, *Bible Defence of Slavery*, 415.

7. Blanchard and Rice, *A Debate on Slavery*, 14.

8. William Paley, *Treatise on Moral and Political Philosophy* (1785), quoted in Fletcher, *Studies on Slavery*, 58.

9. Thornwell, *Rights and Duties of Masters*, 22.

10. Lord, *A Letter of Inquiry*, 9.

11. [Mell], *Slavery*, 30.

12. Hoit, *The Right of American Slavery*, 23.

13. Sloan, *The Great Question Answered*, 68.

14. Thornwell, *Rights and Duties of Masters*, 19.

15. Walters, *The Antislavery Appeal*, 15.

16. Lipscomb, *North and South,* from the *New York Daily Times,* 22.

17. Thornwell, *Rights and Duties of Masters*, 30, 34.

18. Clapp, *Slavery*, 45.

19. Thornwell, *Rights and Duties of Masters*, 19.

20. Ker, *Slavery Consistent with Christianity*, 26.

21. Thornwell, *Rights and Duties of Masters,* 12; Henry Hughes, *A Report on the African Apprentice System* (Vicksburg, 1859), 2 (see also his *Treatise on Sociology* [Philadelphia: Lippincott, 1854], 89); Justice, *The Slavery Question*, 5.

22. Wilson, *Mutual Relations*, 9.

23. Justice, *The Slavery Question*, 9.

24. Thornwell, *Rights and Duties of Masters,* 21.

25. Fuller and Wayland, *Domestic Slavery*, 222.

26. Smith, *Lectures*, 43.

27. Mitchell, *A Bible Defence of Slavery*, 11.

28. Thornton, *An Inquiry*, 67–68.

29. Buck, *The Slavery Question*, 16 (my emphasis).

30. *Pro-slavery Argument*, 263.

31. Tyson, *The Institution*, 36.

32. Smith, *Lectures*, 39.

33. [Mell], *Slavery*, 29.

34. [Hobby], *Remarks Upon Slavery*, 20; Priest, *Bible Defence of Slavery*, 488.

35. Priest, *Bible Defence of Slavery*, 392, 542; McTyeire, Sturgis, and Holmes, *Duties of Masters to Servants,* 80; Clapp, *Slavery*, 38; Baker, *Life,* 148, 286; [Capers], *Bondage,* 60.

36. Thornton Stringfellow, *Stringfellow on Slavery,* in Elliott, ed., *Cotton is King,* 500–502.

37. Fuller and Wayland, *Domestic Slavery*, 81.

38. Jonathan Glickstein, "Poverty is not Slavery," in Perry and Fellman, *Antislavery Reconsidered,* 201.

39. William Goodell, "Slavery Tested by Its own Code," *Quarterly Antislavery Magazine* 1 (Oct. 1835), 29.

40. Elliott, ed., *Cotton is King,* vi.

41. Clapp, *Slavery*, 38.

42. Fuller and Wayland, *Domestic Slavery*, 151.

43. Brookes, *A Defence of Slavery*, 47, 45.

44. Thornton Stringfellow, *Stringfellow on Slavery,* in Elliott, ed., *Cotton is King,* 495.

45. Smith, *Lectures*, 300.

46. Thornton, *An Inquiry,* 113, 104.

47. Quoted in Paulding, *Slavery,* 204–13.

48. McKay, *Slavery and the Obligations of Masters,* 8: "If they do not improve their privileges it is their own fault." See also Sloan, *The Great Question Answered,* 288.

49. Boles, *Black Southerners, 1619–1869* (Lexington: Univ. Press of Kentucky, 1983), 74–92.

50. *Pro-slavery Argument,* 263.

51. Williams, *The South Vindicated,* 66–67; Stearns, *Notes on "Uncle Tom's Cabin,"* 12–17; Woodward, *A Review of "Uncle Tom's Cabin,"* 22; Warren, *Nellie Norton,* ii; Eastman, *Aunt Phillis's Cabin;* J. Thornton Randolph (Pseudonym of Charles Jacobs Peterson), *The Cabin and the Parlor; or, Masters and Slaves* (Philadelphia: T.B. Peterson, 1852). For a famous southern savaging of *Uncle Tom's Cabin* see Holmes, "Review," in McKitrick, ed., *Slavery Defended,* 99–111. Louisa S. McCord, the most famous southern woman proslavery propagandist, also savaged Harriet Beecher Stowe. See McCord, "Stowe's Key to Uncle Tom's Cabin," *Southern Quarterly Review* 8 (July 1853): 214–54; and "Uncle Tom's Cabin," *Southern Quarterly Review* 8 (Jan. 1853): 81–120.

52. Ross, *Slavery Ordained of God,* 38.

53. Albert T. Bledsoe, *Liberty and Slavery,* in Elliott, ed., *Cotton is King,* 416. See also Stringfellow and Goodloe, *Information for the People,* 10.

54. Pringle, *Slavery in the Southern States,* 53.

55. Smith, *Lectures,* 199–200.

56. Smith, *Lectures,* 186–87.

57. Fletcher, *Studies on Slavery,* 216.

58. Buck, *The Slavery Question,* 22.

59. Buck, *The Slavery Question,* 16.

60. Priest, *Bible Defence of Slavery,* 388.

61. Thornton, *An Inquiry,* 153.

62. Lipscomb, *North and South,* from the *New York Daily Times,* 22. See also *Christian Index,* 11 June 1857.

63. Estes, *Defence of Negro Slavery,* 186.

64. Estes, *Defence of Negro Slavery,* 229.

65. Estes, *Defence of Negro Slavery,* 186.

66. Cobb, *A Scriptural Examination,* 22. See Elliott, ed., *Cotton is King,* 613. See also the complex argument that fits both ministers and economists into a conservative (and dominant) wing of proslavery thought in Genovese, *The Slaveholders' Dilemma,* 33–40.

67. *Pro-slavery Argument,* 122–23.

68. Longstreet, *A Voice from the South,* 17.

69. Ross, *Slavery Ordained of God,* 280. See also page 30.

70. Glickstein, *Concepts of Free Labor,* 199–206, 212–13.

71. Fuller and Wayland, *Domestic Slavery,* 231, 234.

72. Fuller and Wayland, *Domestic Slavery,* 240.

73. Stephen Colwell, *The Five Cotton States and New York: or Remarks upon the Social and Economical Aspects of the Southern Political Crisis* (N.P., January 1861), 6. See also Henry Carey, *A Memoir of Stephen Colwell* (Philadelphia: Loomis, 1971), 4–35; Stephen Colwell, *The South* (Philadelphia, 1856), 4, 41.

74. Gerteis, *Morality and Utility,* 150.

75. Foner, *Free Soil,* 66–69; see also 43–48, 266–67.

76. Josiah Nott and Joseph Cartwright led this project. See Elliott, ed., *Cotton is King,* 719.

77. Jenkins, *Proslavery,* 210–65; Genovese, *The Slaveholders' Dilemma,* 33–34.

78. *Pro-slavery Argument*, 178.

79. *Pro-slavery Argument*, 265.

80. *Pro-slavery Argument*, 189.

81. *Pro-slavery Argument*, 265.

82. *Pro-slavery Argument*, 167.

83. *Pro-slavery Argument*, 162.

84. Faust, ed., *Ideology*, 20.

85. Brookes, *A Defence of the South*, 45; Thornwell, *Rights and Duties of Masters*, 21; Smith, *Lectures*, 320; Sloan, *The Great Question Answered*, 223.

86. Jonathan Glickstein, "Poverty is not Slavery," in Perry and Fellman, *Antislavery Reconsidered*, 207.

87. Brookes, *A Defence of the South*, 46.

88. Faust, ed., *Ideology*, 20.

89. Justice, *The Slavery Question*, 10.

90. Smith, *Lectures*, 150.

91. Ferguson, *Address*, 20–21.

92. Stringfellow and Goodloe, *Information for the People*, 24–33; Brookes, *A Defence of the South*, 12.

93. Sloan, *The Great Question Answered*, 223–24.

94. Sloan, *The Great Question Answered*, 207, 225. See also 68.

95. Thornwell, *Rights and Duties of Masters*, 30.

96. Thornwell, *Rights and Duties of Masters*, 24.

97. Genovese, *The Slaveholders' Dilemma*, 33–35; Genovese, *The World the Slaveholders Made*, 24–63.

98. See, for example, Fuller and Wayland, *Domestic Slavery*, 147; Lipscomb, *North and South*, from the *New York Daily Times*, 15–18; Fletcher, *Studies on Slavery*, 203.

99. Ross, *Slavery Ordained of God*, 54–55.

100. Elliott, ed., *Cotton is King*, 554.

101. Thornwell, *Rights and Duties of Masters*, 43.

102. Palmer, *The South*, 7.

103. See Adger, *Doctrine*, 13, for a subtle and ingenious version of this proslavery argument.

104. Elliott, ed., *Cotton is King*, 337–38.

105. Paulding, *Slavery in the United States*, 252, 262, 265.

106. Stringfellow and Goodloe, *Information for the People*, 32.

107. Thornton, *An Inquiry*, 86. See the same argument in Heman Packard Papers, Packard to North Bridgewater Committee, 2.

108. Thornton, *An Inquiry*, 227.

109. Estes, *Defence of Negro Slavery*, 185, 228.

110. Estes, *Defence of Negro Slavery*, 29.

111. Hoit, *The Right of American Slavery*, 34.

112. Williams, *The South Vindicated*, 102–4.

113. Williams, *The South Vindicated*, 154.

114. Reprinted in Priest, *Bible Defence of Slavery*, 527.

115. McKay, *Slavery and the Obligations of Masters*, 7; Brownlow and Pryne, *Ought American Slavery*, 165; Elliott, ed., *Cotton is King*, 495.

116. Smith, *Lectures*, 318, 320, 278–320, and passim; Priest, *Bible Defence of Slavery*, 347.

117. Bertram Wyatt-Brown, "Modernizing Southern Slavery: The Proslavery Argument Reinterpreted," in Finkelman, ed., *Proslavery Thought*, 492.

118. McTyeire et al., *Duties of Masters to Servants*, 66; Thornwell, *Rights and Duties of Masters*, 49.

119. Thornwell, *Rights and Duties of Masters*, 46.

120. Sloan, *The Great Question Answered*, 233. Estes, *Defence of Negro Slavery*, 257. See also Thornwell, *Rights and Duties of Masters*, 25; Thornton, *An Inquiry*, 66.

121. Wilson, *The Mutual Relations*, 19; Calvin Wiley Henderson, "The Christian Duty of Masters" (unpublished), Wiley MSS, Southern Historical Collection, University of North Carolina.

122. McTyeire et al., *Duties of Masters to Servants*, 80–81. See also Thomas Clay, *Detail of a Plan for the Moral Improvement of Negroes on Plantations* (N.P.: 1833), 9–22; Thornton, *An Inquiry*, 93.

123. Ferguson, *Address*, 17; Wilson, *Relations and Duties*, 25; Clapp, *Slavery*, 56; [Capers], *Bondage*, 29; Wilson, *The Mutual Relations*, 19. The colonization society was the inspiration for this idea, which reappeared in some "Rights and Duties" sermons in the 1850s.

124. Thornwell, *Rights and Duties of Masters*, 19, 21.

125. Blake Touchstone, "Planters and Slave Religion in the Deep South," in Boles, ed., *Masters and Slaves*, 103–33.

126. Hamilton, *The Duties of Masters and Slaves Respectively*, 20–21; Sloan, *The Great Question Answered*, 240. See also Wilson, *The Mutual Relations*, 17–19; Thornwell, *Rights and Duties of Masters*, 47; Nathaniel Bowen, D.D., *A Pastoral Letter on Religious Instruction of Slaves* (Charleston: Gabriel M. Bounetheau, 1835), 4–7; [Lucy Kenny] "A Lady of Fredericksburg," *A Death Blow to the Principles of Abolition* (Washington, D.C., 18??), 4.

127. Wilson, *Relations and Duties*, 17.

128. See Clarence Mohr, "Slaves and White Churches in Confederate Georgia," in Boles, ed., *Masters and Slaves*, 153–72.

129. Bertram Wyatt-Brown, "Modernizing Southern Slavery: The Proslavery Argument Reinterpreted," in Finkelman, ed., *Proslavery Thought*, 493, 498–99.

130. Hamilton, *The Duties of Masters and Slaves Respectively*, 22; Wilson, *Masters and Slaves*, 19.

131. Palmer, *The South*, 12.

132. Palmer, *The South*, 8.

133. Henry Ward Beecher, *Freedom and War* (Boston: Ticknor and Fields, 1863), 33–35.

134. Fredrickson, *The Inner Civil War*.

135. *Augusta Chronicle*, May 17, 1849.

136. Stewart, *Holy Warriors*, 72–3.

137. DeBow, *The Interest in Slavery*, 8.

6. The Proslavery Formula and the Test of War, 1860–1865

1. Richard Carawardine, *Evangelicals and Politics in Antebellum America* (New Haven: Yale Univ. Press, 1993), 313; Mitchell Snay, *Gospel of Disunion: Religion and Separatism in the Antebellum South* (New York: Cambridge Univ. Press, 1993).

2. Linderman, *Embattled Courage*, 102–5.

3. Priest, *Bible Defence of Slavery*, 350–51.

4. McCaine, *Slavery Defended*, 21.

5. Brookes, *A Defence of the South*, 21.

6. Brookes, *A Defence of the South*, 22.

7. McCaine, *Slavery Defended*, 27.

8. *Pro-slavery Argument*, 111–12.

9. Longstreet, *A Voice from the South,* 22.

10. Longstreet, *A Voice from the South,* 23.

11. Vernor, *A Sermon,* 10, 13.

12. Palmer, *The South,* 7.

13. Estes, *Defence of Negro Slavery,* 187.

14. Shannon, *An Address,* 32.

15. Brownlow and Pryne, *Ought American Slavery,* 254. See also Smectymnuus, *Slavery and the Church,* 43.

16. *Pro-slavery Argument,* 25–26; Williams, *The South Vindicated,* 47.

17. Brownlow and Pryne, *Ought American Slavery,* 183.

18. Brownlow and Pryne, *Ought American Slavery,* 190.

19. Brownlow and Pryne, *Ought American Slavery,* 167.

20. Dumond, *Southern Editorials,* 154 and passim.

21. James Rowland, ed., *Jefferson Davis, Constitutionalist,* vol. 1 (Jackson, Miss.: Printed for the Mississippi Department of Archives and History, 1923), 50, 72, 357.

22. Steven Channing, *Crisis of Fear: Secession in South Carolina* (New York: Simon and Schuster, 1970), 287; *Columbia Daily South Carolinian,* 3 August 1860.

23. William A. Clebesch, "Christian Interpretation of the Civil War," *Church History* 30 (1961), 4.

24. Tyler Dennett, ed., *Lincoln and the Civil War in the Diaries and Letters of John Hay* (New York: Dodd, Mead and Company, 1939), 180; Roy P. Basler and Christian O. Basler, eds., *The Collected Works of Abraham Lincoln,* vol. 7 (New Brunswick, N.J.: Rutgers Univ. Press, 1990), 393.

25. James McPherson, *Abraham Lincoln and the Second American Revolution* (New York: Oxford Univ. Press, 1990), chapters 2 and 5; Ahlstrom, *A Religious History,* 686.

26. See Freehling, *The Road to Disunion;* William Freehling and Craig Simpson, eds., *Secession Debated: Georgia's Showdown in 1860* (New York: Oxford Univ. Pres, 1992); Edward Crowther, "Mississippi Baptists, Slavery, and Secession, 1806–1861," *Journal of Mississippi History* 56 (May 1994), 129–48.

27. Palmer, *The South,* 7 and passim.

28. Cheesebrough, ed., *"God Ordained This War."*

29. Ahlstrom, *A Religious History,* 97.

30. Gardiner H. Shattuck, *A Shield and a Hiding Place: The Religious Life of the Civil War Armies* (Macon, Ga.: Mercer Univ. Press, 1983); Joseph Cross, *Camp and Field: Papers from the Portfolio of an Army Chaplain* (Macon, Ga.: Burke, Boykin, 1864); Philip Tucker, *The Confederacy's Fighting Chaplain* (Tuscaloosa: Univ. of Alabama Press, 1992).

31. Herman Norton, *Rebel Religion: The Story of Confederate Chaplains* (St. Louis: The Bethany Press, 1961); Sidney J. Romero, *Religion in the Rebel Ranks* (Lanham, Md.: Univ. Press of America, 1983).

32. George Rable, *Civil Wars: Women and the Crisis of Southern Nationalism* (Urbana: Univ. of Illinois Press, 1989), 203. Silver, *Confederate Morale,* 96. Silver documents the widely held belief—also accepted by current historians—that ministers did more to sustain the morale of the Confederacy in the Civil War than any other group. See David Cheesebrough, "The Civil War and the Use of Sermons as Historical Documents," *Magazine of History* 81 (fall 1991), 26–29, for an excellent discussion of interpreting these documents.

33. Sledd, *A Sermon,* 19.

34. *Columbus (Ga.) Weekly Times,* 30 December 1861, reports ministers passing out guns at troop mustering ceremonies where they spoke. See also Cheesebrough and Silver cited in note 32.

35. Winkler, *Duties of Christian Soldiers,* 3–4 and passim.

36. McCurry, *Masters of Small Worlds,* 210, 296. McCurry's book has one of the best descriptions of how evangelicalism, proslavery, and a broad spectrum of gender values and other cultural values (including physical intimidation) united the classes in the South, especially at the crisis of secession. She accurately describes secession as a popular revolt in which yeomen demonstrated their ideological and cultural prowess in the region. For another excellent use of evangelicalism and proslavery to demonstrate how the region resisted planter cultural hegemony see Sparks, *On Jordan's Stormy Banks,* 15. A broader chronological and theoretical discussion of regional values is available in Joseph Reidy, *From Slavery to Agrarian Capitalism in the Cotton Plantation South: Central Georgia, 1800–1880* (Chapel Hill: Univ. of North Carolina Press, 1992). For a range of arguments on this issue see Orville Burton, *In My Father's House Are Many Mansions: Family and Community in Edgefield, South Carolina* (Chapel Hill: Univ. of North Carolina Press, 1985); McKenzie, *One South or Many?;* Collins, *White Society in the Antebellum South;* Harry L. Watson, "Conflict and Collaboration: Yeoman, Slaveholders, and Politics in the Antebellum South," *Social History* 10 (October 1985), 273–98; Robert C. Kenzer, *Kinship and Neighborhood in a Southern Community: Orange County, North Carolina, 1849–1881* (Knoxville: Univ. of Tennessee Press, 1987); Bill Cecil-Fronsman, *Common Whites: Class and Culture in Antebellum North Carolina* (Lexington: Univ. Press of Kentucky, 1992).

37. *Resolution Adopted by McGowan's Brigade. South Carolina Volunteers* (Richmond, 1865).

38. Sledd, *A Sermon,* 20.

39. Wilson, *The Mutual Relations,* 10.

40. McPherson, *What They Fought For,* 51; Michael Barton, *Goodmen: The Character of Civil War Soldiers* (University Park: Pennsylvania State Univ. Press, 1981), 33, 40; Linderman, *Embattled Courage,* 97.

41. Larry M. Logue, "Who Joined the Confederate Army? Soldiers, Civilians, and Communities in Mississippi," *Journal of Social History* 26 (spring 1993), 611–25.

42. Jamerson, *The Private Civil War.*

43. Sledd, *A Sermon,* 12, 17.

44. Sledd, *A Sermon,* 17.

45. Samuel J. Watson, "Religion and Combat Motivation in the Confederate Armies," *Journal of Military History* 58 (Jan. 1994), 29–55.

46. Reid Mitchell, "The Perseverance of the Soldiers," in Gabor S. Borritt, ed., *Why the Confederacy Lost* (New York: Oxford Univ. Press, 1992); Mitchell, *Civil War Soldiers;* Bell I. Wiley, *The Life of Johnny Reb: The Common Soldier of the Confederacy* (Indianapolis: Bobbs-Merrill, 1943).

47. Donna Rebecca Dondes Krug, "The Folks Back Home: Confederate Homefront during the Civil War" (Ph.D. dissertation, University of California, Irvine, 1990), 229–300; Linderman, *Embattled Courage,* 2.

48. Vernor, *A Sermon,* 10.

49. Sledd, *A Sermon,* 19.

50. Sledd, *A Sermon,* 20.

51. Sledd, *A Sermon,* 22.

52. Drew Gilpin Faust, "Christian Soldiers: The Meaning of Revivalism in the Confederate Army," *Journal of Southern History* 53 (February 1987), 64; Wilson, *Baptized in Blood,* 6; G. Clinton Prim, "Revivals in the Armies of Mississippi During the Civil War," *Journal of Mississippi History* 44 (August 1982), 223–28; James Nisbet, *Four Years on the Firing Line* (Wilmington, N.C.: Broad Foot Pub. Co., 1914), 81; (Petersburg, Virginia) *Daily Register,* 22 March 1864; J. William Jones, *Christ in the Camp, or Religion in Lee's Army*

(Richmond: B.F. Johnson and Co., 1887); William W. Bennett, *A Narrative of the Great Revival in the Southern Armies* (Philadelphia: Sprinkle Publications, 1877).

53. Dumond, *Southern Editorials,* 154. See Osthaus, *Partisans of the Southern Press,* 110, 129, for excellent examples of belligerence and the influence of racist values.

54. *Christian Observer,* 6 March 1862. See also Charles H. Read of Richmond's statement in *Observer,* 8 May 1862, and *South Western Baptist* quoted in Frank Moore, ed., *The Rebellion Record,* vol. 1 (New York: G.P. Putnam, 1861–1865), 183.

55. Quoted in Parker, *The United Synod,* 243. See also similar collective statements from the Presbyterians in *Minutes of the Assembly of the Presbyterian Church in the Confederate States of America,* vol. 1 (Augusta: The Assembly of the Presbyterian Church, 1861), 51–60.

56. *Southern Christian Advocate,* 8 May 1862.

57. Wilson, *Baptized in Blood,* 61–66, best explains the southern turn to apocalyptics during and after the War.

58. Williams, *The South Vindicated,* 438.

59. Williams, *The South Vindicated,* 443.

60. Williams, *The South Vindicated,* 156–57.

61. Michelbacher, *A Sermon,* 3.

62. Michelbacher, *A Sermon,* 13.

63. Michelbacher, *A Sermon,* 12; "The Hebrews and Slavery," (Richmond) *Dispatch,* 16 Jan. 1861, p. 2, column 1. Blacks were often called on to offer prayers and homage to the cause at special days of fast or humiliation. See a startling example in *Southern Field and Fireside,* 8 January 1862.

64. Tichenor, *Fast Day Sermon.*

65. Seat, *The Confederate States,* 52.

66. Seat, 64.

67. Seat, 81–82.

68. Seat, 84, 92.

69. Seat, 105.

70. Seat, 132.

71. Seat, 116.

72. Seat, 142.

73. Seat, 134.

74. Seat, 36.

75. Seat, 143.

76. Seat, 143.

77. See Pamela Colbenson, "Millennial Thought Among Southern Evangelicals, 1830–1860" (Ph.D. diss., Georgia State University, 1980), 1, 49, 59, 63, 68–72, for a discussion of southern millennialism and how it related to proslavery and how it compared to northern millennialism.

78. Beringer, et al., *Why the South Lost the Civil War,* 102, 368, chapters. 5, 7, 12, 14.

79. Elliot, *Vain is the Help of Man,* 9.

80. Elliot, *Samson's Riddle,* 18.

81. See William Gilmore Simms, *Sack and Destruction of Columbia* (Columbia, S.C.: Power Press of Daily Phoenix, 1865), for an excellent example of an elitist "positive good" proslavery publicist facing Sherman's wrath.

82. Elliot, *Vain is the Help of Man,* 4.

83. For strong examples of a wartime embrace of evangelical proslavery formulas see James L. Roark, *Masters without Slaves: Southern Planters in the Civil War and Reconstruction*

(New York: W.W. Norton, 1977), 99–100. Roark later argues that planters abandoned proslavery after the War (104–5), but many southerners—especially ministers—did not and continued to espouse and even publish proslavery when there was no slavery left to defend. See Wilson, *Baptized in Blood,* 103.

84. Elliot, *Samson's Riddle,* 21. See, for the similar prewar Episcopal views, *Constitution of the Protestant Episcopal Church in the Confederate States of America* (Columbia, S.C.: Cogswell, 1861).

85. Elliot, *Samson's Riddle,* 19–20.

86. James L. Roark, *Masters without Slaves: Southern Planters in the Civil War and Reconstruction* (New York: W.W. Norton, 1977), 90.

87. Quoted in Emory Thomas, *Robert E. Lee: A Biography* (New York: W.W. Norton, 1995), 152.

88. "A Prayer by Robert E. Lee," General Order, No. 83, the Army of Northern Virginia, n.p., 1863.

89. Elliot, *Vain is the Help of Man,* 8.

90. Elliot, *Vain is the Help of Man,* 21.

91. See a nearly identical description of the rewards that would come from reforming slavery in Thornwell, *Life and Letters,* 444.

92. Elliot, *Samson's Riddle,* 17.

93. Robert J. Burdette, *The Drums of the 47th,* quoted in Linderman, *Embattled Courage,* 150.

94. Wilson, *Baptized in Blood,* 66–67; James L. Roark, *Masters without Slaves: Southern Planters in the Civil War and Reconstruction* (New York: W.W. Norton, 1977), 104; Faust, *Mothers of Invention,* 187–95.

95. Caldwell, *Slavery and Southern Methodists,* iii.

96. Daniel W. Stowell, "'We Have Sinned and God Has Smitten Us!': John H. Caldwell and the Religious Meaning of Confederate Defeat," *Georgia Historical Quarterly* 78 (spring 1994), 1–38.

97. Caldwell, *Slavery and Southern Methodists,* xii.

98. Caldwell, *Slavery and Southern Methodists,* 19.

99. Caldwell, *Slavery and Southern Methodists,* 26.

100. Caldwell, *Slavery and Southern Methodists,* 31.

101. Caldwell, *Slavery and Southern Methodists,* 35.

102. Caldwell, *Slavery and Southern Methodists,* 65.

103. Faust, "Evangelicalism and the Meaning of the Proslavery Argument," 3–17.

104. Benjamin Morgan Palmer, *National Responsibilities Before God* (New Orleans: Price-Current Steson Book and Job Print Office, 1861), 22; Benjamin Morgan Palmer, "A Vindication of Secession and the South," *Southern Presbyterian Review* 14 (1861–62), 162; Benjamin Morgan Palmer, *A Discourse Before the General Assembly of South Carolina on December 10, 1863: Appointed by the Legislature as a Day of Fasting, Humiliation and Prayer* (Columbia, S.C.: C.P. Pelham, 1864), 7–24. See for the continuation of Palmer's views, James Hickey, "Benjamin Morgan Palmer" (Ph.D. diss., Duke University, 1962), 74–77, 183–93, 234.

105. Wilson, *Baptized in Blood,* 102–6; Thornwell, *Life and Letters,* 345.

106. Conser, *God and the Natural World,* 190–97.

107. Wiley, *Scriptural Views,* 8

108. Wiley, *Scriptural Views,* 172. See also Rable, *Civil Wars: Women and the Crisis of Southern Nationalism* (Urbana: Univ. of Illinois Press, 1989), 216.

109. Wiley, *Scriptural Views,* 60.

110. Wiley, *Scriptural Views,* 61.

111. Wiley, *Scriptural Views,* 213.

112. William Martin, *With God on Our Side: The Rise of the Religious Right in America* (New York: Broadway Book, 1996), 14.

Epilogue

1. Charles Storey to Henry Wilson, 26 April 1862, Henry Wilson Papers, Library of Congress, quoted in Louis Gerteis, *Morality and Utility,* 188.

Selected Bibliography

Primary Sources, Manuscripts

Historical Foundation of the Presbyterian and Reformed Churches, Montreat, N.C.
    Daniel Baker Papers
    Amasa Converse Papers
    Robert Lewis Dabney Collection
    William Flinn Papers
    William Henry Forsythe Papers
    Neill McKay Sermon Folder
    Heman Packard Papers
    Benjamin Morgan Palmer Papers
    Abner Addison Porter Papers
    Thomas Smyth Papers
    James Henley Thornwell Collection
University of North Carolina, Southern Historical Collection, Chapel Hill, N.C.
    Iveson Brookes Papers
    Moses Curtis and Ashley Curtis Papers
    James Henley Thornwell Papers
    Calvin Henderson Wiley Papers
Duke University. Perkins Library. Durham, N.C.
    Iveson Brookes Papers
    James Warley Miles Collection
    William Plumer Papers

Primary Sources, Newspapers and Periodicals

Christian Index (Baptist)
Christian Observer
DeBow's Review
The Religious Herald (Baptist)
The Southern Christian Advocate (Methodist)
Southern Presbyterian Review
Southern Quarterly Review
Southern Watchman and General Intelligencer (Baptist)

Published Sources

Adams, Eldon. "The Biblical Defense of Slavery in the Antebellum South." *The Mirror* 5 (May 1983): 1–29.

Adams, Nehemiah. *A South-Side View of Slavery; or Three Months at the South, in 1854*. Boston: T.R. Marvin, 1854.

Adger, John. *The Doctrine of Human Rights and Slavery*. Columbia: I.C. Morgan, 1849.

———. *My Life and Times, 1810–1890*. Richmond: Presbyterian Committee of Publications, 1899.

Ahlstrom, Sydney. *A Religious History of the American People*. New Haven: Yale Univ. Press, 1972.

Ambercrombie, Nicholas. *Sovereign Individuals of Capitalism*. London: Allen and Unwin, 1986.

Armstrong, George Dodd. *The Christian Doctrine of Slavery*. New York: Charles Scribner, 1857.

———. *A Discussion of Slaveholding: Three Letters to a Conservative*. Philadelphia: Joseph Wilson, 1858.

Bailey, David T. *Shadow on the Church: Southwestern Evangelical Religion and the Issue of Slavery*. Ithaca: Cornell Univ. Press, 1985.

Baker, Daniel. *Daniel Baker's Talk to Little Children*. Philadelphia: Presbyterian Board of Education, 1856.

Baker, William. *The Life and Letters of Reverend Daniel Baker*. Philadelphia: Alfred Martin, 1859.

Baldwin, Samuel. *Dominion; or the Unity and Trinity of the Human Race; with the Political Constitution of the World, and the Divine Rights of Shem, Ham, and Japheth*. Nashville: E. Steveson and F.A. Owen, 1858.

Barnes, Albert. *An Inquiry into the Scriptural Views of Slavery*. New York: Negro Univ. Press, 1969 [1857].

Bartlett, Irving. *The American Mind in the Mid-Nineteenth Century*. New York: Thomas Crowell Company, 1967.

Bateman, Fred, and Thomas Weiss. *A Deplorable Scarcity: The Failure of Industrialization in the Slave Economy*. Chapel Hill: Univ. of North Carolina Press, 1981.

Bender, Thomas, ed. *The Antislavery Debate: Capitalism and Abolitionism as a Problem in Historical Interpretation*. Berkeley: Univ. of California Press, 1992.

Bercovitch, Sacvan. *American Jeremiad*. Madison: Univ. of Wisconsin Press, 1978.

Beringer, Richard E., et al. *Why the South Lost the Civil War*. Athens: Univ. of Georgia Press, 1986.

Blanchard, Jonathan, and N.L. Rice. *A Debate on Slavery*. Cincinnati: William H. Moore and Co., 1846.

Bledsoe, Albert T. *Liberty and Slavery*. Philadelphia: J.B. Lippincott and Co., 1856.

Bodo, John. *The Protestant Clergy and Public Issues*. Princeton: Princeton Univ. Press, 1954.

Boles, John B. *The Great Revival, 1787–1805: The Origins of the Southern Evangelical Mind*. Lexington: Univ. of Kentucky Press, 1972.

————. *Religion in Antebellum Kentucky.* Lexington: Univ. Press of Kentucky, 1976.

Boles, John B., ed. *Masters and Slaves in the House of the Lord: Race and Religion in the American South, 1740–1870.* Lexington: Univ. Press of Kentucky, 1988.

Bowen, James L. *Speech of James L. Bowen: Showing the South-side View of the Institution of Negro Slavery.* N.p.: 1860.

Bozeman, Theodore Dwight. *Protestants in the Age of Science: The Baconian Ideal and Antebellum Religious Thought.* Chapel Hill: Univ. of North Carolina Press, 1977.

Brock, William. *Parties and Political Conscience: American Dilemmas, 1840–1850.* Millwood, N.Y.: KTO Press, 1979.

Brookes, Iveson. *A Defence of the South Against the Reproaches and Inchroachments of the North: In Which Slavery is Shown to be an Institution of God Intended to form the Basis of the Best Social State and the Only Safeguard to the Permanence of a Republican Government.* Hamburg, S.C.: Printed at the Republican Office, 1850.

[————]. *A Defence of Southern Slavery Against the Attacks of Henry Clay and Alexander Campbell.* By "A Southern Farmer." Hamburg S.C.: Robinson and Carlisle, 1851.

Brown, Edward. *Origin and Necessity of Slavery.* Charleston: A.E. Miller, 1826.

Brown, Robert. *Modernization: The Transformation of American Life, 1600–1865.* New York: Hill and Wang, 1976.

Brownell, Blaine, and David R. Goldfield, eds. *The City in Southern History: The Growth of Urban Civilization in the South.* Port Washington, N.Y.: Kennikat Press, 1977.

Brownlow, William G., and A. Pryne. *Ought American Slavery to be Perpetuated? A Debate.* Philadelphia: J.B. Lippincott and Co, 1858.

————. *A Sermon on Slavery: A Vindication of the Methodist Church South.* Knoxville: Kinsloe and Rice, 1857.

Bruce, Dickinson. *The Rhetoric of Conservatism: The Virginia Convention of 1829–30 and the Conservative Tradition of the South.* San Marino: Huntingdon Library, 1982.

————. *Violence and Culture in the Antebellum South.* Austin: Univ. of Texas Press, 1977.

Buck, William. *The Slavery Question.* Louisville: Harney, Hughes and Hughes, 1849.

Caldwell, John H. *Slavery and Southern Methodism.* Augusta, Georgia: Printed for the author, 1865.

Calhoon, Robert. *Evangelicals and Politics in Antebellum America.* Columbia: Univ. of South Carolina Press, 1988.

[Capers, Gabriel]. *Bondage a Moral Institution, Sanctioned by Scriptures of the Old and New Testaments, and the Preaching and Practice of the Savior and his Apostles.* By a Southern Farmer. Macon: Griffin and Purse, 1837.

Carlyle, Thomas. "Occasional Discourse on the Nigger Question." In *English and Other Critical Essays.* London: Dent and Sons, 1915.

Cash, Wilbur. *The Mind of the South.* New York: Knopf, 1941.

Cashdollar, Charles D. "Social Implications of the Doctrine of Divine Providence: A Nineteenth Century Debate in American Theology." *HTR* 71 (1978): 265–84.

Censer, Jane. *North Carolina Planters and Their Children, 1800–1860*. Chapel Hill: Univ. of North Carolina Press, 1984.

Cheesebrough, David B., ed. *"God Ordained This War": Sermons on the Sectional Crisis*. Columbia: Univ. of South Carolina Press, 1991.

Clapp, Theodore. *Autobiographical Sketches and Reflections During a Thirty-Five Years Residency in New Orleans*. Boston: Phillips, Sampson and Co., 1857. Reprinted in John Duffy, ed., *Parson Clapp of the Strangers' Church, New Orleans*. Baton Rouge: Louisiana State Univ. Press, 1957.

———. *Slavery: A Sermon*. New Orleans: John Gibson, 1838.

Clay, Clement. *Speech*. Courthouse, Huntsville, Ala.: N.p., Sept. 5, 1859.

Clough, Simon. *A Candid Appeal to the Citizens of the United States*. New York: A.K. Berton, 1834.

Cobb, Howell. *A Scriptural Examination of the Institution of Slavery in the United States*. Perry, Ga.: By the Author, 1856.

Cohen, Charles Lloyd. *God's Caress: The Psychology of Puritan Religious Experience*. New York: Oxford Univ. Press, 1986.

Cole, Charles C. *The Social Ideas of the Northern Evangelists, 1826–1860*. New York: Columbia Univ. Press, 1954.

Cole, C. Robert, and Michael E. Moody, eds. *Godly People: Essays on Protestantism and Puritanism*. London: Oxford Univ. Press, 1983.

Collins, Bruce. *White Society in the Antebellum South*. London: Longman, 1985.

Conkin, Paul. *Prophets of Prosperity: America's First Political Economists*. Bloomington: Indiana Univ. Press, 1980.

———. *Puritans and Pragmatists: Eight Eminent Thinkers*. New York: Dodd, Mead and Company, 1968.

Conser, Walter H., Jr. *God and the Natural World: Religion and Science in Antebellum America*. Columbia, S.C.: Univ. of South Carolina Press, 1993.

Cook, J.W. "Albert Taylor Bledsoe: An American Philosopher and Theologian of Liberty." *Southern Humanities Review* 8 (1874): 215–28.

Cooper, Thomas. *Lectures on the Elements of Political Economy*. 2nd ed. Columbia, S.C.: Morris and Wilson Printers, 1830.

Cross, Whitney. *The Burned Over District: The Social and Intellectual History of Enthusiastic Religion in Western New York, 1800–1850*. Ithaca: Cornell Univ. Press, 1950.

Cunliffe, Marcus. *Chattel Slavery and Wage Labor*. Athens: Univ. of Georgia Press, 1979.

Dabney, R.L. *A Defence of Virginia (and Through Her of the South) in Recent and Pending Contests against the Sectional Party*. New York: E.J. Hale and Son, 1867.

Dagg, John L. *Elements of Moral Science*. New Orleans: 1857.

[Dalcho, Frederick]. *Practical Considerations Founded on Scripture, Relative to the Slave Population of South Carolina*. Charleston: A.E. Miller, 1823.

Davis, David Brion. *The Problem of Slavery in the Age of Revolution, 1770–1823*. Ithaca: Cornell Univ. Press, 1975.

———. *The Problem of Slavery in Western Culture*. Ithaca: Cornell Univ. Press, 1966.

———. *Slavery and Human Progress*. New York: Oxford Univ. Press, 1984.

Davis, David Brion, et al. *The Great Republic.* Toronto: D.C. Heath and Co., 1985.

Davis, Jefferson. *Speech of Mr. Davis of Mississippi on the Subject of Slavery in the Territories.* (February 13, 14, 1850). N.p., 1850.

DeBow, J.D.B. *The Interest in Slavery of the Southern Non-Slaveholder: and the Right of Slavery and Peaceful Secession in the Bible.* Charleston: Steam Power Press of Evans and Cogswell, 1860.

Degler, Carl. *Place over Time: The Continuity of Southern Distinctiveness.* Baton Rouge: Louisiana State Univ. Press, 1977.

Dehon, Theodore. *A Sermon on the Death of Little Children.* Charleston: A.E. Miller, 1833.

Dew, Thomas Roderick. "Review of the Debate in the Virginia Legislature." In *Pro-slavery Argument: As Maintained by the Most Distinguished Writers of the Southern States, Containing the Several Essays, on the Subject, of Chancellor Harper, Governor Hammond, Dr. Simms, and Professor Dew.* Charleston: Walker, Richard and Co., 1852.

———. "Review of the Debate in the Virginia Legislature." In *Slavery Defended: The Views of the Old South.* Ed. Erik McKitrick. Englewood Cliffs, N.J.: Prentice Hall, 1963.

———. *Review of the Debate in the Virginia Legislature of 1831 and 1832.* Richmond: T.W. White, 1832.

Donald, David. "The Proslavery Argument Reconsidered." *Journal of Southern History* 37 (Feb. 1971): 3–18.

Dorfman, Joseph. *The Economic Mind in American Civilization, 1606–1865.* New York: Viking Press, 1946.

[Drayton, William]. *The South Vindicated from the Treason and Fanaticism of the Northern Abolitionists.* Philadelphia: H. Manly, 1836.

Dumond, Dwight. *Southern Editorials on Secession.* New York: The Century Co., 1931.

Dunwoody, Samuel. *Foreknowledge and the Decrees of God: A Sermon.* Charleston: B. Jenkins, 1846.

———. *A Sermon upon the Subject of Slavery.* Columbia: S. Weir, 1837.

Eastman, Mary. *Aunt Phillis's Cabin: or Southern Life as it Really Is.* Philadelphia: Lippincott, 1852.

Eaton, Clement. *The Freedom of Thought Struggle in the Old South.* New York: Harper and Row, 1964.

———. *The Mind of the South.* Baton Rouge: Louisiana State Univ. Press, 1964.

Eighmy, John Lee. *Churches in Cultural Captivity: A History of the Social Attitudes of Southern Baptists.* Knoxville: Univ. of Tennessee Press, 1972.

Eisenstadt, S.N., ed. *The Protestant Ethic and Modernization.* New York: 1968.

Elkins, Stanley. *Slavery: A Problem in American Institutional and Intellectual Life.* Chicago: Chicago Univ. Press, 1959.

Elliot, Stephen. *Samson's Riddle: A Sermon.* Macon: Boyken and Co., Steamboat and Job Printers, 1863.

———. *Vain is the Help of Man: A Sermon.* Macon: Burke, Boykin and Company, 1864.

Elliott, E.N., ed. *Cotton is King and Pro-slavery Arguments: Comprising the Writings of Hammond, Harper, Christy, Stringfellow, Hodge, Bledsoe, and Cartwright, on this Important Issue.* Augusta, Ga.: Pritchard, Abbott and Loomis, 1860.

England, John. *Letters of the Late Bishop England to the Honorable John Forsyth, on the Subject of Domestic Slavery.* Baltimore: John Murphy, 1844.

Essig, James. *The Bonds of Wickedness: American Evangelicals Against Slavery 1770–1808.* Philadelphia: Temple Univ. Press, 1982.

Estes, Matthew. *Defence of Negro Slavery.* Columbus, Miss.: Press of the "Alabama Journal," 1846.

Ewart, David. *A Scriptural View of the Moral Relations of African Slavery.* Charleston: Walker, Evans and Co., Steam printers, 1849.

Farley, Charles A. *Slavery: A Sermon Delivered in the Unitarian Church, Richmond.* Richmond: James Walker, 1835.

Farmer, James O., Jr. *The Metaphysical Confederacy: James Henley Thornwell and the Synthesis of Southern Values.* Macon: Mercer Univ. Press, 1985.

Faust, Drew Gilpin. *The Creation of Confederate Nationalism: Ideology and Identity in the Civil War South.* Baton Rouge: Louisiana State Univ. Press, 1988.

———. "Evangelicalism and the Meaning of the Proslavery Argument: The Reverend Thornton Stringfellow of Virginia." *Virginia Magazine of History and Biography* 85 (Jan. 1977): 3–17.

———. *James Henry Hammond and the Old South: A Design for Mastery.* Baton Rouge: Louisiana State Univ. Press, 1982.

———. *Mothers of Invention: Women of the Slaveholding South in the American Civil War.* Chapel Hill: Univ. of North Carolina Press, 1996.

———. *A Sacred Circle: The Dilemma of the Intellectual in the Old South, 1840–1860.* Baltimore: Johns Hopkins Univ. Press, 1977.

Faust, Drew Gilpin, ed. *The Ideology of Slavery: Proslavery Thought in the Antebellum South, 1830–1860.* Baton Rouge: Louisiana Univ. Press, 1981.

Ferguson, J.B. *Address on the History, Authority and Influence of Slavery.* Nashville: John T.S. Fall, 1850.

Finkelman, Paul, ed. *Proslavery Thought, Ideology, and Politics.* New York: Garland, 1989.

Fletcher, Jonathan. *Studies on Slavery: In Easy Lessons.* Natchez, Miss.: Jack Warner, 1852.

Fliegelman, Jay. *Prodigals and Pilgrims: The American Revolution against Patriarchal Authority, 1750–1800.* Cambridge: Cambridge Univ. Press, 1982.

Fogel, Robert William, and Stanley Engerman. *Time on the Cross: The Economics of American Negro Slavery.* Lanham, Md.: Univ. Press of America, 1984.

Foner, Eric. *Free Soil, Free Labor, Free Men: The Ideology of the Republican Party Before the Civil War.* New York: Oxford Univ. Press, 1970.

Foster, Charles I. *An Errand of Mercy: The Evangelical United Front, 1790–1837.* Chapel Hill: Univ. of North Carolina Press, 1960.

Fox, Richard, and T.J. Jackson Lears. *The Culture of Consumption.* New York: Pantheon Books, 1983.

Fox-Genovese, Elizabeth, and Eugene Genovese. *Fruits of Merchant Capital: Sla-*

very and Bourgeois Property in the Rise and Expansion of Capitalism. New York: Oxford Univ. Press, 1983.

Fredrickson, George. The Black Image in the White Mind: The Debate on Afro-American Character and Destiny, 1817–1914. New York: Harper and Row, 1971.

———. The Inner Civil War: Northern Intellectuals and the Crisis of the Union. New York: Harper, 1965.

Freehling, William. "James Henley Thornwell's Mysterious Antislavery Moment." Journal of Southern History 57 (Aug. 1991): 383–406.

———. Prelude to the Civil War. New York: Bancroft, 1966.

———. The Road to Disunion: Secession at Bay, 1776–1854. New York: Oxford Univ. Press, 1990.

Freeman, G.W. The Rights and Duties of Slaveholders. Raleigh: J. Gales and Son, 1836.

Fuller, Richard. Address Before the American Colonization Society. Baltimore: Office of the True Union, 1851.

Fuller, Richard, and Francis Wayland. Domestic Slavery Considered as a Scriptural Institution. New York: Lewis Colby, 1845.

Furman, Richard. Exposition of the Views of Baptists. Charleston: A.E. Miller, 1822.

———. Human Accountability: A Discourse Delivered Before the Graduating Class of Erskine College. N.p., 1860.

Genovese, Eugene D. A Consuming Fire. Athens: Univ. of Georgia Press, 1999.

———. "The Divine Sanction of the Social Order: Religious Foundations of the Southern Slaveholder's World View." Journal of the American Academy of Religion 55 (1987): 211–33.

———. The Political Economy of Slavery: Studies in the Economy and Society of the Slave South. New York: Pantheon, 1965.

———. The Slaveholders' Dilemma: Freedom and Progress in Southern Conservative Thought, 1820–1860. Columbia: Univ. of South Carolina Press, 1992.

———. "Slavery Ordained of God": The Southern Slaveholders' View of Biblical History and Modern Politics. Gettysburg: Gettysburg College, 1985.

———. The Southern Tradition: The Achievement and Limitations of an American Conservatism. Cambridge, Mass.: Harvard Univ. Press, 1994.

———. Western Civilization Through Slaveholding Eyes: The Social and Historical Thought of Thomas Roderick Dew. New Orleans: The Graduate School of Tulane University, 1986.

———. The World the Slaveholders Made: Two Essays in Interpretation. New York: Pantheon, 1969.

Gerteis, Louis. Morality and Utility in American Antislavery Reform. Chapel Hill: Univ. of North Carolina Press, 1987.

Gillespie, Neal C. The Collapse of Orthodoxy: The Intellectual Ordeal of George Frederick Holmes. Charlottesville: Univ. of Virginia Press, 1972.

Glickstein, John. Concepts of Free Labor in Antebellum America. New York: Oxford Univ. Press, 1992.

Glock, Charles Y., and Phillip Hammonds, eds. Beyond the Classics? New York: Free Press, 1973.

Goen, C.C. *Broken Churches, Broken Nation: Denominational Schisms and the Coming of the American Civil War.* Macon: Mercer Univ. Press: 1985.

Graham, William. *The Contrast, or the Bible and Abolitionism: An Exegetical Argument.* Cincinnati: *Daily Cincinnati Atlas* Office, 1844.

Green, Robert W., ed. *Protestantism, Capitalism, and Social Science: The Weber Thesis Controversy.* Lexington: Univ. of Kentucky Press, 1973.

Greven, Philip, ed. *Child-Rearing Concepts, 1628–1861.* Itsaca, Ill.: 1973.

Hamilton, W.T. *The Duties of Masters and Slaves Respectively or Domestic Servitude as Sanctioned by the Bible.* Mobile: F.H. Brooks, 1845.

Harrell, David E., Jr., ed. *Varieties of Southern Evangelicalism.* Macon: Mercer Univ. Press, 1981.

Hartz, Louis. *The Liberal Tradition in America: An Interpretation of American Political Thought Since the Revolution.* New York: Harcourt and Brace, 1955.

Hatch, Nathan O. *The Democratization of American Christianity.* New Haven: Yale Univ. Press, 1989.

Helper, Hinton Rowan. *The Impending Crisis of the South: How to Meet It.* New York: Burdick Brothers, 1857.

Hesseltine, William B. "Some New Aspects of the Proslavery Argument." *Journal of Negro History* 21 (Jan. 1936): 1–15.

Higham, John. "The Changing Loyalties of William Gilmore Simms." *Journal of Southern History* 9 (May 1943): 210–23.

———. *From Boundlessness to Consolidation: The Transformation of American Culture, 1848–1860.* Ann Arbor: Univ. of Michigan Press, 1969.

Hill, Samuel. *The North and South in American Religion.* Athens: Univ. of Georgia Press, 1980.

Hilton, Boyd. *The Age of Atonement: The Influence on Social and Economic Thought, 1795–1865.* Oxford: Clarendon Press, 1988.

Hindus, Michael. *Prison and Plantation: Crime, Justice, and Authority in Massachusetts and South Carolina.* Chapel Hill: Univ. of North Carolina Press, 1980.

[Hobby, William]. *Remarks Upon Slavery; Occasioned by Attempts to Circulate Improper Publications in the Southern States. By a Citizen of Georgia.* Augusta, Ga.: Printed at the S.R. Sentinel Office, 1835.

Holder, Ray, ed. "On Slavery: Selected Letters of Parson Winans, 1820–1844." *Journal of Mississippi History* 566 (Nov. 1984): 320–75.

Hoit, T.W. *The Right of American Slavery.* St. Louis: L. Bushnell, 1860.

Holifield, E. Brooks. *The Gentlemen Theologians: American Theology in Southern Culture, 1795–1860.* Durham: Duke Univ. Press, 1978.

[Holland, Edwin Clifford]. *A Refutation of the Calumnies Circulated Against the Southern and Western States Respecting the Institution and Existence of Slavery Among Them.* Charleston: A.E. Miller, 1822.

Holmes, George Frederick. "Review." In *Slavery Defended: The Views of the Old South.* Ed. Eric McKitrick. Englewood Cliffs, N.J.: Prentice Hall, 1963. 99–111.

Holt, Michael. *The Political Crisis of the 1850s.* New York: Wiley, 1978.

Hopkins, John Henry. *Scriptural, Ecclesiastical and Historical View of Slavery, From the*

Days of the Patriarch Abraham to the Nineteenth Century. New York: W.I. Pooley and Co., 1864.

How, Samuel. *Slavery Not Sinful.* New Brunswick, N.J.: J. Terhune's Press, 1856.

Howard, Victor B. *Conscience and Slavery: The Evangelical Calivinist Domestic Missions, 1837–1861.* Ohio: Kent State Univ. Press, 1990.

Howe, Daniel Walker. "The Evangelical Movement and the Political Culture in the North during the Second Party System." *Journal of American History* (Mar. 1991): 1216–39.

———. *The Political Culture of the American Whigs.* Chicago: Univ. of Chicago Press, 1979.

Hunter, James Davison. *American Evangelicalism: Conservative Religion and the Quandary of Modernity.* New Brunswick: Rutgers Univ. Press, 1983.

Isaac, Rhys. *The Transformation of Virginia, 1740–1790.* Chapel Hill: Univ. of North Carolina Press, 1982.

Jamerson, Randall C. *The Private Civil War: Popular Thought During the Sectional Conflict.* Baton Rouge: Louisiana State Univ. Press, 1988.

Jarratt, Devereaux. *Thoughts on Some Important Subjects in Divinity; in a Series of Letters to a Friend.* Baltimore: Warner and Hanna, 1806.

Jenkins, William Sumner. *Proslavery Thought in the Old South.* Chapel Hill: Univ. of North Carolina Press, 1935.

Jeter, Jeremiah. *The Recollections of a Long Life.* Richmond: Richmond Religious Herald and Co., 1891.

Johnson, Michael. *Toward a Patriarchal Republic: The Secession of Georgia.* Baton Rouge: Louisiana State Univ. Press, 1977.

Johnson, Paul E. *A Shopkeeper's Millennium: Society and Revivals in Rochester, New York, 1815–1837.* New York: Hill and Wang, 1978.

Johnson, Thomas C., ed. *Life and Letters of Robert L. Dabney.* Richmond: The Presbyterian Committee of Publications, 1903.

Jordan, Winthrop. *White over Black: American Attitudes toward the Negro, 1550–1812.* Chapel Hill: Univ. of North Carolina Press, 1968.

Junkin, George. *The Integrity of Our National Union vs. Abolitionism: An Argument from the Bible.* Cincinnati: R.P. Donogh, 1843.

Justice. *The Slavery Question: Comprising the Doctrine of the Bible on the Subject of Slavery.* Spartansburg, S.C.: Printed at the "Spartan Office," 1849.

Kaufman, Allen. *Capitalism, Slavery, and Republican Values: Antebellum Political Economists, 1819–1848.* Austin: Univ. of Texas Press, 1982.

Kaufman, Walter. "Suffering in the Bible." In *Faith of a Heretic.* Garden City: Doubleday, 1961. 137–69.

Ker, Leander. *Slavery Consistent with Christianity.* Baltimore: Sherwood and Co., 1840.

Kerber, Linda. *Federalists in Dissent: Imagery and Ideology in Jeffersonian America.* Ithaca: Cornell Univ. Press, 1970.

Klauser, Samuel Z., ed. *The Quest for Self-Control.* New York: Free Press, 1965.

Kohl, Lawrence. *The Politics of Individualism: Parties and the American Character in Jacksonian America.* New York: Oxford Univ. Press, 1989.

Kousser, J. Morgan, and James M. McPherson, eds. *Region, Race, and Reconstruction: Essays in Honor of C. Vann Woodward.* New York: Oxford Univ. Press, 1982.

Lawrence, John. *The Slavery Question.* Dayton: Published for the United Brethren of Christ by Vonnieda and Kulmer, 1854.

Levi-Strauss, Claude. *The Savage Mind.* Chicago: Univ. of Chicago Press, 1968.

Lewis, Jan. *The Pursuit of Happiness: Family and Values in Jefferson's Virginia.* Cambridge, England: Cambridge Univ. Press, 1983.

Linderman, Gerald. *Embattled Courage: The Experience of Combat in the American Civil War.* New York: The Free Press, 1987.

Lipscomb, Andrew A. *North and South: Impressions of Northern Society upon a Southerner.* Mobile, Ala.: Carver and Ryland, 1853.

———. *North and South: Impressions of Northern Society upon a Southerner,* from the *New York Daily Times,* October 16, 1852.

Lloyd, Arthur Young. *The Slavery Controversy, 1831–1860.* Chapel Hill: Univ. of North Carolina Press, 1935.

Longstreet, A.B. *Letters on the Epistle of Paul to Philemon on the Connection of Apostolical Christianity and Slavery.* Charleston: B. Jenkins, 1845.

———. *A Voice from the South: Comprising Letters from Georgia to Massachusetts and to the Southern States.* Baltimore: Samuel E. Smith: 1848.

Lord, Nathan. *A Letter of Inquiry to Ministers of the Gospel of All Denominations on Slavery.* Boston: Petridge and Co., 1854.

Lounsbury, Richard C., ed. *Louisa S. McCord: Selected Writings.* Charlottesville: Univ. Press of Virginia, 1997.

Loveland, Anne C. "Richard Furman's 'Questions on Slavery.'" *Baptist History and Heritage* 10 (July 1975): 177–81.

———. *Southern Evangelicals and the Social Order, 1800–1860.* Baton Rouge: Louisiana State Univ. Press, 1980.

MacLeod, Duncan. *Slavery, Race, and the American Revolution.* London: Cambridge Univ. Press, 1974.

MacPherson, C.B. *The Political Theory of Possessive Individualism: Hobbes to Locke.* London: Oxford Univ. Press, 1962.

Maddex, Jack P., Jr. "'The Southern Apostasy' Revisited: The Significance of Proslavery Christianity." *Marxist Perspectives* 2 (fall 1979): 132–54.

Marsden, George. *The Evangelical Mind and the New School Presbyterian Experience: A Case Study in Thought and Theology.* New Haven: Yale Univ. Press, 1970.

———. *Fundamentalism in American Culture: The Shaping of Twentieth Century Evangelicalism, 1870–1925.* New York: Oxford Univ. Press, 1980.

Marty, Martin. "Paradox Lost: Order in Evangelical Thought in Mid-Nineteenth Century America." *Church History* 44 (September 1975): 352–66.

———. *Righteous Empire: The Protestant Experience in America.* New York: Holt, Reinhart, and Winston, 1970.

Matthews, Donald. *Religion in the Old South.* Chicago: Univ. of Chicago Press, 1977.

———. *Slavery and Methodism : A Chapter in American Morality, 1780–1845.* Princeton: Princeton Univ. Press, 1965.

May, Henry. "The Decline of Providence?" In *Ideas, Faiths and Feelings: Essays in American Intellectual and Religious History, 1752– 1982*. New York: Oxford Univ. Press, 1983. 130–45.

———. *The Enlightenment in America*. New York: Oxford Univ. Press, 1974.

McCaine, Alexander. *Slavery Defended from Scripture*. Baltimore: Wm. Woody, 1842.

McCardell, John. *The Idea of a Southern Nation: Southern Nationalists and Southern Nationalism, 1830–1860*. New York: W.W. Norton, 1979.

McCord, Louisa. *Political and Social Essays*. Charlottesville: Univ. Press of Virginia, 1995.

McCray, Drew. *The Elusive Republic: Political Economy in Jeffersonian America*. Chapel Hill: Univ. of North Carolina Press, 1980.

McCurry, Stephanie. *Masters of Small Worlds: Yeoman Households, Gender Relations, and the Political Culture of the Antebellum South Carolina Low Country*. New York: Oxford Univ. Press, 1995.

McKay, Neill. *Slavery and the Obligations of Masters*. N.p.: N.d.

McKenzie, Robert. *One South or Many? Plantation Belt and Upcountry in Civil War–Era Tennessee*. New York: Cambridge Univ. Press, 1994.

McKivigan, John R. *The War Against Proslavery Religion: Abolitionism and the Northern Churches, 1830–1865*. Chapel Hill: Univ. of North Carolina Press, 1984.

McLoughlin, William. "Evangelical Child-Rearing in the Age of Jackson: Francis Wayland's View of When and How to Subdue the Willfulness of Children." *Journal of Social History* 9 (fall, 1975): 23–31.

McPherson, James. "Slavery and Race." *Perspectives in American History* 3 (1969): 460–73.

———. *What they Fought For, 1861–1865*. Baton Rouge: Louisiana State Univ. Press, 1994.

McTyeire, H.N., C.F. Sturgis, and A.T. Holmes. *Duties of Masters to Servants: Three Premium Essays*. Charleston: Southern Baptist Convention, 1851.

[Mell, Patrick Hues]. *Slavery: A Treatise, Showing that Slavery is Neither a Moral, Political nor Social Evil*. Penfield, Ga.: Benj. Brantly, 1844.

Meredith, Robert. *The Politics of the Universe: Edward Beecher, Abolition and Orthodoxy*. Nashville: Vanderbilt Univ. Press, 1968.

Meredith, Thomas. *Christianity and Slavery: Strictures on Rev. William Hague's Review of Doctors Fuller and Wayland on Domestic Slavery*. Boston: Gould, Kendall and Lincoln, 1847.

Meyers, Marvin. *The Jacksonian Persuasion*. New York: Vintage Books, 1957.

Michelbacher, M.J. *A Sermon: Preached on the Day of Prayer C.S.A. at the German Hebrew Synagogue, Bayth Ahabah*. 27 March 1863. Richmond: MacFarlane and Ferguson, 1863.

Miles, James Warley. *God in History: A Discourse Delivered before the Graduating Class of the College of Charleston on Sunday*. Charleston: Steam-power Press of Evans and Cogswell, 1863.

Miller, Perry. *Errand into the Wilderness*. Cambridge, Mass.: Harvard Univ. Press, 1956.

———. *The Life of the Mind in America: From the Revolution to the Civil War*. New York: Harcourt, Brace and World, 1965.

———. *The New England Mind: From Colony to Province.* Cambridge, Mass.: Harvard Univ. Press, 1953.

———. *The New England Mind: The Seventeenth Century.* New York: Harvard Univ. Press, 1939.

Miller, Randall M., Harry Stout, and Charles Reagan Wilson, eds. *Religion and the American Civil War.* London: Oxford Univ. Press, 1998.

A Mississippian. "Slavery: The Bible and 'Three Thousand Parsons.'" *DeBow's Review* 26 (Jan. 1859): 43–54.

Mitchell, J.C. *A Bible Defence of Slavery, and the Unity of Mankind.* Mobile: J.Y. Thompson: 1861.

Mitchell, Reid. *Civil War Soldiers: Their Expectations and Experiences.* New York: Viking, 1988.

Moore, R. Laurence. *Religious Outsider and the Making of Americans.* Cornell: Cornell Univ. Press, 1986.

Moorehead, James. *American Apocalypse: Yankee Protestants and the Civil War.* New Haven: Yale Univ. Press, 1978.

———. "Between Progress and the Apocalypse." *Journal of American History* 88 (Dec. 1984): 524–42.

Morgan, Edmund. *American Freedom, American Slavery.* New York: W.W. Norton, 1975.

Morrow, Ralph. "The Proslavery Argument Revisited." *Mississippi Valley Historical Review* (June 1961): 79–94.

Oakes, James. *The Ruling Race: A History of American Slaveholders.* New York: Knopf, 1982.

O'Brien, Michael. *All Clever Men Who Make Their Way.* Fayetteville: Univ. of Arkansas Press, 1982.

———. "The Nineteenth Century American South." *Historical Journal* 24 (September 1981): 751–63.

———. *Rethinking the South: Essays in Intellectual History.* Baltimore: Johns Hopkins Univ. Press, 1988.

Osthaus, Carl. *Partisans of the Southern Press: Editorial Spokesmen of the Nineteenth Century South.* Lexington: Univ. Press of Kentucky, 1994.

Palmer, Benjamin Morgan. *The South: Her Peril and Her Duty. A Discourse Delivered in the First Presbyterian Church, New Orleans.* New Orleans: Office of the True Witness and Sentinel, 1860.

Parker, Harold M. *The United Synod of the South: The Southern New School Presbyterian Church.* New York: Greenwood Press, 1988.

[Parsons, Theodore, and Eliphalet Pearson]. *A Forensic Dispute on the Legality of Enslaving Africans.* Boston: Printed by John Boyle for Thomas Leverett, 1773.

Paskoff, Paul, ed. *The Cause of the South: Selections from "DeBow's Review,"* Baton Rouge: Louisiana State Univ. Press, 1982.

[Patterson, George]. *The Scripture Doctrine with Regards to Slavery.* Pottsville, Pa.: Benjamin Bannan, 1856.

Patterson, Orlando. *Freedom: Volume I, Freedom in the Making of Western Culture.* New York: Basic Books, 1991.

Paulding, James. *Slavery in the United States.* New York: Harper and Brothers, 1836.

Perry, Lewis, and Michael Fellman, eds. *Antislavery Reconsidered: New Perspectives on the Abolitionists.* Baton Rouge: Louisiana State Univ. Press, 1979.

Pessen, Edward. "How Different Were the Antebellum North and South?" *American Historical Review* 85 (Dec. 1980): 119–40.

Peterson, Thomas Virgil. *Ham and Japheth: The Mythic World of Whites in the Antebellum South.* Metuchen, N.J.: Scarecrow Press, 1978.

Phillips, Ulrich Bonnel. *Life and Labor in the Old South.* Boston: Little, Brown, 1929.

Poggi, Gianfranco. *Calvinism and the Capitalist Spirit.* Amherst: Univ. of Massachusetts Press, 1983.

Porter, A.A. *Our Danger and Our Duty.* Charleston: E.C. Councell, 1850.

Potter, David M. *The Impending Crisis.* New York: Harper and Row, 1976.

Priest, Josiah. *Bible Defence of Slavery.* Glasgow, Ky.: Walker and Richard, 1852.

Pringle, Edward. *Slavery in the Southern States.* Cambridge, England: J. Bartlett, 1852.

Pro-slavery Argument: As Maintained by the Most Distinguished Writers of the Southern States, Containing the Several Essays, on the Subject, of Chancellor Harper, Governor Hammond, Dr. Simms, and Professor Dew. Charleston: Walker, Richard and Co., 1852.

Purifoy, Lewis. "The Southern Methodist Church and the Proslavery Argument." *Journal of Southern History* 32 (August 1966): 325–41.

Remini, Robert. *The Revolutionary Age of Andrew Jackson.* New York: Harper and Row, 1976.

Rhett, Robert Barnwell. *Address to the People of Beaufort and Collection Districts, Upon the Subject of Abolition.* N.p.: 1838.

Rice, David. *Slavery Inconsistent with Justice and Good Policy.* Lexington, Ky.: J. Bradford, 1792.

Rice, Madeleine. *American Catholic Opinion in the Slavery Controversy.* Gloucester: Peter Smith, 1964.

Rice, Nathan L. *Ten Letters on the Subject of Slavery: Addressed to the Delegates from the Congregational Associations to the Last General Assembly of the Presbyterian Church.* St. Louis: Keith, Woods and Co., 1855.

Rivers, Richard Henderson. *Elements of Moral Philosophy.* Nashville, Tenn.: Southern Methodist Publishing House, 1860.

Rogers, Tommy W. "Dr. F.A. Ross and the Presbyterian Defense of Slavery." *Journal of Presbyterian History* 45 (June, 1967): 112–24.

Rogers, William. *The Call to Seriousness: The Evangelical Impact on the Victorians.* New York: Macmillan, 1976.

Ross, Frederick. *Position of the Southern Church in Relation to Slavery, as Illustrated in a Letter of F.A. Ross to Rev. Albert Barnes.* New York: N.p., 1857.

———. *Slavery Ordained of God.* Philadelphia: Lipincott and Co., 1857.

Rothman, David. *The Discovery of the Asylum: Social Order and Disorder in the New Republic.* Boston: Little, Brown, 1971.

Rubin, Louis, Jr. *The Edge of the Swamp: A Study in the Literature and Society of the Old South.* Baton Rouge: Louisiana State Univ. Press, 1989.

Ruffner, William H., ed. *Lectures on the Evidences of Christianity, Delivered at the University of Virginia, During the Session of 1850–1851.* New York: Robert Carter and Brothers, 1856.

Salhope, Robert E., ed. *Individualism in the Early Republic.* Cambridge, Mass.: Harvard Univ. Press, 1991.

Sandeen, Ernest R. *The Roots of Fundamentalism: British and American Millenarianism, 1800–1930.* Chicago: Chicago Univ. Press, 1970.

Saum, Lewis O. *The Popular Mind of Pre-Civil War America.* Westport, Conn.: Greenwood Press, 1980.

Sawyer, George. *Southern Institutes.* Philadelphia: J.B. Lippincott and Co., 1858.

Scherer, Lester B. *Slavery and the Churches in Early America, 1619–1819.* Grand Rapids: Eerdmans, 1975.

Scott, Donald. *From Office to Profession: The New England Ministry 1750–1850.* Philadelphia: Univ. of Pennsylvania Press, 1978.

Seat, William. *The Confederate States of America in Prophecy.* Nashville: Southern Methodist Publishing House, 1861.

Sellers, Charles. *The Market Revolution: Jacksonian America, 1815–1846.* New York: Oxford Univ. Press, 1991.

———. "The Travail of Slavery." In *The Southerner as American.* Ed. Charles Sellers. Chapel Hill: Univ. of North Carolina Press, 1960. 40–71.

Shannon, James. *An Address Delivered Before the Proslavery Convention of the State of Missouri.* St Louis: Republican Book and Job Office, 1855.

Shore, Lawrence. *Southern Capitalists: The Ideological Leadership of an Elite, 1832–1885.* Chapel Hill: Univ. of North Carolina Press, 1986.

Silver, James. *Confederate Morale and Church Propaganda.* Tuscaloosa: Confederate Pub. Co., 1957.

Simmel, George. *On Individuality and Social Forms.* Chicago: Univ. of Chicago Press, 1971.

Simpson, Lewis. *The Man of Letters in New England and the South: Essays on the History of the Literary Vocation in America.* Baton Rouge: Louisiana State Univ. Press, 1973.

———. *Mind and the American Civil War: A Meditation on Lost Causes.* Baton Rouge: Louisiana State Univ. Press, 1989.

Sledd, R.N. *A Sermon.* Petersburg: A.F. Crotchfield and Co., Printers, Bank Street, 1861.

Sleigh, William. *Abolitionism Exposed, Corrected: By a Physician; Formerly Resident of the South.* Philadelphia: J. Sharp, 1838.

Sloan, James. *The Great Question Answered, or Is Slavery a Sin in Itself (Per Se)?* Memphis: Hutton, Galloway, and Co., 1857.

Smectymnuus. *Slavery and the Church: Two Letters Addressed to N.L. Rice.* Boston: Crocker and Brewster, 1856.

Smith, E. *Bible Servitude.* Mansfield, Ohio: By the Author, 1852.

Smith, H. Shelton. *In His Image But . . . . : Racism in Southern Religion, 1780–1850.* Durham: Duke Univ. Press, 1972.

Smith, Mark M. *Debating Slavery: Economy and Society in the Antebellum American South*. London: Cambridge Univ. Press, 1999.

———. *Mastered by the Clock: Time, Slavery, and Freedom in the American South*. Chapel Hill: Univ. of North Carolina Press, 1997.

Smith, Timothy L. *Revivalism and Reform: American Protestantism on the Eve of the Civil War*. Baltimore: Johns Hopkins Univ. Press, 1980.

Smith, William A. *Lectures on the Philosophy and Practice of Slavery*. Nashville: Stevenson and Evans, 1856.

Smylie, James. *A Review of a Letter, from the Presbytery of Chillicothe, to the Presbytery of Mississippi, on the Subject of Slavery*. Woodville, Miss.: William A. Norris and Co., 1836.

Smyth, Thomas. *The Unity of Human Races: Proved to be the Doctrine of Scripture, Reason, and Science*. New York: George P. Putman, 1850.

Snay, Mitchell. "American Thought and Southern Distinctiveness: The Southern Clergy and the Sanctification of Slavery." *Civil War History* 35 (Dec. 1989): 311–28.

Sparks, Randy. "Mississippi's Apostle of Slavery: James Smylie and the Biblical Defense of Slavery." *Journal of Mississippi History* (fall 1989): 89–106.

Sparks, Randy. *On Jordan's Stormy Banks: Evangelicalism in Mississippi, 1773–1876*. Athens: Univ. of Georgia Press, 1994.

Stannard, David. *The Puritan Way of Death*. New York: Oxford Univ. Press, 1984.

Stearns, E.J. *Notes on "Uncle Tom's Cabin": Being a Logical Answer to its Allegations and Inferences Against Slavery as an Institution*. Philadelphia: Lippincott, Grambo and Co., 1853.

Stewart, James. *Holy Warriors: The Abolitionists and American Slavery*. New York: Hill and Wang, 1976.

Stirling, James. *Letters from the Slave States*. London: H.H.W. Parker and Son, 1857.

Stringfellow, B.F., and Dr. Goodloe. *Information for the People: Two Tracts for the Times*. Boston: Alfred Mudge and Son, 1855.

Stringfellow, Thornton. *A Brief Examination of Scripture Testimony on the Institution of Slavery*. Washington: Congressional Globe Office, 1850.

———. *Scriptural and Statistical Views in Favor of Slavery*. 4th ed. Richmond, Va.: J.W. Randolph, 1856.

———. *Slavery: Its Origin, Nature, and History, Considered in the Light of Bible Teachings, Moral Justice, and Political Wisdom*. New York: John F. Trow, 1861.

Stroupe, Henry. *The Religious Press in the Southern and Atlantic States, 1802–1865*. Durham: Duke Univ. Press, 1956.

Swaney, C.B. *Episcopal Methodism and Slavery with Sidelights on Ecclesiastical Politics*. Boston: R.G. Badger, 1926.

Sweet, William Warren. *Religion in the Development of American Culture, 1765–1840*. New York: Harper, 1952.

Taylor, Thomas J. *Essay on Slavery; As Connected with the Moral and Providential Government of God*. New York: Joseph Longking, 1851.

Taylor, William R. *Cavalier and Yankee: The Old South and National Character*. New York: George Braziller, 1961.

Thornton, J. Mills. *Politics and Power in a Slave Society: Alabama, 1800–1860.* Baton Rouge: Louisiana State Univ. Press, 1978.

Thornton, Thomas C. *An Inquiry into the History of Slavery; Its Introduction into the United States; Causes of Continuance; and Remarks upon the Abolition Tracts of William E. Channing.* Washington: William M. Morron, 1841.

Thornwell, James Henley. *The Life and Letters of James Henley Thornwell.* Edited by B.M. Palmer. Richmond: Whittel and Shepperson, 1875.

———. *The Rights and Duties of Masters.* Charleston: Steam-power Press of Walker and James, 1850.

Thrasher, John B. *Slavery a Divine Institution.* Port Gibson, Miss.: Southern Reveille Book and Job Office, 1861.

Tichenor, I.T. *Fast Day Sermon.* Montgomery: General Assembly of the State of Alabama, 1863.

Tise, Larry. *Proslavery: A History of the Defense of Slavery in America, 1701–1840.* Athens: Univ. of Georgia Press, 1987.

Towner, Lawrence. "The Sewall-Saffin Dialogue on Slavery." *William and Mary Quarterly* 21 (Jan. 1964): 41–2.

Tuveson, Ernest L. *Redeemer Nation: The Idea of America's Millennial Role.* Chicago: Univ. of Chicago Press, 1968.

Tyson, Bryan. *The Institution of Slavery in the Southern States, Religiously, and Morally Considered in Connection with our Sectional Troubles.* In *A Defence of Southern Slavery and Other Pamphlets.* New York: Negro Univ. Press, 1969.

Ushur, A.P. "Domestic Slavery." *Southern Literary Messenger* 5 (Oct. 1839): 681–701.

Vernor, W.H. *A Sermon: Delivered before the Marshall Guards No. 1, on Sunday, May 5, 1861.* Lewisburg, Tenn.: Southern Messenger Office, 1861.

Walters, Ronald C. *The Antislavery Appeal: American Abolitionism after 1830.* Baltimore: Johns Hopkins Univ. Press, 1976.

Ward, John William. *Andrew Jackson: Symbol for an Age.* New York: Oxford Univ. Press, 1962.

Warren, E.W. *Nellie Norton: Or Southern Slavery and the Bible. A Scriptural Presentation of the Principal Arguments upon which the Abolitionists Rely. A Vindication of Southern Slavery from the Old And New Testaments.* Macon: Burke, Boykin, and Company, 1864.

Watson, Harry L. *Liberty and Power: The Politics of Jacksonian America.* New York, Hill and Wang, 1990.

Wayland, Francis. *Elements of Moral Science.* Boston: Gould, Kendall and Lincoln, 1835.

Weber, Max. *The Protestant Ethic and the Spirit of Capitalism.* New York: Scribners, 1930.

———. *General Economic History.* Glencoe, Ill.: Free Press, 1927.

Welter, Rush. *The Mind of America: 1820–1860.* New York: Columbia Univ. Press, 1975.

Whitefield, George. *Three Letters from the Rev. George Whitefield.* Philadelphia: B. Franklin, 1740.

Wiley, Calvin Henderson. "The Christian Duty of Masters." N.p.: N.d.

———. *Scriptural Views of National Trials: Or the True Road to the Independence and Peace of the Confederate States of America.* Greensboro, N.C.: Sterling, Campbell and Albright, 1863.

Williams, James. *The South Vindicated; Being a Series of Letters Written for the American Press during the Canvas for the Presidency in 1860.* London: Longman, Roberts and Green, 1862.

Winkler, E.T. *Duties of Christian Soldiers.* Charleston: Evans and Cogswell, 1861.

Wilson, Charles Reagan. *Baptized in Blood: The Religion of the Lost Cause, 1865–1920.* Athens: Univ. of Georgia Press, 1980.

———, ed. *Religion in the Old South.* Jackson: Univ. of Mississippi Press, 1985.

Wilson, Joseph. *The Mutual Relations of Masters and Slaves as Taught in the Bible.* Augusta, Ga.: Steam Press of the Chronicle and Sentinel, 1861.

Wilson, Joshua Lacy. *Relations and Duties of Servants and Masters.* Cincinnati: Isaac Hefley and Co., Printers, 1834.

Wish, Henry. *George Fitzhugh, Propagandist of the Old South.* Gloucester, Mass.: 1962.

Wishy, Bernard. *The Child and the Republic: The Dawn of Modern American Child Nurture.* Philadelphia: Univ. of Pennsylvania Press, 1972.

Woodward, A. *A Review of "Uncle Tom's Cabin"; Or, An Essay on Slavery.* Cincinnati: Applegate, 1853.

Woodward, C. Vann. *American Counterpoint: Slavery and Racism in the North-South Dialogue.* Boston: Little, Brown, 1964.

———. *The Burden of Southern History.* Baton Rouge: Louisiana State Univ. Press, 1968.

Wright, Gavin. *The Political Economy of the Cotton South.* New York: Norton, 1978.

Wyatt-Brown, Bertram. *Southern Honor: Ethics and Behavior in the Old South.* New York: Oxford Univ. Press, 1982.

———. *Yankee Saints and Southern Sinners.* Baton Rouge: Louisiana State Univ. Press, 1985.

Wylie, Irvin. *The Self-Made Man in America.* New York: Free Press, 1954.

Index